D1393402
Hava
Withdrawn

Palgrave Key Concepts

Palgrave Key Concepts provide an accessible and comprehensive range of subject glossaries at undergraduate level. They are the ideal companion to a standard textbook, making them invaluable reading for students throughout their course of study and especially useful as a revision aid.

The key concepts are arranged alphabetically so you can quickly find terms or entries of immediate interest. All major theories, concepts, terms and theorists are incorporated and cross-referenced. Additional reading or website research opportunities are included. With hundreds of key terms defined, **Palgrave Key Concepts** represent a comprehensive must-have reference for undergraduates.

Published

Key Concepts in Accounting and Finance
Key Concepts in Business Practice
Key Concepts in Human Resource Management
Key Concepts in International Business
Key Concepts in Management
Key Concepts in Marketing
Key Concepts in Operations Management
Key Concepts in Politics
Key Concepts in Strategic Management
Linguistic Terms and Concepts
Literary Terms and Criticism (*third edition*)

Further titles are in preparation

www.palgravekeyconcepts.com

Palgrave Key Concepts
Series Standing Order ISBN 1–4039–3210–7
(*outside North America only*)

You can receive future titles in this series as they are published by placing a standing order. Please contact your bookseller or, in case of difficulty, write to us at the address below with your name and address, the title of the series, and the ISBN quoted above.

Customer Services Department, Macmillan Distribution Ltd,
Houndmills, Basingstoke, Hampshire RG21 6XS, England

Key Concepts in Operations Management

Jonathan Sutherland and Diane Canwell

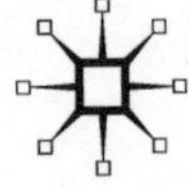

First published 2004 by
PALGRAVE MACMILLAN
Houndmills, Basingstoke, Hampshire RG21 6XS and
175 Fifth Avenue, New York, N.Y. 10010
Companies and representatives throughout the world

PALGRAVE MACMILLAN is the global academic imprint of the Palgrave Macmillan division of St. Martin's Press, LLC and of Palgrave Macmillan Ltd. Macmillan® is a registered trademark in the United States, United Kingdom and other countries. Palgrave is a registered trademark in the European Union and other countries.

ISBN 1–4039–1529–6 paperback

This book is printed on paper suitable for recycling and made from fully managed and sustained forest sources.

A catalogue record for this book is available from the British Library.

A catalog record for this book is available from the Library of Congress.

10 9 8 7 6 5 4 3 2 1
13 12 11 10 09 08 07 06 05 04

Printed in China

Contents

Introduction

Operations management may be considered, as a discipline, to be one of the orphans of the business world. It attracts, comparatively speaking, little interest either from graduates or from the press and public in general. Operations management extends beyond the area of manufacturing and includes the management of service industries, distribution, quality control and other disciplines.

In terms of world coverage, operations management only ever seems to attract the attention of the public when serious problems are encountered such as environment issues or the automation of systems, leading to mass unemployment in a given region. Yet the story of operations management is one of continuous change and quest for perfection. This quest has led operations management down several cul-de-sacs in the past, through a series of trends which have transformed the manufacturing and service industry base across the world, and continues to create systems and individuals who are determined to strive for perfect production methods.

Indeed, operations management was once known as 'production management', but it is now a far more all-embracing discipline that encompasses all of the areas already mentioned and many of those allied to these areas of business. From the extraction of raw materials, through their processing to finished goods, their storage and their distribution, to the complexities of service-based operations management, there are systems, processes, checks and controls to ensure quality and adherence to standards.

Operations management is not a discipline solely concerned with the maintenance of robotic systems which make, move and store products. It is a discipline deeply involved with innovation, quality, performance and, above all, those who design, run and maintain the systems of factories, call centres, distribution centres and a host of other organizations concerned with the discipline.

The structure of the glossary

Every attempt has been made to include all of the key concepts in this discipline, taking into account currently used terminology and jargon common throughout operations management in organizations around the world. There are notable differences in legislation and procedure when we compare production and manufacturing, warehousing and storage, supply chains and distribution and the other subdivisions of the discipline in the United Kingdom, Europe, the United States and Japan. Increasingly in Europe, for example, there is a harmonization process in train which is gradually seeking to standardize regulations and procedures.

Each of the key concepts has been placed alphabetically in order to ensure that the reader can quickly find the term or entry of immediate interest. It is normally the case that a brief description of the term is presented, followed by a more expansive explanation.

The majority of the key concepts have the following in common:

- They may have a reference within the text to another key concept, identified by a word or phrase that is in **bold** type – this should enable readers to investigate a directly implicated key concept should they require clarification of the definition at that point.
- They may have a series of related key concepts, which are featured at the end of the definition – this allows readers to continue their research and investigate subsidiary or allied key concepts.
- They may feature book or journal references – a vital feature for the reader to undertake follow-up research for more expansive explanations, often written by the originator or a leading writer in that particular field of study.
- They may include website references – it is notoriously difficult to ensure that websites are still running at the time of going to print, let alone several months beyond that time, but in the majority of cases long-established websites or governmental websites that are unlikely to be closed or to have a major address change have been selected.

Glossary terms – a guide

Whilst the majority of the key concepts have an international flavour, readers are cautioned to ensure that they have accessed the legislation, in particular, which refers to their native country or to the country in which they are working.

It is also often the case that there are terms which have no currency in a particular country as they may be allied to specific legislation of another country. Therefore readers are cautioned to check whether the description does not include a specific reference to such law, and not to assume that the key concept is a generic one and that it can be applied universally to operations management.

In all cases, references to other books, journals and websites are based on the latest available information. It was not always possible to ensure that the key text or printed reference is in print, but the majority of well-stocked college or university libraries should have access to the original materials. In the majority of cases, when generic operations management books have been referenced, these are, in the view of the writers, the best and most readily available additional reading texts.

ABC

See **activity-based costing**.

ABC analysis

ABC analysis is a precursor to **ABC classification**. It uses a **Pareto analysis** to determine the inventory value for each group of products. The analysis usually involves multiplying the annual demand by the unit cost. In this way the whole inventory of an organization can be ranked in descending order of cost. Not all organizations use this form of analysis; some prefer to use the rate of turnover of groups of products as the basis of their analysis, rather than using an annual-demand value.

ABC classification

Having carried out an **ABC analysis**, the organization can now create three broad bands of product groups. 'A' classified products have the highest annual cash volume, whilst those in the 'C' category have the lowest cash volume. These classifications allow the organization to ensure that 'A' classified products are given closer attention. This means that the products should always be in stock, that the orders should be more frequent, that stock checks should be carried out on a regular basis, that the goods should be conveniently located on the premises for easier despatch and that periodically a forecast of sales is recalculated, in order to adjust any of the other features. 'C' rated products, or product groups, represent rather less value and importance to the organization. They therefore do not receive the same degree of attention as 'A' or 'B' class products.

Typically, 'A' class products will represent up to 80% of the annual demand for products from the organization. As the related turnover of these products is so high, they will normally not represent more than 20% of the stock at any one time, hence the importance of stock control and planning. 'B' rated items can represent up to 10% of the annual demand and may, at any time, represent up to 25% of the production or the stock. 'C' rated items may account for up to 65% of the stock, but only around 10% of the annual demand and production. These items need less forward planning than the other two categories.

Acceptable quality level (AQL)

A manufacturing organization will invariably set a maximum proportion or percentage of defects allowable in any given **batch** or lot. This percentage or proportion is known as AQL and is a measure of whether or not the process as a whole is producing an acceptable or satisfactory level of quality and performance.

Acceptance sampling

Acceptance sampling is the means by which an organization or its customers determine whether a **batch** or a 'lot' of finished products have a reasonable number of defects. Acceptance sampling is the basis for the fundamental decision as to whether to accept or reject a specific batch. A figure will be set and a random sample will be chosen from the batch. If defects within the sample exceed the acceptance sample figure that was set then the whole batch will be rejected.

Activity-based costing (ABC)

Essentially, activity-based costing is an accounting method, or information system, that seeks to link costs with activities which generate those costs. The key aspect is the identification and measurement of cost drivers. Each complex activity is broken down into specific activities, which could include how long it might take to set machinery up to begin producing a product, any associated delays whilst production is under way, movement of materials to and from the machine during production, and all other activities associated with that production period.

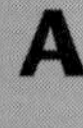

Activity-based costing can be applied to all types of activities, including, for example, the delivery of products to customers, which may include time taken to load the vehicle, the number of miles between each delivery point, the number of stops made and any known or predicted hold-ups during the delivery process. Each of these individual activities contributes to the accumulated costs for the whole process. Each activity can then be assessed in terms of its cost in order to identify ways in which the costs can be driven down.

Activity-based management (ABM) is the process of controlling and improving factors identified during activity-based costing. Typically, an organization may consider approaches to specific activities which defy attempts to drive down costs. **Outsourcing**, for example, may be a solution. ABM also considers the impact on costs if operations are expanded or reduced, and attempts to discover whether the costs will be constant, regardless of the level of operation, or whether they are related directly to the levels of operation.

Cokins, Gary, *Activity-based Cost Management: An Executive's Guide.* Chichester: John Wiley, 2001.

Activity-based management (ABM)

Activity-based management (ABM) is the application of the results from activity-based costing (ABC) for process and profit improvement. ABM aims to generate a number of improvement initiatives and provide the business with a clearer view of the profitability of its products or services. The associations can be best described in the diagram in Figure 1.

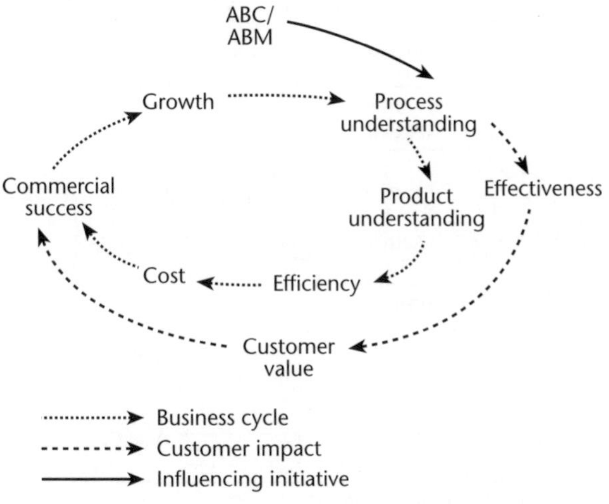

Figure 1 Activity-based management

Whilst ABC is calculated by the finance department, ABM needs to be a more widespread concern as it can identify the main factors driving resource-consumption. In most cases, teams are deployed to undertake ABM activities.

See also **activity-based costing.**

A

Activity-on-arrow (AOA)

An activity-on-arrow is a project management arrow diagram, where the arrows symbolize the activities the project involves. The diagrams are constructed using arrows, with each arrow representing a task which needs to be completed or is waiting to be completed. Normal activities are depicted as straight lines with arrows attached, and dummy activities represent events which have to occur, but which do not use any resources. Typically, the activity-on-arrow diagrams can be illustrated as in Figure 2.

There are some general conventions regarding the creation of the diagrams, in that the diagrams are read from left to right, and that the length of the arrows does not imply the length of time it takes to complete the activity. As the activity develops, successive activities are given a higher number on the diagram to reinforce the order of events.

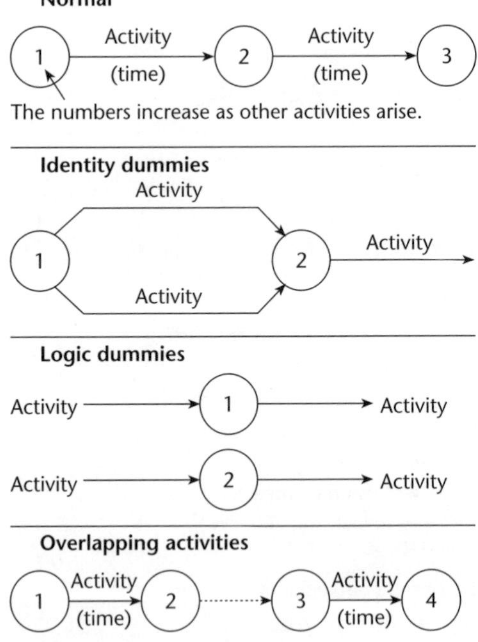

Figure 2 Examples of activity-on-arrow diagrams

Activity-on-node (AON)

An activity-on-node network is essentially a precedence diagram in which the nodes symbolize activities. In many respects the network is similar to an **activity-on-arrow** network, except that instead of using circles in the diagram, rectangles (or nodes) are used.

There are several different ways of using this form of diagram, as can be seen in Figure 3.

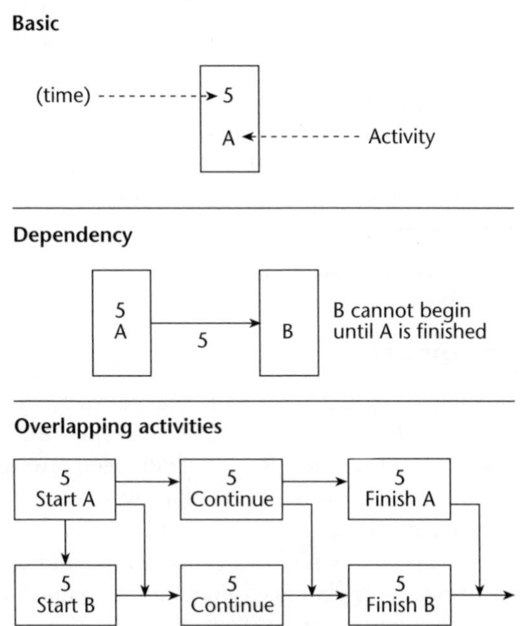

Figure 3 Examples of activity-on-node diagrams

The nodes contain an activity, a description of the activity and the duration of that activity. The dependencies are shown as relationships between the activities.

Advanced planning and scheduling (APS)

Essentially, advanced planning and scheduling (APS) is a software system which creates detailed schedules for orders. Unlike **material requirements planning (MRP)** and **enterprise resources planning (ERP)**, which produce basic plans largely based on fixed **lead times**, APS combines both manufacturing and scheduling to create very detailed schedules.

Gunther, H. and Beek P., *Advanced Planning and Scheduling Solutions in Process Industry.* Heidelberg: Springer Verlag, 2003.

A

Aggregate inventory management (AIM)

Aggregate inventory management (AIM) is vital to organizations which have thousands of individual items in their inventory. It would prove to be extremely difficult, not to mention time consuming, to devote inventory management time to each specific item. The solution is to group items which have commonalities, such as similar levels of turnover, value or space required to store them.

A standard or aggregate set of management parameters is set for each identified group and the items within that group are managed in the same way. Periodically, however, the system needs to be reviewed in order to ensure that the products or items contained within each group still share the same characteristics.

See also **average aggregate inventory value (AAIV).**

Aggregate planning

Aggregate planning, or an aggregate plan, is a means by which an organization can convert its business or marketing plan into a workable production plan. There is a considerable difference between the generalizations contained within a business plan, which tends to focus on costs, revenue and profit, and a production plan. A production plan, however, needs to break down units by production, and quantify inputs and outputs. A production plan is essential for a complex organization which is producing a variety of different products. There will be differences, particularly in costs, associated with each type of product. Typically, the production plan will need to incorporate the costs associated with holding stock, the costs associated with changes in capacity, and any **opportunity costs**.

Aggregate planning is intermediate-range planning of general levels of employment and output to balance supply and demand. In this respect, the term 'aggregate' implies that the planning is carried out for groups of products (or product types) rather than individual products.

A planner would take into account the projected demand, capacity, and costs of various options in devising an aggregate plan. Typically, the variables considered would be the output rate, employment level, overtime/under-time, and subcontracting. The primary focus of aggregate planning is to achieve output objectives at the lowest possible cost.

It is rarely possible to structure a plan that guarantees optimal conditions, therefore planners often resort to trial-and-error methods to achieve an acceptable plan. The strategies which aggregate planners might try are to:

- maintain a level workforce and meet demand variations in some other manner;
- maintain a steady rate of output, and use some combination of inventories and subcontracting to meet demand variations (although varying employment levels are costly, disruptive, and result in low employee morale);
- match demand period by period with some combination of workforce variations, subcontracting, and inventories;
- use a combination of decision variables.

In order to plan effectively, estimates of the following issues must be available to planners:

- demand for each period;
- capacity for each period;
- costs (regular time, overtime, subcontracting, **back orders**, etc.).

However, in order to translate an aggregate plan into meaningful terms for production, it must be disaggregated (broken down into specific product requirements). This will assist in the determination of requirements in respect of labour, materials and inventories.

Brandimarte, Paolo and Villa, A., *Modeling Manufacturing Systems: From Aggregate Planning to Real-time Control*. Heidelberg: Springer Verlag, 1999.

Aggregation

Aggregation is the process of identifying the total value of a variable or measure by adding up or summing those variables or measures.

The term is especially used in macroeconomics as the most common items which are aggregated are demand, supply and expenditures on gross domestic product, which result in aggregate demand, aggregate supply, and aggregate expenditures.

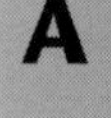

A business can use aggregation to make calculations into the aggregate values of demand, supply and expenditure across the broad range of its activities (especially if the business has multiple manufacturing and production facilities).

Agile manufacturing

The term 'agile' describes a manufacturing organization which aims to be as competitive as possible in what is often an unpredictable environment. An agile manufacturer is able to use its resources and adapt to change and uncertainty very quickly. Agile manufacturers aim to turn changes in the market into positive opportunities by producing a wide variety of different products which directly match the requirements of customers. Above all, these organizations are rapid in their responses and in their deployment of resources in order to achieve these goals. Generally an agile manufacturer would have empowered teams who are able to quickly adapt and use their skills, applying **multi-skilling** and understanding to immediate opportunities and customer demands.

Goldman, S. L., Nagel, R. N. and Preiss, K., *Agile Competitors and Virtual Organizations.* New York: Van Nostrand Reinhold, 1995.

Allocated stock

Allocated stock refers to parts, components or finished products which have been reserved either for a particular job, or for a particular customer, but have not yet been issued or despatched.

Allowance/allowance factor

During the calculation of an employee's performance rating, which would include their skills, effort, the working conditions and their consistency, it would be necessary to make some allowances to compensate for factors affecting the overall rating. Because the basic time in the calculation does not contain any allowances, these are usually calculated as a percentage (normally between 15% and 20%) of the basic times involved in each aspect of the work activity. Allowances will be given for:

- *Relaxation*, in order that employees can visit the toilets and rest areas and so that they can be given time to recover from the efforts of the job.
- *Contingency*, to compensate for the fact that many activities require additional tasks which were not incorporated into the basic time allocated to the specific job.
- *Tools and machines*, to compensate the employee for the amount of time required for machinery and equipment adjustments and the initial setting up of vital equipment.
- *Rejects*, which is not always considered, but would be essential in a production process that has a regular proportion of rejected or defective products.
- *Interference*, which compensates for time lost when one or more of the machines for which the employee is responsible has a breakdown.

- *Excess work*, which compensates for the additional workload thrust on the shoulders of the employees because of temporary or unexpected changes in their working conditions.

All-time order

'All-time order' is a term used to describe the very last order for a product which is in the last phase of its life cycle. The all-time order seeks to be large enough to cover any anticipated demand for that product, in the certain knowledge that it will no longer be available as a stock item.

Alternative work arrangements

Increasingly, management has looked for ways in which productivity, lower levels of sick and family leave, improved morale, recruitment and employee retention can be achieved. One such way is to introduce alternative work arrangements. The system, when applied to situations where the employer still requires the workforce to attend work at a specific location, helps reduce traffic and parking pressures, as well as extending hours of cover and service to customers or clients.

Typically, there has been a shift from standard working hours, with fixed arrival and departure times, to a more flexible approach. Alternatively, employees can work longer shifts for up to four days a week under **compressed working week** systems.

Clearly there is also an opportunity here within the scope of alternative working arrangements to offer employees the opportunity to work at home, perhaps engaged in telecommuting or tele-work.

The normal procedure in setting up a system of alternative working arrangements requires the cooperation of both the employees and their immediate manager. Normally decisions will be based on the job function for which the individual is responsible, taking into account staffing needs, budgetary considerations and the availability of space in the office. Work schedules still need to be maintained and there needs to be a degree of supervision in all cases of alternate working arrangements. The introduction of such arrangements needs to be advantageous both to the business and to the employees in question and should be viewed in consideration of any associated advantages and disadvantages to both parties.

Estess, Patricia Schiff, *Work Concepts for the Future: Managing Alternative Work Arrangements*. Los Altos, CA: Crisp Publications, 1996.

Andon

Andon is a Japanese term which refers to a system that picks up on defects which have occurred on an **assembly line**. Warning lights are activated when a defect is found and the assembly line is then stopped until the cause of the defect has been identified and dealt with.

See also ***jidoka***.

Annualized hours

An annualized hours scheme is an agreement between an employer and an employee to establish the total number of hours worked by that employee within a given year. The system is often applied to industries which have recognizable seasonal peaks and troughs in terms of demand. It can be seen as a way of obviating the need for overtime and has increasingly become prevalent in banking and financial services, as they have moved towards call-centre-based operations. The system itself is fairly straightforward in as much as a calculation is made as to the total number of annual hours worked, based on an agreed number of hours per week. This figure is then amended, taking into account public holidays and annual leave. The remaining number of hours is then scheduled as a pattern throughout the year.

In other industries, such as offshore drilling operations, annualized hours schemes accommodate a pattern of intensive two-week periods onsite and two-week periods off on leave. As far as businesses operating in Europe are concerned, there is a requirement to adhere to the **Working Time Regulations**. These state that the number of hours worked per week should not exceed 48 hours and that minimum rest periods must be incorporated into the system.

The gradual introduction of annualized hours has caused considerable difficulties and **trade unions** have been keen to ensure that intensive working does not undermine health and safety, overtime opportunities and other fundamental rights. Annualized hours can also be applied to part-time workers, where the system is applied on a pro-rata basis.

A

Grant-Garwood, Carole and Grisenthwaite, Michael, *Tolley's Practical Guide to the Working Time Directive and Regulations*. Oxford: Tolley Publishing, 1998.

Applied research

Applied research, as opposed to **basic research**, offers immediate commercial application in operations management. Typically, applied research will take place in order to analyse a particular process system, or related activity, with the specific intention of identifying and recommending potential improvements. The use of applied research can be considered to be an ongoing process by which an organization, a university or a commercial research organization, systematically investigates key aspects of a manufacturing business's operations.

Appraisal costs

Appraisal costs are ongoing costs associated with activities aimed at determining and monitoring current quality levels. The investigations will include checks, tests, inspections, the monitoring of customer views, and **benchmarking** activities.

An organization will place a considerable emphasis on appraisal. However, the system does need to be stable and sophisticated. In other words, if the appraisal system can cope with increased and widespread checking, measuring and monitoring procedures, quality improvements can be obtained. Typically, the appraisals will draw attention to weaknesses such as areas where performance has deteriorated and which therefore need specific attention. If appraisals are not carried out in relation to quality issues, then the level of quality will deteriorate. A business will try to balance the amount of time, effort and costs associated with appraisal, as more effective systems will pick up on all of the key issues and a situation of diminishing returns may occur.

AQL

See **acceptable quality level.**

Arrow diagram

An 'arrow diagram' is another way of describing a **Project (Program) Evaluation and Review Technique (PERT)** or **critical path method (CPM)** chart.

An arrow diagram is a graphic description of sequential steps that must be completed before a project can be completed. The arrow diagram method which is utilized in PERT or CPM is a network of lines that connect all the elements related to the execution of a plan. Typically, it is represented graphically using either a horizontal or a vertical tree structure connecting all of the elements.

See also **activity-on-arrow** and **activity-on-node.**

Assemble to order (ATO)

Assemble to order (ATO) is a customer-driven production method. Normally a business will have a series of standard components, or bolt-ons, which create, in effect, a bespoke product for the customer. The customer chooses from the available components, which make up the overall product. The organization arranges its production methods to ensure that all of the most commonly requested components of the product are close at hand, enabling the business to produce a wide range of different product variations in a relatively short time. The key to the system is the ability to offer the customer the shortest possible **lead time**. An organization which uses ATO does not have any finished goods in stock; all products are made to order. Typical high street examples would include sandwich bars, which can create, using a range of readily available ingredients, a specified meal for the customer while they wait. In manufacturing, Dell Computers have geared much of their production system around ATO, enabling them to assemble, pack and ship customer-specified computer products in a comparatively short period of time.

Assembly line

An assembly line is an arrangement of machines, equipment and employees designed to produce a continuous flow, usually in **mass production** operations. The exact sequence of the operations is determined by the organization in order to provide the most economic and effective means of manufacturing the final product. The concept certainly appeared around the time of the Industrial Revolution, changing the entire work situation for employees. Some of the first assembly lines were used in the nineteenth century in the US in the meat-packing industries in Ohio and Chicago. However, assembly lines are most associated with Henry Ford, who designed his own assembly line in 1913. His three basic principles still hold true:

- The system should provide a planned, orderly and continuous progression of the product through the factory.
- Work is delivered to each employee, rather than the business relying on them and their initiative to find work.
- The components and their order of fitting determines the structure of the manufacturing process.

See also **Fordism**.

Assignable variation

Assignable variation is a form of variation in a process which occurs as a result of causes which can be identified. The principles of variation state that no two items are exactly alike, therefore there needs to be a degree of tolerance in accepting the fact that it is impossible to make two items exactly the same. However, the differences between two items can be measured and the reasons for those variations can be determined. An assignable variation is one which is due to a specific cause, whereas a chance variation is a random variation that does not have a specific cause.

Associative forecasting

Associative forecasting can be used when historical observations indicate that there is a relationship between a dependent variable, y (for example, demand), and an independent variable, x (selected by the analyst), i.e., when x changes, y changes. The relationship will be expressed as an equation, such as a straight line ($y = a + b\,x$).

Using the historical observations, the coefficients in the equation are determined using regression analysis:

$$b = \frac{n(\Sigma xy) - (\Sigma x)\,(\Sigma y)}{n(\Sigma x^2) - (\Sigma x)^2}$$

$$a = \frac{\Sigma y - b\Sigma x}{n}$$

The resulting equation is used to develop the forecast.

Attribute

An attribute is a property or characteristic that is common to some or all of the instances of an entity. In terms of a product or a process, an attribute is a component feaure, which is usually qualitative, rather than quantitative in nature.

Attribute data, then, are qualitative data, which can be counted for recording and analysis. Control charts based on attribute data can deal with the number of affected units, count-per-unit, or quality score. An attribute may be a negative quality, such as a defect.

Attributes sampling

'Attributes sampling' is a term used in quality assurance. When a business is sampling, a 'yes or no' attribute is measured (such as 'defective' or 'not defective').

Automatic guided vehicle (AGV)

An automatic guided vehicle is a driverless machine which is used in warehouses and factories to move materials around. In essence, an AGV replaces the traditional manned forklift truck for some of these tasks.

Increasingly, materials are packed onto standard pallets (this is necessary as the AGV requires this degree of standardization in the form of the items that it can move). The AGV system is informed of the location of the pallet which needs to be moved and is then instructed as to where the pallet is required to be placed in the factory or the warehouse. The AGV will move to pick up the pallet and then, by means of wires or magnets set into the floor (or laser beams), the AGV navigates around the premises to the desired location. An AGV may be managed by a **warehouse management system (WMS)**.

Automation

'Automation' refers to manufacturing processes which are largely controlled by machinery driven by software and monitored (and amended) by employees.

There are, generally, three different forms of automation, as can be seen in Table 1.

Autonomation

Autonomation is a ***jidoka***-related term which refers to the act of stopping a production line when an employee identifies a defective part or product.

Autonomous maintenance

Autonomous maintenance is a **total preventive/productive maintenance (TPM)**-related issue. Each employee is allocated a specific machine to both operate and maintain. He or she is responsible for the inspection and repair of that machine, as well as routine adjustments, cleaning and lubrication as and when it is required, according to a fixed set of instructions and criteria.

Table 1 Types of automation

Type of automation	Features	Considerations
Fixed automation	Uses high-cost and specialized equipment for a fixed sequence of operations, offering low cost and high volume. The main limitations are the lack of variety of the units and high costs associated with major changes in products or processes.	The most rigid of the three types as it uses high-cost equipment in a series of fixed processes. Ideal for high-volume, low-cost units where there is little variation.
Programmable automation	Effectively, **computer-aided design/manufacturing (CAD/CAM) or computer numerical control (CNC)**. The main limitations of these machines are the employee skills needed to program them and the machines' inability to detect wear and variations in materials. The system could also incorporate Directed Numerical Control (DNC) machines, which are controlled by a computer. Alternatively, robots which are powered pneumatically, hydraulically or electronically could be used.	Highly flexible, but uses high-cost and general purpose machinery. Process sequence changing is relatively simple and the automation process should be capable of producing a wide variety of low-volume products in small batches. The use of CNC and robots is typical. Computer-aided design/manufacturing (CAM) ranges from robots to fully automated quality control.
Flexible automation	Essentially three options, which include: a **manufacturing cell (MC)** in which a small number of CNC are used to produce similar products; a **flexible manufacturing system (FMS)**, where a group of machines can be reprogrammed to produce a variety of similar products; or a system of **computer-integrated manufacturing (CIM)**, which deploys an integrated computer system to link a range of manufacturing processes.	These systems are derived from programmable automation, except that they use more customized equipment. FMS requires shorter change-over periods, allowing the organization to have almost continuous operation and the ability to produce a wide variety of products. FMS typically uses supervisory computer control, automatic material handling as well as robots.

Available-to-promise (ATP)

The available-to-promise (ATP) is a business function which sets the capabilities that support responses to customer orders. Traditionally, ATP involved a simple database lookup using a **master production schedule**.

With the advent of **e-business**, **make-to-order** production and high-variety product offerings, ATP functionality has become a critical component of business strategy and now requires a far more sophisticated and complex model, not to mention information technology support services. ATP can be typified as being either a push-based model (push system), which allocates resources and prepares information based on forecasted demand, or a pull-based model (pull system), which generates responses to actual customer orders.

See **push and pull systems.**

Average aggregate inventory value (AAIV)

AAIV measures the total value of all the items currently held in an organization's inventory. It can be expressed in the following manner:

$$\text{Average aggregate inventory value} = \text{Total value of all items held in inventory}$$

The organization can use this data in order to calculate the number of weeks' supply currently held:

$$\text{Weeks of supply} = \frac{\text{Average aggregate inventory value}}{\text{Weekly sales (at cost)}}$$

The AAIV also has applications for a business wishing to calculate the inventory turnover:

$$\text{Inventory turnover} = \frac{\text{Annual sales (at cost)}}{\text{Average aggregate inventory value}}$$

Back flush

Back flush or back flushing aims to simplify the management of an organization's inventory. An organization may adopt the policy of noting a reduction in the inventory when components are taken from stock in order to be incorporated into another product. Technically, the components, until they are shipped, are still within the inventory system and until they are shipped there may be a requirement for the organization to select more of those components to go into the current production process. Back flushing means that the organization only reduces the number of components on the inventory once the finished products containing those components have been shipped and they are no longer in stock.

The system does mean that the organization will not have a clear idea of how many of the relevant components are still physically within the organization, and it may not take into account the fact that components, having been removed from stock for production, are subsequently not all used. However, providing the organization is aware of how many components are being used to create a particular product and then multiplies that by the number of products in a given shipment, it can arrive at an accurate estimation of how many of those components need to be removed from the inventory count. This means that back flushing reduces the requirement for the organization to carry out data collection exercises to track the progress and location of components while they are still within the organization's premises.

Back office/front office

A business will often determine which part of the organization will have contact with customers. The front office is the customer interface area which aims to deal with customer demands and expectations, allowing the back office to continue to concentrate on tasks which support the running of the organization as well as supporting the efforts of the front office.

The front office handles the delivery of service systems to the customer, allowing the back office not to be exposed and pressurized by customer demands, thereby spreading the demands and managing the capacity of the organization.

Back order

Back orders occur when a business is unable to fulfil a customer order immediately. The customers are informed that items from their order are at present unavailable, but that their order will be fulfilled as soon as the manufacturer is in a position to place additional stock at their disposal.

Backward loading

Backward loading or back loading is a production planning methodology. As the term implies, the production plan is calculated backwards from the date by which the product or products are required. The production plan is then inserted into the overall production schedule of the organization, taking into account available slack periods in production capacity. In other words, the time on machinery, or employees' time, is allocated to that particular production on the basis of available gaps. By slotting in the requirements of the production to available machine or man hours, the organization is able to identify a precise start date for the production. Backward loading does not aim to create a detailed schedule, but simply seeks to ensure that either machines or employees are working to full capacity on any given day by the addition of this extra work.

Backward scheduling

Backward scheduling can be differentiated from **backward loading** as it aims to create a detailed schedule for each stage in the production process and then matches available periods of under-capacity, in which particular stages of the production could be allocated. Like backward loading, as the term implies, backward scheduling begins with the date by which the product is required and then, by allocating each operation from the detailed schedule, a start date can be determined.

Balance delay

'Balance delay' is a term associated with line-balancing problems. Line balancing itself is one of the most important problems in the preliminary design stage for flow-line production systems.

For a given set of manufacturing operations and a given cycle time, the line-balancing problem is the assigning of each operation to a work station in such a way that the number of work stations is minimized and precedence constraints are satisfied. The work station time (which is the sum of the times required for all operations at this work station) must not exceed the given cycle time.

The difference between the cycle time and work station time is called 'idle time' and the sum of idle time for all work stations is called 'balance delay time'. The balance delay time will be minimal in cases where the number of workstations is kept to a minimum. A generalized line-balancing problem consists of distributing operations among work stations while minimizing criteria different from the number of work stations (i.e. costs, productivity, reliability, maintainability) and then taking into account some additional constraints.

Balanced scorecard

A balanced scorecard is an integrated means of measuring organizational performance. Aside from looking at the organization's ability to innovate, manage finances and deal with customers, it also addresses internal operations, including human resource management.

Very few organizations are able to effectively align their strategies and thus operate at maximum efficiency. Using the concept of a balanced scorecard, a business can seek to understand, all the way down to individuals within the organization, the exact nature of the key performance indicators that need to be controlled, and facilitate the understanding of relationships within the organization. Whilst the deployment of a balanced scorecard system can help in this understanding, its true value is in enabling a business to implement and track key initiatives. This means providing across the length and breadth of the business a greater vision and utilization of resources.

Kaplan, Robert S., Lowes, Arthur and Norton, David P., *Balanced Scorecard: Translating Strategy into Action*. Cambridge, MA: Harvard Business School Press, 1996.

Kaplan, Robert S. and Norton, David P., *Strategy-focussed Organization: How Balanced Scorecard Companies Thrive in the New Business Environment*. Cambridge, MA: Harvard Business School Press, 2000.

Baldrige Award

The Baldrige Award is based on an analysis of the factors which contribute towards the creation and running of an effective organization.

The critical factors are identified as being leadership, a people focus, a customer focus, a supplier focus, planning for improvement, process optimization and organizational performance. In this respect, the Baldrige Award examines the quality of an organization's activities in seven categories:

- Leadership
- Information and Analysis;
- Strategic Planning;
- Human Resource Development and Management;
- Process Management;
- Business Results;
- Customer Focus and Satisfaction;

The seven categories are examined in terms of 'Examination Items' and 'Areas to Address'. Examination Items consist of sets of Areas to Address; there are 24 Examination Items. Although the award was designed primarily for the private sector, it is equally applicable for the public sector.

www.quality.nist.gov
European Federation for Quality Management (EFQM) at www.efqm.org

Bar code

See **electronic point of sale (EPOS)**.

Basic research

Basic research is typified as being an attempt to increase general knowledge of production and manufacturing issues, without this necessarily having any immediate application. Basic research investigates key areas of operations management, principally fundamental issues which affect a number of different industries across a number of sectors. The results of the research do not offer either the research organization or the organizations which contribute towards the investigations during the research any short-term expectation of commercial gain.

Batch

A batch is a defined quantity of a product or material produced under uniform conditions.

The term 'batch', when applied to a system or a mode of production, implies that all of the necessary operations are collected and processed at one time. This is as opposed to them being processed as they arrive.

Once a batch is under way it proceeds to completion without additional input or user interaction.

Batch processing

Batch processing is a somewhat traditional means by which an organization periodically produces a set amount of a particular product, before switching production to the processing of another product. In this respect the processing of a batch of items aims to build up a stock which can meet subsequent demand. One of the biggest problems that a business faces in using batch processing is to work out exactly how large each batch should be. There are implications related to whether the batch sizes are small or large. Clearly every time the manufacturing process is reconfigured in order to produce a batch of a particular product there are associated set-up costs and delays. However, when an organization is tempted to produce larger batches, there are implications with regard to the value of that stock, which may not be sold to customers immediately, and equally, the fact that the business cannot be processing other products while the larger batch is being processed. On the one hand larger batches offer lower costs in terms of set-up, as the change-overs are less frequent, but on the other hand there is the problem of having to carry excess inventory until such a time as it is sold. Increasingly businesses try to be flexible and adaptable in the way they configure their processing equipment and switch from one batch to another. Characteristically, a **flexible manufacturing system (FMS)** is now applied to most traditional batch manufacturing situations.

It is generally held that there are four types of batch processing operations; these are shown in Table 2.

Central to the planning of batch processing are three key factors:

- The sequence of the batches, which will determine the order in which the batches of different items or customers are processed.
- The decision regarding batch sizes or **lot sizing**. In other words the quantity of each item, or customer, that is processed or dealt with at any one time.
- The scheduling of the batches, which aims to determine how the batches are to be processed using the available equipment, and the implications of processing a particular product or customer, in relation to other customers or products which need to be processed.

Hansen, Per Brinch (ed.), *Classic Operating Systems: From Batch Processing to Distributed Systems*. New York: Springer Verlag, 2001.

B

Table 2 Batch processing systems

Type of operation	Description
Supply	There are considerable cost benefits in being able to deliver to several customers simultaneously. Using batch processing in supplying situations, the business will accumulate customers, probably by geographical area, until such a time as it is cost effective to load the customers' orders into a single vehicle for delivery. In this application the customers are dealt with in batches rather than the products themselves.
Service	In some service situations, particularly in the entertainment or leisure industries, customers are also batched. A particular event, such as the departure of a tour, or the beginning of a ride, will not commence until sufficient customers warrant the activity to begin.
Transport	Increasingly some transport systems operate on a batch processing basis. Rather than running scheduled and timed routes, transport will leave a location (within given parameters) once a specified number of passengers have arrived and await transportation. This is an increasing trend, notably in the 'route-less hopper-style' bus transportation within city centres.
Manufacture	In manufacturing situations batch processing is often used to create output stock which is produced in anticipation of future demand. Batch processing can also be applied to situations when the organization has received sufficient orders from a variety of customers which then warrants the setting up of a batch process.

Batch shop

The term 'batch shop', when used of a manufacturing facility, may describe the entire manufacturing organization or a part of that organization which is designed to undertake **batch processing**. Typically a batch shop is an ideal manufacturing process set-up for products which warrant neither **mass production** nor small-scale production.

Bay

A 'bay' is a term most closely associated with a specified area within a warehouse. Normally each bay will be located between pillars or supporting structures within the overall building. In other words, a facility would have *n* number of interior sections, each of which would be called a bay. For organizational purposes the warehouse may choose to identify specific bays with the storage of specific products or ranges of products.

Bays may also be situated adjacent to a production line, either at the beginning of the line or at the end, as, in effect, holding areas or 'holding bays', with parts and components being held at one end and finished products housed at the other.

The term 'bay' is also associated with the process of loading and unloading vehicles, either at warehouses or at factories or retail outlets. Again, specific parts of an area which have vehicular access will be designated as loading or unloading bays for incoming or outgoing products or waste materials.

Benchmarks/benchmarking

Benchmarking is a process of identifying and learning from the best practices of similar activities being undertaken by other organizations. Benchmarking is used to:

- improve the business's understanding of the external environment;
- learn from the successes and failures of others;
- identify and compare elements of a competitor's strategy;
- learn best practices from any industry, to apply to and improve your own internal processes;
- minimize complacency; in other words, recognize that internal progress may not be apace with that of competitors;
- learn to be creative or proactive and not reactive.

It is generally believed that there are five steps towards benchmarking:

1 *Identifying what is to be benchmarked*. As it is not possible to benchmark everything at once, benchmarking should be applied to the most critical areas. A detailed study and measurement should be undertaken in the selected areas to identify base data as well as ensuring managerial support and the involvement of staff within those areas.
2 *Determining who to benchmark with*. It is essential to determine which other organization should be approached. Direct competitors are unlikely to be responsive, but non-direct competitors may be more willing to exchange information. Benchmarking candidates should encompass both small and large businesses, as well as those in the public or private sector.
3 *Data collection*. Face-to-face interviews and visits to other busi-

nesses often provide the best quality information. The correct questions need to be asked and cross-checked. Inaccuracy at this point may invalidate the whole process.

4 *Data analysis*. Meaningful comparisons need to be made between the business and the benchmarked organization. Steps should be taken to identify dissimilar or divergent issues, as well as entrepreneurial or novel ideas.
5 *Identifying and implementing proposals*. Having identified desirable components, the business now needs to plan how these will be implemented, ensuring clear communication. Changes may result in a need for training and for new criteria to be understood. There will be a period before full efficiency is achieved, and a monitoring system needs to be implemented to provide feedback.

The benchmarking process may reveal more valuable information to a potential competitor than the business may receive from that competitor. It requires a fundamental trust which reflects the rights and legalities of both parties. There are key ethical aspects in relation to benchmarking:

- dealing with individuals and organizations in an honest manner;
- ensuring that other parties understand how information will be used;
- promptly informing other parties if the use of information is to be changed;
- ensuring that all activities are carried out with integrity;
- the establishment of precise ground rules if a competitor is used in the benchmarking process.

Bogan, Christopher E. and English, Michael J., *Benchmarking for Best Practices: How to Define, Locate and Emulate the Best in Business*. New York: McGraw-Hill Education, 1994.

B

Best operating level

Given the fact that the term 'capacity' implies an attainable rate of output, it does not consider how long that rate can be sustained. In other words, if a manufacturing facility has a capacity of *x* units, it is unclear whether this refers to an average over a period of time or a peak performance at some point in the past.

In order to work around this problem, the concept of the best operating level is used as this is the level of capacity for which the process was designed. In addition, it is also the volume of output at which average unit cost is at a minimum.

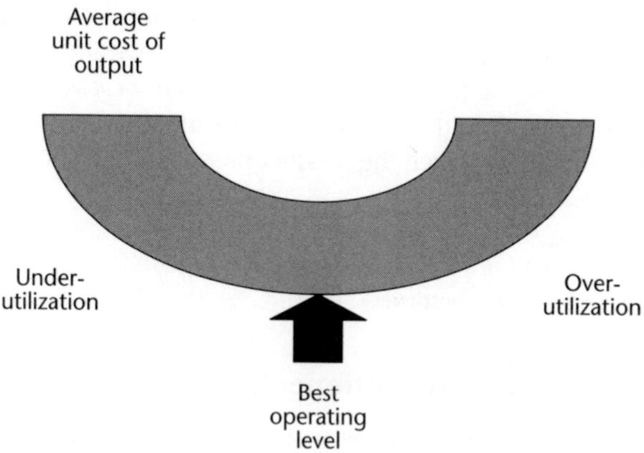

Figure 4 Best operating level

The best operating level can be shown as in Figure 4. If the output falls below this level, there is an instance of under-utilization and the average unit cost will increase as overheads must be allocated to fewer units. If the output goes above this level, there is an instance of over-utilization and the average unit cost also increases, due to the fact that there are overtime payments to made, increased equipment wear and tear, as well as higher levels of defects.

Bill of lading (BOL)

A bill of lading is a contract issued to a transportation company (a shipper), listing the goods shipped, acknowledging their receipt and promising delivery to the person or business named. Bills of lading are also known as manifests or waybills.

Bools, Michael, *The Bill of Lading – Document of Title*. London: LLP Professional Publishing, 1997.

B

Bill of materials (BOM)

A bill of materials (BOM) aims to list all of the parts, components and individual items which were used to create or manufacture a specific product. In essence, a bill of materials is rather like a list of parts, but it goes one stage further than this as the components, parts and other items are listed as they were added to the product. In other words, a careful examination of a BOM indicates how a product was assembled. Some organizations refer to a BOM as a formula or recipe. Careful examination of the BOM should indicate to the organization the precise ordering of production units and processes within the premises. Assuming that most products are constructed or assembled in this manner, a BOM should help the organization to identify the most common route along which the product passes on the shop floor.

Blocking

See **bottleneck and non-bottleneck.**

Bottleneck and non-bottleneck

'Bottleneck' and 'non-bottleneck' are terms associated with the management of the production process. A bottleneck is effectively a system which cannot, for a variety of reasons, reach the levels of capacity which are demanded. A bottleneck can, therefore, seriously limit the total amount of production on a given production line because production is limited to the total capacity which the bottleneck is able to achieve.

A non-bottleneck is part of a production process that does not appear to have an inherent limit on its ability to produce. In other words, its capacity is considerably higher than the demands placed upon it. Normally an organization would choose to block a non-bottleneck process in order to ensure that it only produces the level of output required. There are a number of reasons for this, the most important of which is that partly finished products produced by a non-bottleneck process consume items from the inventory, and therefore increase the amount of **work in progress**. A non-bottlenecked process will normally be limited to a defined level of output, usually controlled by a specified storage area. Once this storage area is full, production in the non-bottlenecked process is temporarily terminated.

Clearly, organizations seek to avoid blocking a bottleneck process because the bottleneck is already unable to reach the desired capacity levels and this would simply further limit the production capability.

See also **theory of constraints.**

Brainstorming

Brainstorming sessions would be carried out as a group activity. Individual members of the group are encouraged to put forward their first ideas about a problem and how it might be solved, in order to generate as many ideas as possible, even if they are not always usable alternatives. Brainstorming would involve members from various parts of the organization and is seen as a way of encouraging creativity and innovation. Sometimes the members of the group are required to literally shout out their first thoughts about a subject.

Breakeven analysis and the breakeven point

In order to identify an organization's breakeven point, it is necessary to consider the relationships between the various costs and sales in an integrated manner. The breakeven point is defined as being the point at which the level of sales is not great enough for the business to make a profit and yet not low enough for the business to make a loss. In other words, earnings from sales are just sufficient for the business to cover its total costs. This occurs when total revenue from sales exactly equals the total cost of production.

Breakeven point occurs when total cost = total revenue

From this it can be assumed that if total revenue from sales is greater than the total costs, then the organization concerned will make a profit. Conversely, if the opposite is true, and the total revenue is less than the total costs, then the organization can make a loss. It is essential that organizations take this very important factor into account. The organization will find that it is essential to determine how many units of output it must produce and sell before it can reach its breakeven point.

The total cost of the unit of production is made up of two factors, the fixed and variable costs, where:

Total cost = fixed costs + variable costs

And the total revenue is given by the number of products sold, multiplied by the selling price:

Total revenue = price × quantity

The drawing up and labelling of a breakeven chart makes the calculation of the breakeven point easier. The breakeven chart requires a considerable amount of labelling in order to be able to identify exactly what the chart is describing about the breakeven point.

As can be seen in Figure 5, the breakeven chart will include:

- Units of production – which is considered to be the number of completed products and not, importantly, the components which make up those products.
- Fixed costs (FC) – which are the costs that do not alter in relation to changes in demand or output. They have to be paid regardless of the business's trading level.

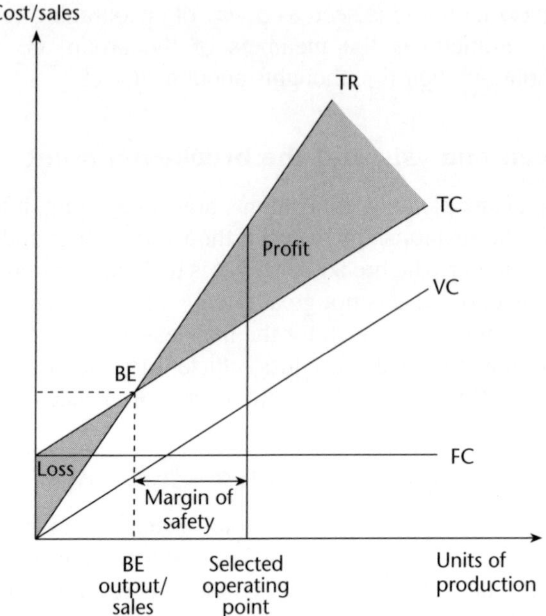

Figure 5 A breakeven chart

- Variable costs (VC) – which change in direct proportion to changes in output, such as the cost of raw materials, components, labour and energy. Breakeven charts require the assumption that some costs vary in direct proportion to changes in output. In fact, it is unlikely that any costs are totally variable as raw materials, for example, are likely to cost less per unit if the organization buys in bulk. In this instance, it cannot be assumed that the cost of raw materials will double if output doubles.
- Total costs (TC) – these are simply the sum of all fixed and variable costs.
- Sales and costs – sales are the income generated from the selling of the units of production to customers. Costs, on the other hand, are expenses incurred by the organization in the purchase of raw materials, other fixed costs and variable costs.
- Breakeven point (BE) – this is the point at which sales levels are high enough for the organization not to make a loss, but not high enough for it to make a profit. In other words, this is the point where total sales equal total costs.
- Profit – in terms of the breakeven chart, and the breakeven point, this is achieved when sales exceed total costs.

- Loss – in terms of the breakeven chart, and the breakeven point, this occurs when the total revenue (TR) from sales has not met the total costs.
- Selected operating point – this is the planned production and sales level.
- Margin of safety – this is the amount by which the selected operating point exceeds the breakeven point. This indicates the amount by which sales could fall from the planned level before the organization ceases to make a profit.

Bucket brigade

Bucket brigades are a means of organizing the workforce on a flow line so that the line actually balances itself.

Products move progressively down the production line, gradually being added to and processed until they are completed. The products physically move and the employees remain (relatively) static. It is notoriously difficult to balance the workloads; this is usually undertaken by precise identification of the work elements, and estimates of standard work-content. Many assembly lines are balanced by engineers, who define task elements and then conduct time-and-motion studies so that the work can be divided equally among operatives on the line.

Bucket brigades, however, are designed to be self-organizing as each worker carries a product towards completion; when the last worker finishes his or her product it is sent it off and the worker moves back upstream to take over the work of his or her predecessor, who moves back and takes over the work of the next predecessor and so on, until after relinquishing the product, the first worker moves back to the start to begin a new product.

If operatives are sequenced from slowest to fastest, then the operatives will spontaneously gravitate to the optimal division of work so that throughput is maximized. It is imperative that the operatives maintain their sequence; no passing is allowed, which sometimes means that one worker is blocked by a successor and has to wait before work can resume (the successor having moved out of the way).

The primary benefits of the system are:

- there is a reduced need for planning and management;
- production becomes more flexible and agile;
- throughput is increased;
- secondary labour is reduced and quality improved;
- there is minimal work-in-process;
- training and coordination are simplified.

Buffering

Buffering is a means by which an organization attempts to ensure that it has a safe level of stock in addition to its base stock. The organization will attempt to ensure that there is sufficient inventory available to satisfy the average demand over a given period of time. The buffer stock is the extra amount which the organization holds to protect it against uncertain situations. The eternal problem is where this buffer stock should be stored and by whom. Clearly no organization in the **supply chain** wants to have the responsibility and the associated costs of holding buffer stock. None the less, at each level of the supply chain there may be an immediate need for stock in excess of the base stock. Therefore either the organization itself has to take the responsibility for holding that buffer stock, or it has to come to some arrangement with the suppliers, who will hold the buffer stock on its behalf. How complex and time-consuming the transformation of stock received from suppliers is before it can be sold on to the organization's customers, is a major determinant in who will hold the buffer stock. Manufacturers who require long **lead times** to produce a product would not consider the option of requiring their suppliers to hold buffer stock to be a viable option. In this respect there may be no other alternative but to **build to forecast** a certain percentage of their output, which can then be transferred and earmarked as buffer stock. Organizations which simply **build to customer order** may not have the facility to set aside products as buffer stock. They will need to be more flexible and more reliant on their suppliers to ensure that necessary parts and components are immediately available in the event of unexpected levels of demand.

The way in which many businesses approach the concept of buffering reflects the ways in which operations management has developed over the past few years. Examples of systems in differing businesses are shown in Figure 6. In the past, a business believed that it was unable to deal with the fluctuations which occurred external to the organization. Physical buffering had to be in place (in the form of finished products) to ensure that demand could be satisfied. This was a standard practice regardless of the fact that the business might be able to increase its output to cope with an increase in demand.

Operations managers were not considered to be expert enough to deal with organizational issues outside their immediate area of involvement. To this end, human resources managers were deployed to deal with employees who would work in operations. Operations management itself is, in effect, buffered from the outside by supporting functions within the organization, as can be seen in Figure 7.

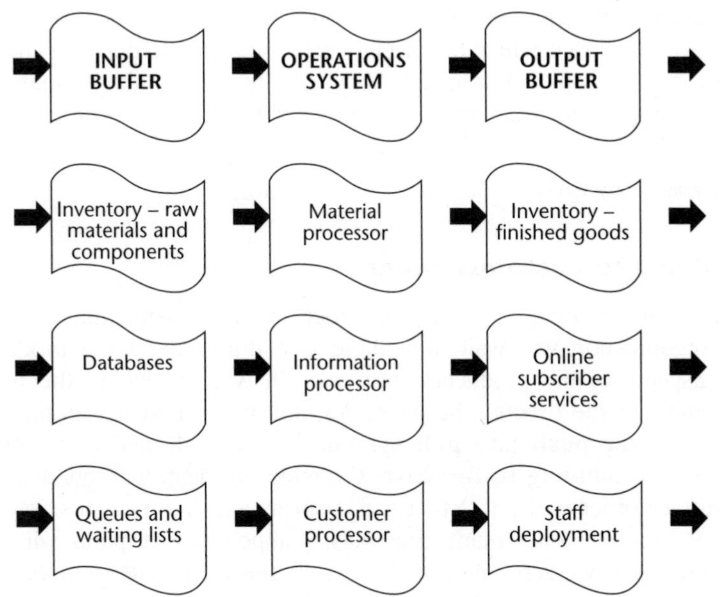

Figure 6 Physical buffering system

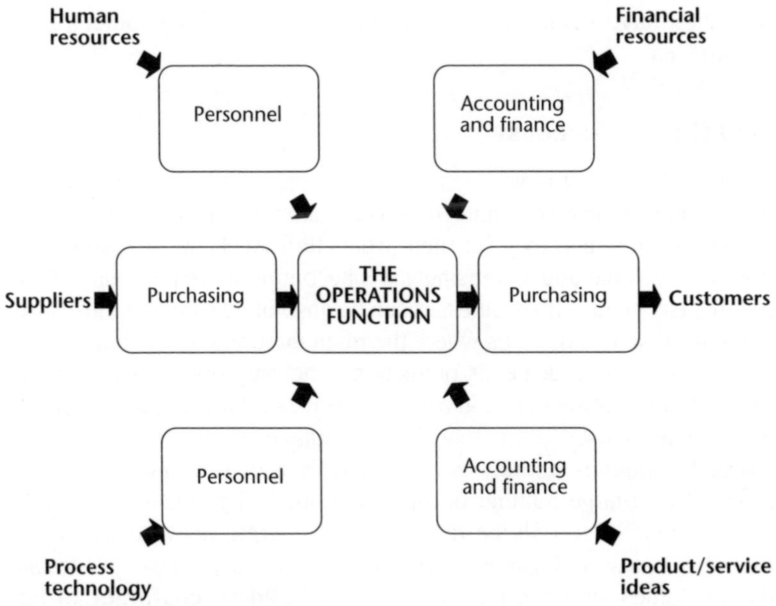

Figure 7 External buffering systems

This continued process means that operations fail to get to grips with the external issues which may well affect their ability to operate, and to learn how to cope with change. Above all, they are unable to manage their own resources as so many other elements of the organization have an input.

See also **safety stock.**

Building to customer order

The term 'building to customer order' refers to situations where an organization will wait until there is a firm order for a product. All aspects of the production process will wait, including the final assembly of the product, its packaging and its despatch. This pulling aspect of the **push and pull system**, by the customer, is in direct contrast to **building to forecast**. The major problem with building to customer order is the fact that the business is never in a position to know precisely how many materials, components or parts will be required at any given time in order to fulfil these customer orders. The problem, of course, extends to the suppliers, who may be expected to deliver the necessary supplies to the manufacturer at extremely short notice. It is often the case that manufacturing organizations which build to order actually order to forecast from their suppliers, in order to ensure that they have sufficient stock should they receive customer orders themselves.

Building to forecast

In the past, the vast majority of manufacturers built to forecast. In other words, they made an estimate, based on historical data and trends in the market, from which they set their production levels. Most markets are now very volatile and increasingly it is becoming more perilous to build to forecast because no businesses can be absolutely sure that these forecasts are real. In situations where the manufacturers do not have timely or accurate customer-needs predictions, the only option is to build to forecast and run the risk, and associated costs, of holding the inventory in their warehouses. Ultimately, if the manufacturers get the building-to-forecast estimates entirely wrong, then they may be faced with the prospect of a large number of unwanted finished goods in their warehouses, which can only be dealt with by offering heavy discounts or clearance sales. No business wishes to do this and increasingly, despite the difficulties, they are moving across to **build to customer order**, with all of the necessary implications related to their own production schedules and those of their suppliers.

Bullwhip effect

The bullwhip effect occurs in a **supply chain** and is caused by differing perceptions of demand. In complex supply chains, which may involve a raw materials supplier, a manufacturer, a distributor, a series of retailers and a wide number of customers, there will always be differences, or variations, in demand. The bullwhip effect occurs when a part of the supply chain interprets the demand or forecasted demand from its customers at a different rate from the level at which the next organization in the chain had anticipated demand from them. Generally there are four reasons why the bullwhip effect occurs (these are listed in Table 3).

The bullwhip effect is sometime referred to as the Forrester effect. The Forrester effect is, similiarly, where small changes in one part of the supply chain cause wild fluctuations elsewhere.

Lee, Hau L., Padmanabhan, V. and Whang, Seungjin, 'The Bullwhip Effect in Supply Chains', *Sloan Management Review*, Spring 1997, pp. 93–102.

Business process re-engineering (BPR)

BPR makes a fundamental and systematic reappraisal of the way in which an organization operates. For many organizations this is a painful experience which may lead to considerable downsizing. BPR aims to identify and then eliminate any aspect of the business which does not add value. This would include reducing the level of employment, flattening the organization chart, and a reappraisal of any reward systems. One of the major outcomes of BPR is **job enlargement**. Generally, BPR is associated with an impersonal management approach, purely focused on profitability and productivity.

Champy, James and Hammer, Michael, *Re-engineering the Corporation: A Manifesto for Business Revolution*. London: Nicholas Brealey Publishing, 2001.

Business requirements planning (BRP)

Business requirements planning is a holistic approach which incorporates business, sales and production plans, ensuring that they are consistent with one another and that the management has seen to it that resources, where needed, are made available. Once this has been achieved, the BRP then incorporates a **master production schedule**

Table 3 Reasons for the bullwhip effect

Cause	Description and effect	Solution
Updating demand forecast	Normally a business will tend to base its forecasts of demand with reference to its own customers and demand history. Each member of the supply chain will identify different fluctuations in demand and thus amplify the bullwhip effect up and down the supply chain.	Theoretically, the members of the supply chain could attempt to use the same demand forecasts, based on the forecasts predicted by those who sell to the end-user. However, technology has begun to deal with these differences in demand forecasting, specifically through the collection of information from **electronic point of sale** systems, **electronic data interchange (EDI)** and **vendor managed inventory** systems.
Periodic ordering, or batch ordering	Normally organizations will place orders with their suppliers in order to ensure that they have sufficient products or components to last them for a specified period of time. These orders are made in the knowledge that the business will not necessarily consume them by production or sell all of the order immediately. It is done to reduce the costs of each transaction and associated transportation costs. Because organizations which supply these businesses cannot necessarily predict the frequency of the batch orders, demand fluctuations occur.	Electronic ordering systems, cumulative discounts and other methods aimed at reducing transaction costs can be used, as can the outsourcing of deliveries to businesses set up to transport smaller quantities of products or components.

⇒

Table 3 Reasons for the bullwhip effect (*continued*)

Cause	Description and effect	Solution
Price changes	It is in a business's nature to wish to purchase products or components when prices are low, thereby having sufficient stock in order to cover periods when prices have increased. When prices are low an enormous level of demand is generated, which causes a huge bullwhip effect further up the supply chain.	Price stability is the key, and by using **activity-based costing**, a supplier can identify factors which may cause a fluctuation in price. In dealing with these aspects of production, the supplier can seek to offer a much more predictable and stable pricing level.
Rationing	In many areas of business there are inevitable periods of under-supply and over-supply caused by a variety of factors, notably seasonal trends. Customers who are aware that a period of under-supply is about to be entered will inflate their orders to ensure that they have their own sufficient supplies to last them over the under-supply period. This simply increases the under-supply problem, causing a bullwhip effect up the supply chain.	The clearest solution is to advise customers of periods when there will be shortages, which should allow them, over a period of time, to adjust their orders to compensate.

and **capacity requirements planning** in order to ensure that the overall levels of capacity are sufficient to meet expected demand. Naturally this would include an investigation into the level of supply, warehousing availability and any associated production schedules.

Schultz, Terry R., *BRP: The Journey to Excellence*. Milwaukee, WI: Forum, 1984.

Call centres

A sales, customer service and direct marketing term used to describe a location or facility designed to take and make inbound and outbound telephone communications. Call centres are widely used for telemarketing by businesses aiming at direct sales contact with prospects.

Increasingly, call centres are located in areas remote from the regions they directly serve; this is largely due to the enormous cost differentials enjoyed by businesses prepared to relocate their call centres in less developed nations. Costs, in terms of both pay and premises, are considerably lower in countries such as India. Other notable call-centre-orientated countries include the Republic of Ireland, a country to which there has been a considerable exodus because of low pay rates and the fact that English is the primary language, as well as active canvassing towards businesses.

Another major trend in call centres is that many businesses have taken the step to outsource to dedicated call-centre facilities which are able to man the centre continuously. In addition, using the differentials in time zone, call-centre outsourcing allows the business to have total 365-day coverage in normal business hours, again reducing costs by not employing staff during unsocial hours.

Capability and maturity (Hayes and Wheelwright's Four Stages)

Hayes and Wheelwright identified four stages of manufacturing competitiveness, as illustrated in Figure 8. The implications and descriptions of these four stages are summarized in Table 4.

Hayes, Robert H., and Wheelwright, Steven C., *Restoring our Competitive Edge: Competing through Manufacturing*. New York: John Wiley, 1984.

Capacity

Simply, capacity is the maximum rate of output for a given process. It is usually measured in output per unit of time. Businesses will tend to use

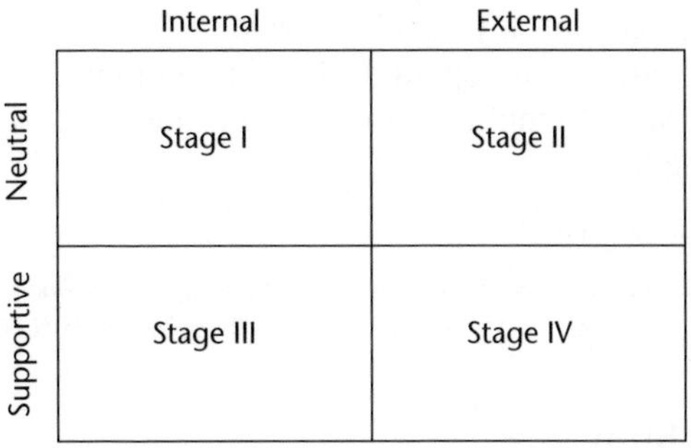

Figure 8 The four stages of manufacturing competitiveness

Table 4 The four stages of manufacturing competitiveness

Stage	Description and implications
I	Businesses consider their manufacturing organization to be internally neutral; their purpose is to manufacture products without a hitch. Their designs are very innovative and providing that the marketing department does it job, then the products will sell well.
II	Businesses look beyond the internal, yet are externally neutral in terms of manufacturing. The business follows standard manufacturing processes and standards, buying components and production equipment from the same suppliers as its competitors. It has similar ways of dealing with employees and similar standards in terms of quality and control systems.
III	These are businesses with an internally supportive manufacturing base; systems are coordinated and aim to achieve a degree of competitive advantage.
IV	These businesses have externally supportive manufacturing systems which aim to gain a competitive edge over their rivals. These businesses do not copy the competitors; they aspire to be as good as the competitors (not necessarily better).

different units of time in order to calculate their capacity, such as reckoning it per minute, per hour, per day or per shift. In truth, the maximum capacity is much better described as being the demonstrated capacity, as this is the true level of capacity which has been achieved. Some organizations and analysts will attempt to calculate a theoretical capacity, which is largely based on the capacity of the machines involved and rarely takes into account any variables which may affect the capacity. Businesses will attempt to operate at their optimum capacity. This means that they will attempt to reduce costs or loss of capacity associated with waiting time.

See also **waiting time in line**.

McNair, C. G. and Vangermeersch, R. (eds), *Total Capacity Management: Optimizing at the Operational, Tactical and Strategic Levels*. Boca Raton, FL: St Lucie Press, 1998.

Capacity cushion

An organization's capacity cushion is equal to the amount of capacity it has in excess of expected demand. It is normally calculated using the following formula:

$$\frac{\textit{Capacity} - \textit{expected demand}}{\textit{expected demanded}}$$

The figure is expressed as a percentage. Normally the higher the level of uncertainty which the organization has in terms of future demand, the larger the capacity cushion. Organizations who wish to be able to respond quickly to customer demand will build in a sizeable capacity cushion, enabling them to quickly increase their productivity of the production lines so as to soak up that new demand. Businesses which have standard products and a high level of capital intensity tend to have smaller capacity cushions, in order to offset the fixed costs of the equipment which they use.

Capacity focus

Capacity focus revolves around the notion that a manufacturing facility tends to believe that it works best when it focuses on a fairly limited set of production objectives. In other words, the organization should not attempt or expect to excel in every aspect of manufacturing performance.

This means that the organization should concentrate on a fairly limited range of goals (such as cost, quality, **flexibility**, new product development, reliability, shorter **lead times** or low investment) and not all of these issues. It should choose the goals that most closely match its organizational objectives.

As manufacturing technology has become more advanced and the competition more fierce, there is an increasing trend for organizations to attempt to do everything well and have multiple objectives. It is, however, also true that in certain sectors a business does not have to be excellent on all issues in order to compete effectively.

The capacity-focus concept can be achieved by having **plants within plants** (PWPs). Each of the PWPs will not only have separate sub-organizations, but will also use different equipment and process policies. They will also be able to institute different workforce management policies and production control methods. In this way, the desire to achieve efficiency and excellence in every area can be achieved in part by excellence in one of the PWPs.

Capacity management

Capacity management is the discipline that ensures that infrastructure is provided at the right time in the right volume at the right price. It also ensures that all of the inputs are used in the most efficient way.

Capacity management also involves input from various areas of the business, including the infrastructure to support the services, contingencies and associated costs. Typically, the inputs related to capacity management include:

- performance monitoring;
- workload monitoring;
- application sizing;
- resource forecasting;
- demand forecasting;
- modelling.

These processes create the results of capacity management: in other words, the plan itself, the forecasts, the data and the level of service guidelines.

Capacity requirements planning (CRP)

Capacity requirements planning (CRP) is the process of determining short-term output demands, either on an organization or on one of its production processes. CRP is a computerized system that projects the load from a **material requirements plan (MRP)** onto the capacity of the system and then identifies underloads and overloads. CRP is used by an organization to assess whether it can start new projects in the future, or whether it can produce an immediate order for a customer. Normally CRP will require information about when orders are required, details of equipment and labour, as well as orders which are already in the pipeline. The CRP will then be able to provide the organization with a profile for each operation in the production system. It will make a comparison between the work that needs to be completed and the work already in progress, in relation to the system's capacity. CRP relies on accurate information, defining capacity as a sum produced using the following formula:

Number of machines or employees × number of shifts × utilization of machines and workers × efficiency

CRP is therefore used to calculate the ability of the organization to meet its orders.

Capacity utilization rate (CUR)

CUR is the ratio of actual production, by business sector factories and other productive establishments, in the economy, compared with the total potential production of these establishments.

CUR can therefore indicate the productiveness or effectiveness of the factories within a specific sector. CUR is used by analysts and the government to make a judgement as to how close to full employment a sector or the country is, taking into account the fact that CUR fluctuates from day to day, month to month and year to year. Ideally, a CUR of 85 per cent is considered healthy in times of expansion as this is taken as a measure indicating being as close to full employment as may be possible. When the economy takes a down-turn and there is contraction in demand, the CUR could drop to as low as 70 per cent.

The CUR of the various sectors is combined to produce an overall picture of the economy, but this aggregate figure does not illustrate the peculiarities of the different sectors and the mixed fortunes which they may be experiencing.

CUR can also be used to determine a single business's capacity utilization, which is indeed the foundation of the CUR for the sector and ultimately the economy as a whole. CUR is, therefore, the percentage of a company's, industry's or country's production capacity which is actually used, over some period of time, otherwise known as the operating rate.

Carousel

A carousel is a storage system which brings the product to the picker in a warehouse, as opposed to the picker having to walk to the storage bin in which the product is being stored.

Typically, the storage bins are mounted on motor-driven chains and brought to the picker via a software management system which requires the picker to input a code relevant to the product or the storage bin. Using automated carousels, a warehouse can contain a much greater volume of products and storage bins as they can be stacked vertically far higher than would be possible if the picking was carried out manually. Not only is the warehousing more cost-effective in terms of stacking and storage ability, but the automated systems make each individual picker more productive (i.e. producing higher picking rates per person).

Carrying charge/cost

The term 'carrying charge' relates to a means by which decisions can be made regarding the inventory. Typically, the organization will take into account the cost of the capital required to hold a certain level of stock, an estimation of the number of items held in the inventory which are now obsolete, as well as the direct storage costs. The generally accepted carrying charge should not exceed 40 per cent of the total value of the inventory.

The carrying cost is calculated by multiplying the carrying charge by the average value of the inventory itself.

Casual labour

The employment of casual labour, or casual employees, is seen as a viable alternative by many employers to provide a degree of **flexibility**, particularly when demand may not be easy to predict. Casual labour is usually taken on a once-off job basis, or the individuals are placed on standby by the employer to come in occasionally and carry out work as and when required.

The term 'casual labour' also implies an employment situation where employees are given low pay, little or no training, no job security, sick or holiday pay, and where they can be discarded as and when the business sees fit. Casual labour has attracted the unfortunate nickname of 'flexploitation', which refers to situations where the lowest, minimum wage payments are made, often to individuals who are desperate for work and are prepared to ignore any associated dangers with the work they are asked to undertake.

Philips, Gordon and Whiteside, Noel, *Casual Labour: The Unemployment Question in the Port Transport Industry, 1880–1970*. Oxford: Oxford University Press, 1985.

Category management

Category management involves the identification of interchangeable or substitute products which could reasonably replace products required by the customer. The identified groups of products are brought together under one category so that they can be offered to the customer as alternatives, should the specific product demanded be unavailable, or if it has been superseded by another product in that category. Category management can be differentiated from an alternative means by which products are managed. In many cases businesses will manage products individually and they will have clearly identifiable differences from other products offered by that business. In this respect it is difficult for customers to perceive the level of substitution of alternative products offered by the same business.

Nielson Marketing Research, *Category Management: Positioning your Organization to Win*. Chicago, IL: Contemporary Books, 1997.

Cause-and-effect diagram

A cause-and-effect diagram is often referred to as a fishbone diagram (*see* **Ishikawa diagram**). The process of creating cause-and-effect diagrams usually has three steps. The first involves drawing the backbone arrow, at the end of which the effect is noted. The individuals involved in creating the diagram now identify the main areas which need to be investigated – which, in their opinion, are a cause of the effect. Once these general areas have been noted, the individuals can then flesh out the diagram, as can be seen in the example in Figure 9.

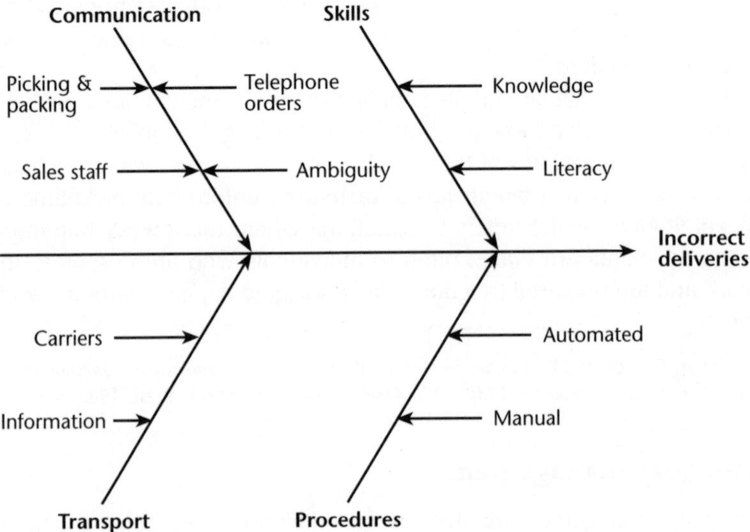

Figure 9 Dispersion analysis-type cause-and-effect diagram.

C

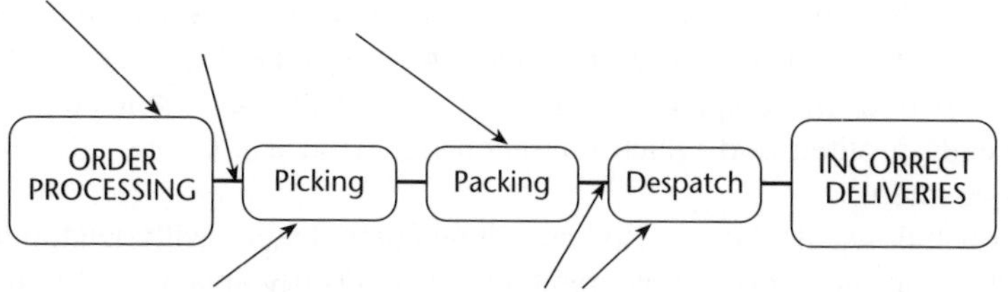

Figure 10 Production-process classification cause-and-effect diagram

Once this procedure has been completed, all of the factors which relate to the effect can be explored and their interrelationships examined. There are, however, two other different styles of cause-and-effect diagram, the first of which is known as the production-process classification cause-and-effect diagram and is shown in the diagram in Figure 10.

In a manufacturing, or **supply chain** environment, this form of cause-and-effect diagram is usually much more straightforward to complete as those involved in the construction of the diagram are intimately acquainted with the processes leading up to the effect. Note that in this example, there are a number of stages which have been independently identified as leading up to the effect. Each of these issues will have its own series of sub-considerations.

The other alternative is a cause-enumeration-type diagram. This type of cause-and-effect diagram is constructed in an entirely different manner. All of the possible causes are noted first and then the chart is drawn, showing the relationship of the causes to one another. This approach is far more flexible as the list of potential causes may be far more comprehensive than when trying to fit them onto a pre-drawn cause-and-effect diagram.

Ishikawa, Kaoru, *Guide to Quality Control.* Tokyo: Asian Productivity Organization, 1991.

C

Cash flow

'Cash flow' is a term used to describe the net funds which have flowed through an organization over a period of time. Traditionally, cash flow is usually defined as earnings. The identification of when those earnings were received and when payments had to be made defines the parameters of cash flow. Estimating cash flow is often complicated by the actual value of the cash received in a given period. The level of cash flow does not take into account expenses which may have been incurred by the organization prior to the period the cash flow covers, yet during this period the organization is benefiting from those costs in the past. Equally, the reverse is true; payments may now be due over the cash flow period on equipment or stock, from which the organization has already profited and which has been noted on a previous cash flow assessment.

Cash flow calculation also has a difficulty in dealing with outstanding debts and money owed by creditors. These do not appear on the cash flow as neither has been paid, yet they are important considerations, as they may have a negative or positive effect on the available working capital of the organization. The available funds which are calculated and identified within the cash flow have enormous implications for the business, particularly as the available working capital determines the organization's immediate ability to pay subsequent debts and to make necessary investments.

Walters, David, *Operations Strategy*. Basingstoke: Palgrave Macmillan, 2002.

C-chart

A C-chart is a **control chart**, which displays the number of defects that have been identified in a given sample.

Cellular manufacturing

Cellular manufacturing is a factory layout in which machines are grouped by products produced, rather than more traditional groupings by function. Manufacturing cells each have a group of machines appropriate for producing a specific product. The system is ideally used for **batch** production, where it substantially reduces **work in progress**. Traditional manufacturing requires both production time and two waiting periods; the first occurs when the parts of a product have to be made elsewhere in the factory. The second occurs when these parts need to be transported to a location for final assembly and construction. Cellular manufacturing eliminates these two waits but, however, machinery within the factory may need to be physically moved and grouped together for each new product, as different products may require a different mix of machinery. Equally, there are problems when specific skills are required in order to operate or maintain the related machinery. Assuming the batch is large enough, it is practical to arrange the machinery and other facilities where they are required for production. Each cellular group producing a different product will have a different layout determined by the needs of that product. **Flow systems** within each cell will differ but the utilization of machines and human resources will be high. Associated benefits of cellular manufacturing are:

- improved product quality;
- earlier identification of potential manufacturing problems;
- improvements in efficiency and productivity;
- increased flexibility;
- greater ability to control process and product quality;
- reduced cost of non-conformance.

Irani, Shahruka A. (ed.) *Handbook of Cellular Manufacturing Systems.* New York: Wiley-Interscience, 1999.

Centre-of-gravity method

The centre-of-gravity method is a statistical technique which is used to determine the ideal location, or locations, of distribution centres which are capable of serving several destinations. The centre-of-gravity method involves placing the existing location on a coordinate grid. The grid may be of any scale, but each location should maintain its relative distance. The *X* and *Y* coordinates are then calculated for the centre of gravity and this should give an ideal location for a new distribution centre. The centre-of-gravity method is designed to minimize transportation costs and is therefore generally used for services using the location of existing destinations. The method takes into account the volumes of products which need to be transported, the distances and the costs related to this, whilst assuming that the shipping costs per unit or per mile are constant.

Centred moving average

A centred moving average is a **moving average** which is positioned in the middle of the group of numbers which it represents.

See **moving average method.**

C

Chase (demand) strategy

Chase strategy, or chase demand strategy, recognizes the reality that many products have seasonal demand. Businesses will set their production rates to match predicted or historical seasonal demand figures. They will aim to ensure that they have built up sufficient stocks of products in order to match the seasonal demand, as the period of demand may be comparatively short, which will not enable them to supply products at short enough notice to hit the peak demand period. Therefore, the businesses will keep a consistent production rate going over the year, building up sufficient stocks to take account of their high peak demand period. During the high peak period their stock levels will be comparatively low as they will have already matched their stock to the fulfilment of orders from their customers in anticipation of that seasonal demand.

An alternative approach, which still uses this type of strategy, is to produce products which are counter-seasonal in terms of demand. For example, a Christmas card manufacturer may choose to develop ranges of cards to match demand for other celebrations, such as Father's Day, Mother's Day or Valentine's Day. In this way, the business does not have the storage problems that an organization geared up for a consistent production rate across the year has, when simply selling during one seasonal demand period.

Check sheet

A check sheet is used for a variety of purposes and is, basically, a document containing a number of predetermined questions to be answered regarding subjects such as an audit inspection, the maintenance of machinery and equipment, current work schedules, productivity and quality issues, as well as a variety of other routine processes or manufacturing-related inspections or audits.

Clicks and mortar

'Clicks and mortar' describes a business which has both an online and and offline presence, as opposed to being a virtual business, which only exists on the internet. Typically, the business may have an online presence in addition to its more traditional high street stores (such as Body Shop).

Pottruck, David and Pearce, Terry, *Clicks and Mortar: Passion-driven Growth in an Internet-driven World.* New York: Jossey Bass Wiley, 2001.

Collaborative planning, forecasting and replenishment (CPFR)

The fundamental concept behind CPFR is the development of data and processing models which enable a business to collaboratively plan, forecast and replenish the supply chain. The planning aspect will involve an agreement between trading partners which states the ways in which they will conduct business between one another. The forecasting aspect will incorporate agreed methods and the timing of marketing and promotional campaigns, which will assist accurate forecasting. The replenishment aspect leads to an agreement between the businesses in relation to the generation and fulfilment of orders.

The common method of ensuring the flow of information in a readily accessible format from the point of sale has been the general acceptance of the sharing of the **electronic point of sale (EPOS)** through **electronic data interchange (EDI)**.

Seifert, Dirk, *Collaborative Planning: Forecasting and Replenishment: How to Create a Supply Chain Advantage*. New York: Amacom, 2003.

Commonality

Commonality is both a measure and a process which aims to identify components that are used in a wide variety of products. Components or parts which have a high degree of commonality are those which will be used in a large number of different products. They will offer the business a considerable number of benefits, as can be seen in Table 5.

Competitive advantage

The term 'competitive advantage' refers to a situation where a business has a commercial advantage over the competition by being able to offer consumers better value, quality or service. Normally, a competitive advantage would be measured in terms of lower prices but in the case of more benefits and greater quality, higher prices are possible as a result of the competitive advantage enjoyed.

Porter, Michael E., *Competitive Advantage: Creating and Sustaining Superior Performance*. New York: Simon & Schuster, 1998.

Competitive priorities

In 1984 Hayes and Wheelwright suggested that an organization's competitive priorities are either one, or more, of quality, **lead time**, cost and **flexibility**. The theory has been much amended over the years since first being written – notably by Foo and Friedman (1992) who added service and manufacturing technology – and can now be typified as in Table 6.

Foo, G. and Friedman, D. J., 'Variability and Capability: The Foundation of Competitive Operations Performance', *AT&T: Technical Journal*, July/August 1992, pp. 2–9.

Hayes, Robert H. and Wheelwright, Steven C., *Restoring our Competitive Edge: Competing through Manufacturing*. New York: John Wiley, 1984.

Table 5 Benefits of commonality

Advantage or benefit	Description
Ordering costs	As a result of the component having a high demand within the organization, each order will be large, which will reduce the associated ordering costs.
Economic order quantity	As large numbers of the component will be used on a daily basis, the order sizes can be fixed to ensure that excess stock is not carried, but that there is always sufficient stock to cope with demand.
Lower stock levels	The organization can more accurately forecast the amount of these components that will be required in any given period. This means that a lower stock level can be maintained in relation to these forecasts.
Reduced forecasting errors	As the component is used in many products, the chances of incorrectly calculating the demand for the product is reduced, as forecasts can be based on production levels which have already been set in relation to orders.
Reduced product design costs	Providing the component is genuinely usable in any new product design, aspects relating to this component and the possibility of it failing or not being suitable are eliminated.
Reduced manufacturing overheads	If the employees are conversant with the component already, then its application in new manufacturing does not have to be a major consideration.
Enhanced customer delivery service	Assuming that the component is compatible across the different markets which the business supplies, there will be a reduction in the **lead time** in respect of this part of the product.
Increased reliability	Assuming that the component has proved to be reliable and robust, the product overall will be more reliable.

Component

The word 'component' is a generic term normally used to describe a part, such as a bolt or screw, which has been obtained from a supplier and is used as a part of the production of a more complex product. Many manufacturing organizations create components as their finished products and it is the sum of all of these components or parts which makes a product, which then moves progressively down the **supply chain**

Table 6 Competitive priorities

Dimension	Detail
Quality	Performance, features, reliability, conformance, technical durability, serviceability, aesthetics, perceived quality, value for money
Time	Manufacturing lead time, due-date performance, rate of product introduction, delivery lead time, frequency of delivery
Price and cost (manufacturing cost)	Value added, selling price, running costs, service costs, profit
Flexibility	Material quality, output quality, new product development, modification of existing products, volume flexibility, product mix, resource mix

towards the end-user. A complex finished product may contain many hundreds or thousands of separate components which have been joined together as a single entity or product, with a purpose and function wholly different from those of the individual component parts.

Compressed working week

The compressed working week is an example of **alternative work arrangements** and is often referred to as a compressed-time option. Some businesses will refer to the compressed working week as a '4/10 schedule', which refers to the most common practice, of employees working 4 × 10-hour days with the 5th day as leave. Alternatively, the system is referred to as a '9-day fortnight' or '9/80' and in some cases a '9/8 schedule'.

The 9-day fortnight means simply that the employee works for 9 working days in each 2-week block. A 9/80 schedule refers to a system where employees work for 80 hours over 9 days (instead of the normal 10). A 9/8 schedule is more complex as employees work for 9 hours on 4 days a week and for 8 hours on the 5th day, or they have a day off.

As far as the US and the UK are concerned, upwards of 25 per cent of private-sector employers offer compressed working weeks. There are a number of advantages associated with these more complicated work schedules, which tend to be centred on two key areas:

- *Customer satisfaction* – a traditional 5 days a week schedule often meant that businesses would be required to take on additional staff to cover periods beyond Monday to Friday. There would be associated breaks in production, coverage and consistency in relation to dealing with customers. Equally, at times when the business needed extra coverage, there would be a requirement to pay employees for overtime. Using a compressed working week, more employees can be deployed at crucial times of the week, with lower staffing levels being maintained when demand is lower. Equally, the timing of the compressed working week can be adjusted to match demand and required turnaround times.

- The other major concern is *employee retention*. It has been a major discovery that a compressed working week actually attracts and adds to the retention strategies of a business. A compressed working week does offer a degree of **flexibility**. Guaranteed additional time sufficient to deal with domestic issues such as childcare, for example, means that a compressed working week is often attractive to employees with young children, or other commitments outside of work.

The compressed working week, however, does have problems associated with it, specifically with reference to issues such as safety and the health of employees. A longer, albeit concentrated, working week does add to the physical strain upon employees, as they will inevitably have shorter breaks between blocks of work within a four-day period. Crucial to the imposition of a compressed working week is the requirement for the business to give employees sufficient time to reschedule their personal lives. Providing the imposition is planned before it is initiated, most employees seem to be receptive to the concept of the compressed working week.

Olmstead, Barney and Smith, Suzanne, *Creating a Flexible Workplace: How to Select and Manage Alternative Work Options*. New York: Pfeiffer Wiley, 1994.

C

Computer-aided design (CAD)

Computer-aided design enables engineers to create a design from predetermined specifications and then to view that design either in minute detail or from different angles. The software allows the designer to see how the changing of one value or variable has an overall impact on the design itself. Most CAD software is capable of being run on a standard computer.

See also **computer-aided design/manufacturing (CAD/CAM).**

Computer-aided design/manufacturing (CAD/CAM)

CAD/CAM puts together design and manufacture. It enables the designer or engineer to not only design the product, but then generate all necessary instructions that are required to control the manufacturing process itself.

Lee, Cunwoo, *Principles of CAD/CAM/CAE Systems*. Reading MA: Addison-Wesley, 1999.

Computer-aided inspection (CAI)

CAI uses systems, such as infrared lights, to detect defects in products passing along a production line. The computer is programmed to carry out an inspection of particular features, specifications, or parameters of the product throughout the production process. This enables the business to make the earliest possible detection of faults before the part-finished product proceeds along the production line. Clearly the earliest identification of defects is cost effective in the sense that it eliminates the completion of products which subsequently prove to be defective.

Nambiar, K. R., *Computer-aided Design: Production and Inspection*. New Delhi: Narosa Publishing House, 1999.

Computer-integrated manufacturing (CIM)

See **computer-aided design (CAD); computer-aided design/manufacturing (CAD/CAM);** *and* **computer numerical control (CNC).**

Computer numerical control (CNC)

CNC is one of the most commonly used forms of flexible automation, where a single machine has many tools and performs many operations, perhaps machining a detailed part from a block of metal. The machine receives instructions from an external source (tape or computer).

Concurrent engineering (CE)

Concurrent engineering aims to take into account and to incorporate the entire life cycle of the product. When a product is being developed the designers and engineers not only consider the inherent purpose and specifications of the product, but also consider how the product will be manufactured, how quality systems will be deployed, the associated costs and even how the product will be finally disposed of at the end of its useful life to the end-user. In other words, CE is an integrated process that encompasses design, manufacture and support and may well incorporate the input of individuals within the organization who would not normally be associated with product development. Typically this means that the development would involve design, production, marketing, sales and customer service and support.

Cusumano, Michael A. and Nobeoka, Kentaro, *Thinking Beyond Lean: How Multi-project Management is Transforming Product Development at Toyota and Other Companies*. New York: Free Press, 1998.

Configuration management

Configuration management (CM) is essentially a means by which an organization can attempt to ensure that in an environment of change, processes, facilities and products continue to conform with one another. CM, therefore, implies the ability of the organization not only to accommodate changes, but also to rapidly adapt and reinvent, and formalize its standards and procedures. The key to CM is the ability to communicate the requirements of conformance to various areas of the organization. At the hub of successful CM is a proven and solid business infrastructure which can initiate and disseminate change and information across the breadth of the organization. It has considerable implications for manufacturing processes as rapid conformance changes may need to be instituted as processes are being executed. In other words, whilst CM attempts to effectively redesign its internal processes, the task of continuing to produce is still paramount.

Configurator

A configurator is an essential precursor for manufacturing organizations who are **building to customer order**. Usually a configurator is a software tool which a salesperson demonstrates and inputs data into in the presence of a customer. The configurator, often used in kitchen or bedroom layout and design, is deployed by sales people to provide a graphic representation of the product or products from a given menu. The salesperson will choose, or attempt to influence the customer to purchase, the higher-valued (higher-margin) items. The configurator will prevent customers from choosing combinations that will not work. Once the configurator and the salesperson have completed the process with the customer, the order, based on the exact specifications, as laid out from the meeting with the customer, can be electronically sent to the manufacturer or supplier.

Configure to order (CTO)

In essence, CTO is a similar approach to **assemble to order (ATO)**. The organization creates standard products that can have adjustments made to suit specific customer needs. The essential difference is that a standard product is generally created and that only minor changes are made, rather than a more significant series of changes which may involve the use of different components, as in 'assemble to order'. Configure to order is also known as 'reconfigure to order'.

Conformance

Conformance or, more properly, quality conformance, measures the degree to which a particular design specification is actually met in the finished article. Conformance is normally measured by comparing the number of products successfully manufactured without defects against those that have passed through the production process yet have defects. It can also be measured by the amount of products or components that have been wasted during the production process, as a result of them being inherently defective, or rendered defective by an error in the process itself.

Taormina, Tom and Brewer, Keith, *Implementing ISO 9000:2000: The Journey from Conformance to Performance*. Englewood Cliffs, NJ: Prentice-Hall, 2001.

Constant work in progress (CONWIP)

CONWIP is a means by which a production line can be managed in a simplistic and almost foolproof manner. Once a completed product has reached the end of a particular assembly line or production line, a signal is relayed to the start of the production line giving the instruction to begin the production process of another product. In this way, the organization is aware precisely of the number of products in the system, or **work in progress**. CONWIP is a more holistic approach than **drum buffer rope (DBR)** as it is applied to the entire process.

CONWIP does not require the same level of complexity as a **just-in-time system (JIT)** or ***kanban*** system as it does not require buffers (**buffering**) to be established between each separate part of the production process.

Continuous flow/processing

In continuous processing, products are processed through a series of stages, being transferred automatically from one process to the next.

Many continuous processing facilities, as a result of the complexity of the manufacturing process, and the associated costs with setting up the process, rarely stop but run without break, except for periodic scheduled maintenance. Many of these production lines are so complex that the shutting down of the line may involve several days of lost production.

Typically, continuous production is used in cases where the products are identical, using precisely the same parts or components each time, with very little variance in quality and style. Much of the system is computer-controlled, with employees running diagnostic checks, carrying out spot **quality control** audits and immediately dealing with issues raised during the inspection process at the end of the production line.

Conventional inventory controls tend to ignore the demands of continuous flow or continuous processing. It is notoriously difficult for an organization to judge, given the high volumes of inputs and outputs on a continuous production line, exactly how much raw materials and how many components and parts will actually be required. There are various options, including estimating an average output over the period, related to the restocking system, but this may not take into account any deficiencies in the parts or components, a need to speed up the continuous production or, indeed, a serious maintenance issue requiring the shutting down of the whole operation for a period of time. If the inventory control system does not match the requirements of the continuous production, then the following may arise:

- The output may be starved. In other words, the output has to be slowed down and the amount of finished products will diminish as a result of there being insufficient raw materials, components or parts to feed the continuous process.
- The precise opposite of this is over-feeding the continuous production process, which produces more finished products than are immediately required. This places a strain upon the storage capabilities of the organization, effectively blocking the storage of raw materials, parts and components which are still required to feed the production process.

Continuous processing is generally used when high volumes of the products are required. The materials themselves are automatically transferred along the production line from stage to stage and rarely are the production lines stopped, because of the cost implications of taking this decision. The most common forms of continuous production are found in the petro-chemical and oil-refining industries.

Nicholas, John, *Competitive Manufacturing Management: Continuous Improvement, Lean Production and Customer-Focussed Quality*. New York: McGraw-Hill Education, 1998.
Rother, Mike and Harris, Rick, *Creating Continuous Flow: An Action Guide for Managers, Engineers and Production Associates*. London: Lean Enterprises Institute, 2002.

Continuous improvement

There are many ways of approaching the handling of continuous improvement. The fundamental concept however remains that in order for an organization to achieve long-term and sustainable improvements, there must be a continuous improvement process which allows the organization to improve over shorter periods of time. The whole continuous improvement system aims to achieve change in the longer term by carefully and consistently measured steps, which address specific problems.

One of the many ways in which this process can be typified is the six-step process, as can be seen in the diagram in Figure 11.

The process begins with a baseline measurement system, which aims to guide the organization through the problem-solving process and identify the areas which require improvement. In the second and third steps the areas requiring immediate improvement are selected and the root causes of substandard performance are evaluated. Having achieved

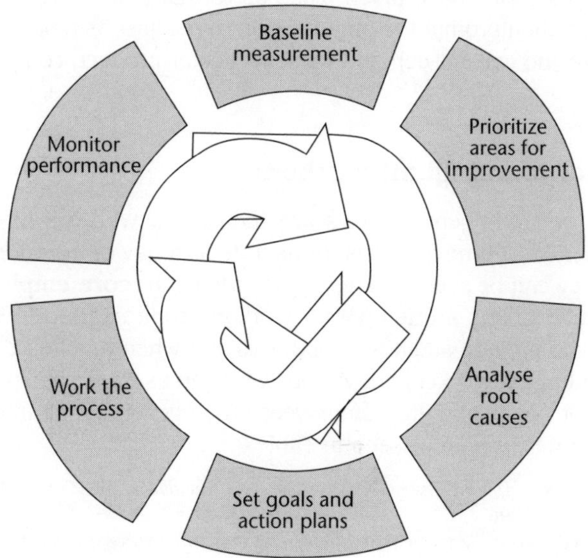

Figure 11 The six-step process

C

some improvement, goals are then developed, importantly both in the long and the short term, enabling the organization to systematically eliminate any barriers to improvement. The performance needs to be measured and tracked and the six-step process returns to the baseline measurement in order to redirect the organization's problem-solving efforts. The circle of related and interdependent issues is a continual one, which systematically addresses issues and barriers, discovering ways in which they can be surmounted.

In order to fully understand the implications of all of the processes, it is prudent to consider the implications of each of the six steps. The fundamentals are examined in Table 7.

See also ***kaizen*** and **total quality management (TQM)**.

Nicholas, John, *Competitive Manufacturing Management: Continuous Improvement, Lean Production and Customer-Focussed Quality*. New York: McGraw-Hill Education, 1998.

Marsh, John, *The Continuous Improvement Toolkit: The A–Z of Tools and Techniques*. London: B. T. Batsford, 1998.

Continuous review

A 'continuous review' is a term associated with the checking of inventory systems. An essential task of a continuous review is to examine the current inventory position compared with the next reorder point and transactions which have taken place up to that point. The continuous review can then prompt the organization to readjust its reorder point in relation to the current demand for a particular product, component or part.

Contract (contingent) workers

Contract or contingent workers are individuals who are hired for a limited period of time, perhaps for as little as a day or even for several years. They can be seen as a necessary adjunct to **core employees** as contingent workers are temporary workers, contractors or other individuals who provide additional labour as and when required by a business. Contingent workers are variously known as transients, peripheral workers or complementary employees. They generally fall into one of five categories, as can be seen in Table 8.

George, Helen, *The Professional Contract Workers' Handbook*. New York: McGraw-Hill Education, 1996.

Macdonald, Lynda, *Managing Fixed-term and Part-term Workers: A Practical Guide to Temporary, Seasonal and Contract Employees*. Oxford: Tolley Publishing, 2002.

Table 7 The six-step process

The six-step process	Description
Baseline measurement	The initial step is for the organization to determine its current operating situation. The organization will identify a number of areas which are affecting the overall operating system. Processes can be measured, analysed and tracked in terms of their effectiveness and productivity. In this model the baseline measurement can be likened to zero in quantifying continuous improvement.
Prioritize improvement areas	The organization will now frame performance standards, possibly through **benchmarking**. This will assist the organization in focusing on the major areas requiring improvement related to productivity, profitability, quality or safety.
Root cause analysis	Once the major areas have been selected the organization must now address any barriers to improvement. Once the root causes have been isolated the solutions can then be framed in order to deal with them individually.
Goal setting and action planning	It is imperative that goals are incremental so that the organization and those involved can reap tangible benefits by seeing parts of the problem successively solved. Without the incremental factor, dealing with complex problems may lead to de-motivation. A series of goals will make up a major goal, each of them progressing the organization along the way to dealing with a specific issue. Alongside the goals, clear, direct and specific action plans must be framed, but these need to be flexible enough to be changed as and when required.
Work the process	Definitive action plans will direct the organization in its efforts to implement the various improvements. The plans need to be logical and must be revised if necessary. At this stage the organization is at the very heart of the problems it faces, and cross-functional teams and brainstorming to overcome issues can be essential tools.
Performance measurement	The final step in the first revolution of the continuous performance model seeks to measure the tangible results. By this stage whatever problems have been tackled should now have been overcome, which will have had a positive impact on the operations of the organization. They should now be compared with the original baseline measurements in order to verify that goals have been achieved. It may be the case that the improvements are more, or less, than had been desired. Therefore the process begins once again, as partially resolved issues may need further improvement.

Table 8 Contract or contingent workers

Category of worker	Description
Part-timer workers	These are individuals whose working week can generally be adapted to suit the needs of the business. They can also include individuals who are working on a temporary or seasonal basis.
Agency workers	Employees who are, in effect, employed by an agency, for which the business pays an additional fee per hour or day worked. The agency is responsible for the wages and for tax and other benefits. These individuals can be hired on a daily, weekly, monthly or other basis.
Contract workers	These are usually individuals who provide a form of professional support under contract, for a fixed period or a fixed number of hours over a given period of time.
Leased workers	These are either temporary or permanent employees who can be taken on on a long-term basis, usually in the form of a whole group of individuals who perform a specific function.
Direct hire workers	These are a business's pool of available individuals who can be called in, usually at short notice, to cover unforeseen gaps in the workforce, and may often be retired workers or former employees.

Control chart

A control chart is a simple graphical and statistical procedure aimed at assisting the identification of controllable aspects of a production process. This means that the manufacturer has a better chance of being able to avoid the production of variable products.

Typical control charts (e.g. Figure 12) will measure the quality of individual products as they are completed on the production line (measures would include weight, colour, diameter etc.). The products are grouped into batches and the mean or standard deviation of the batches is calculated. The control chart is then created with a centre line signifying the mean, along with the upper and lower limits of acceptability. Normally, this is set at around three standard deviations in the upper and lower limits.

Subsequent batches of products can be compared with the control chart parameters and then plotted onto the chart. The business would be seeking to find patterns on the graph to identify a commonality in the deviations. The data may be able to pinpoint a crucial step in the process

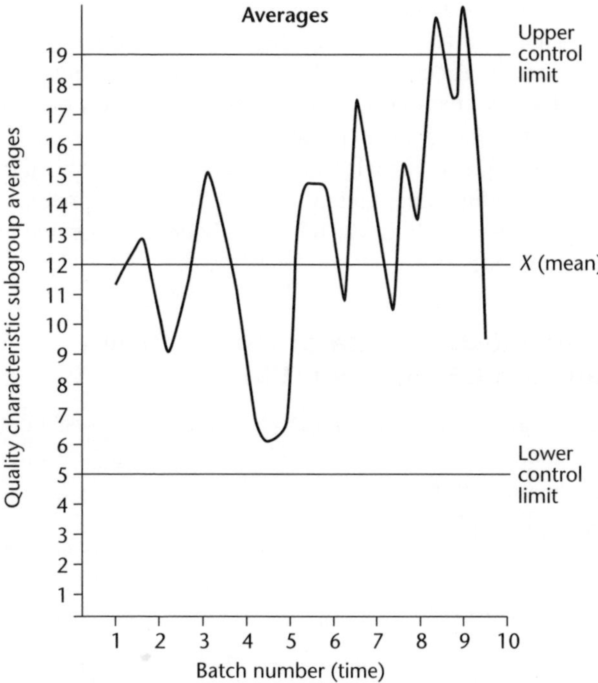

Figure 12 Example of a control chart

which is causing a problem along the whole production line. Engineers can then be sent to the appropriate part of the line in order to rectify the fault, after which there should be a more predictable and closer adherence to the control chart centre line. This methodology is sometimes called **statistical process control**.

C

Control limit

In any form of demand forecasting there will always be a margin of error. To an extent a certain margin of error is not only expected, but it is also accepted. However, there are circumstances when the organization which has made the forecast needs to be alerted to the fact that the forecast has been compromised by real demand figures which do not match predicted patterns. Typically, an organization will establish a series of parameters, taking into account any error in the forecast figures. These are known as control limits, which can be either positive or negative. In the case of a negative control limit being triggered, it alerts the organization to the fact that demand appears to be moving in a direction far below what had been predicted on the forecast. In the case of an upper control limit being triggered, this draws attention to a demand trend far in excess of what had been predicted, thereby alerting them to the fact that their current rate of production may be inadequate to provide a sufficient supply of products to match that demand. In both cases the triggering of control limits should alert the organization to the fact that there is a fundamental flaw in their forecasting methodologies, or perhaps a series of factors which had not been incorporated into their prediction techniques.

Control of Substances Hazardous to Health Regulations (COSHH) 1999 (UK)

These regulations require employers to make regular assessments of the risks from hazardous substances and to ensure that precautions are taken to reduce these risks.

www.hse.gov.uk/hthdir/noframes/coshh

Core competencies

Core competencies have two specific definitions. The first is identical to that of competences, or the identification of the key skills, knowledge and experience required of an individual to carry out a specific job role.

The other definition refers to the ability of employees or managers to be adaptable in the sense that they could work in an alternative remote location, specifically abroad. In these cases core competencies examine the adaptability and resourcefulness of the managers to operate in what might be an unknown overseas environment.

Prahalad and Hamel describe core competencies as the collective learning in the organization. In particular, they are concerned with the coordination of diverse production skills and the integration of multiple streams of technologies. They also cite the importance of the organization of work and the delivery of value (indeed value is essential in the consideration of core competencies).

C

Prahalad, C. K. and Hamel, Gary, *Competing for the Future*. Cambridge, MA: Harvard Business School Press, 1996.

Stone, Florence M. and Sachs, Randi T., *High-value Manager: Developing the Core Competencies for Organizational Demands*. New York: Amacom. 1996.

See also **distinctive competencies**.

Core employees

Core or key employees are individuals who are essential to the running of an organization. Typically, they will be individuals who hold crucial strategic job positions within the organization and have been identified by both the management and human resources department as being vital. These individuals are often provided with additional incentives in order to ensure their retention. Core employees can be distinguished from other employees, and specifically those who are considered to be **contract or contingent workers**.

Correlation

Correlation is a statistical measure which attempts to find a relationship between two values. Correlation is suggested when values between –1 and +1 are recorded and this may mean that the values or variables may move closer together.

A positive correlation exists when product A is said to more reliable than the mean and product B is also considered to be more reliable than the mean. A negative correlation occurs when Product A is more reliable than the mean and Product B is less reliable than the mean.

A positive correlation suggests that there are commonalities in the two values or variables and a negative correlation may mean that there are no commonalities between the two values or variables.

Cost of quality

The term 'cost of quality' is taken to encompass the measurement or framework set up to calculate all quality-related costs. The framework would include the prevention of quality problems, which is notoriously difficult to measure, as it encompasses the design of new products and the training of employees not directly related to the product itself. The framework also incorporates any costs related to inspection or testing, lost capacity in a **bottleneck**, breakdowns in machinery, de-motivation, defective products and any other internal quality issues. Externally, the cost of quality also seeks to quantify deteriorations in customer perceptions due to faulty products; the costs of maintaining customer service, including repairs, warranties and guarantees; and any issues on quality which have affected relationships with suppliers or customers along the **supply chain**.

Crosby, Philip B., *Quality is Free*. New York: Signet Books, 1992.

Cost–volume analysis

Cost–volume analysis focuses on the relationships between cost, revenue and volume of output. Cost–volume analysis is one of the common methods used in the evaluation of capacity planning. Variables used in the analysis are:

FC = Fixed cost
VC = Variable cost per unit
TC = Total cost
TR = Total revenue
R = Revenue per unit
Q = Quantity or volume of output
Q_{BEP} = Break-even quantity
P = Profit

The assumptions of cost–volume analysis are as follows:

- One product is involved.
- Everything produced is sold.
- The variable cost per unit is the same regardless of the volume.
- Fixed costs do not change with volume changes (or they are step changes).
- The revenue per unit is the same regardless of volume.

The cost–volume analysis is therefore the total cost (TC), being the sum of the fixed cost (FC) and the variable cost per unit (VC), times output volume (Q), or:

$$TC = FC + VC \times Q$$

See also **breakeven analysis and the breakeven point.**

C

Craft production

Craft production involves the use of a specific skill or trade, to produce an individual object for a specific customer. In the majority of cases craft production involves making products one at a time to the exact specifications of the customer. In craft production, machines augment the skills of the craftsperson. The craftsperson's skills are often highly specialized and it is the employee or the craftsperson who moves to each project, rather than the project moving to them. Most craft production involves **building to order** and this production system is used when large-scale production or **mass customization** are not appropriate.

Crash

Crash or crashing is an attempt to shorten the duration of a particular activity. The implications are that the performance of the individual tasks involved, or at least some of them, can be concertinaed into a shorter time in order to reduce the overall length of time which the activity will take.

See also **crash time.**

Crash time

Once an organization or project team has decided to **crash** an activity, a re-estimation of the time which the activity will take has to be calculated. This revised time-span for the activity is known as 'crash time'.

Critical activity

A critical activity is a major event on a **critical path**.

See also **critical incident** *and* **critical path method (CPM).**

Critical chain

A critical chain is a means by which an organization can look at the full duration of a particular project, and is considered to be somewhat more all-inclusive than a **critical path**. The critical chain not only addresses the issues which a critical path considers, but also takes into account any factors relating to the supply of products or components prior to the commencement of the production process itself. A critical chain would consider the start and finish times, as well as any slack periods. The longest total time taken through these stages is known as the critical path. The critical chain seeks to assign the resources required for each part of the process and recognizes the fact that the next stage cannot be undertaken until the resources required for that stage are made available. The critical chain, then, identifies all of the stages in the process until the schedule has been completed. In this respect, a critical chain is somewhat longer than a critical path. In addition, the critical chain incorporates time buffers, which aim to protect the activities on the critical chain from beginning later than is desirable.

Alongside a critical chain, a non-critical chain would also be constructed, which would ensure that activities that could have an impact on the critical chain were planned in such a way that they would not interrupt the critical chain.

Leach, Lawrence P., *Critical Chain Project Management*. Norwood, MA: Artech House, 2000.

C

Critical incident

The critical-incident technique involves the identification and investigation of issues which have either a beneficial or a negative impact on customer satisfaction. Critical incidents can be typified as being either advantageous or desirable qualities which the business, or its employees display, or factors which are continual causes for complaint and dissatisfaction. The critical-incident technique can be used to identify aspects not only of the organization's performance, but also of individual employees' performance, by recognizing aspects of how they handle customer service situations and provide a satisfactory or unsatisfactory outcome for the customer.

Latino, R. J. and Latino, K. C., *Root Cause Analysis: Improving Performance for Bottom Line Results*. Boca Raton, FL: CRC Press. 1999.

Critical path

A critical path is the longest possible path through which a project has to pass in order to be completed. A critical path identifies crucial activities in the stages of dealing with, or managing, a particular project, identifying in effect the 'worst case scenario' in order to make a clearer estimation as to the time a project will take to complete. The critical path aims to focus the organization's attention on those activities which are essential to ensure the completion of the project.

See also **critical path method (CPM)**.

Critical path method (CPM)

Unlike **backward scheduling**, the critical path method begins with the start time for a particular project. It then proceeds to identify the earliest possible start times and finish times for each activity which is required to complete the overall project. Once this has been done, the CPM seeks to work backwards from the date by which the project needs to be completed and amends the start times of all of the activities in relation to this date. The critical path is the pathway which has the minimum amount of slack time (see Figure 13). This critical path is then given a priority in terms of attention and allocation of resources, aiming to reduce the overall project time.

The CPM should also assist the business in being able to identify aspects or activities in the process which can either be rolled together or speeded up in order to have a positive impact on the overall project completion time.

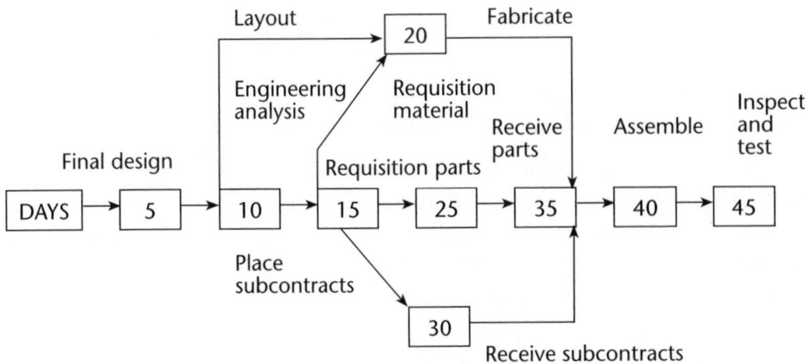

Figure 13 Example of a critical path

Busch, Dennis H., *New Critical Path Method: State of the Art in Project Modelling and Time Reserve Management*. Chicago, IL: Probus Publications, 1990.

Critical ratio (CR)

The critical ratio is often used by an organization to determine which of the various customers' orders should be processed first. Finding the critical ratio involves comparing the time remaining before the due delivery date is reached and the amount of processing time required for the job. The job which has the lowest ratio should be the job which is processed next.

Crosby, Philip B.

One of his first books by the business philosopher and author Philip B. Crosby, *Quality is Free*, was seen as the beginning of the quality-orientated trend in manufacturing. Having worked on an assembly line, he turned to instructing management on the concept of prevention being cheaper and more efficient than fixing problems. This naturally developed into the **zero defects** model.

Crosby argued that doing things wrong affects profit and when products are made incorrectly they have to be either remade or scrapped. Improving the process itself means no waste, assured quality and protection of profits. Crosby suggested that there were four absolutes of quality:

- The definition of quality is conformance to requirements.
- The system of quality needs to be prevention or preventative.
- The cost of quality needs to be measured in terms of failure.
- There is only one performance standard, namely zero defects

Crosby went on to suggest the necessary requirements in order to successfully implement zero defects (see Table 9).

Crosby, P. B., *Quality is Free*. New York: McGraw-Hill, 1979.
Crosby, P. B., *Quality without Tears*. New York: McGraw-Hill, 1984.

Table 9 Crosby's requirements for success

Consideration	Description
Management commitment	Clearly defining the management position regarding quality.
Quality improvement team	Establishment of the team's role in operating quality-improvement programme.
Quality measurement	Establishment of quality measurements which allow for evaluation and correction.
Cost of quality	Quantifying the cost of quality.
Quality awareness	Ensuring all employees are aware of the team's activities.
Corrective action	Establishment of a structured, organized and permanent approach to resolving problems.
Zero defects planning	Completion of the preparation for launching the zero defects programme.
Supervisor training	Determining training which supervisors require in accomplishing quality improvements.
Zero defect day	Major event to inform all employees that a transformation has occurred.
Goal setting	Transformation of the pledges into action by setting goals.
Error > cause > removal	Provision of a method for employees to communicate any problems.
Recognition	The recognition of employees who have participated in the programme and have achieved goals.
Quality council	The promotion of discussion and communication between specialists in quality issues.
Do it over again	Maintenance of the momentum of the improvement programme.

Cross-docking

'Cross-docking' is a term associated with warehouse management and has, in fact, three different applications or definitions.

Generally, cross-docking refers to situations when products arrive at an incoming dock or port and are transferred directly to vehicles, which will then relay the products on directly to the customer. In this way cross-docking is seen as a means by which an organization dealing with trans-shipment and distribution avoids the necessity of warehousing the products themselves for any length of time.

A more precise definition describes cross-docking as fulfilling customer orders direct from a dock, from products which have just arrived, regardless of the fact that there is stock at the supplier's premises which could have fulfilled that order.

The third, even more precise, definition states that cross-docking aims to process shipments for customers, to outgoing vehicles, within between one and twenty-four hours of the products arriving at the port. The process is seen as being ideal, not only for the fulfilment of large orders, which may, in themselves, be whole containers, but also for the transfer of smaller orders into more appropriate vehicles, which can then proceed on their delivery rounds from the dock rather than the organization's warehouse.

The key aspect is that cross-docking allows an organization to reduce its stockholding by almost simultaneously taking possession of the stock and then disposing of the stock to customers, without the need for storage or further handling.

Croston's forecasting method

Croston's forecasting method is a means by which a business can carry out forecasting for 'lumpy demand'. Lumpy demand occurs when a number of periods have been typified by a zero demand. Using standard forecasting methods would prove useless in such cases as methods such as **exponential smoothing** would produce results which told the business very little.

The Croston method uses exponential smoothing three times: when there is no demand, there is no update, but when a positive demand is noted, three exponential smoothing updates are performed. These are:

1 *Tbar* = the time between positive demands;
2 *Dbar* = the amount of demand when it is positive;
3 The absolute deviation in positive demand.

C

The Croston forecast of expected demand per period is, therefore, *Dbar/Tbar*.

Croston, J., 'Forecasting and Stock Control for Intermittent Demands', *Operational Research Quarterly*, vol. 23, no. 3 (1972), pp. 289–303.

Cumulative graph

Cumulative graphs can be used by organizations to track their ability to deal with demand fluctuations. In the majority of cases **capacity** is set at a level that will satisfy an estimated or measured demand, but these capacity calculations are not always as accurate as the organization would wish. Therefore there is always a disparity between demand and capacity. Using a cumulative graph, the cumulative capacity and the cumulative demand over a period of time can both be plotted. The organization would seek to see those two lines on the graph as closely matched as possible and, if anything, the cumulative capacity line should always be marginally higher than the cumulative demand line. In these cases the graph would indicate that at certain times over the period, the organization has had excess stock (although given the cumulative nature of this capacity calculation, it does not necessarily mean that they have capacity stock at this moment). Should the cumulative demand line pass, or cross, the cumulative capacity line, then the organization has a clear indication that at some point over the period they were unable to satisfy demand, and consequently have lost sales.

In analysing a cumulative graph, an organization can seek to discover ways in which it can adjust its capacity and thus affect its cumulative capacity, in order to more closely match the cumulative demand. Typically, both the cumulative capacity and the cumulative demand will measure finished products (both produced and demanded) over a set period, perhaps one year.

Customer relationship management (CRM)

Customer relationship management is based on the assumption that there is a relationship between a business or brand and its customers. This is a relationship that needs to be managed, both through the individual buying stages and in the longer term. CRM is very much related to fostering customer loyalty and, in the longer term, customer retention.

For the organization, CRM can provide up-to-date information regarding its customers, including the status of their orders and the need to deploy any support services. Close CRM can also reduce the transaction costs for the customer and ultimately provide the business with a clearer indication as to demand levels.

Harvard Business Review, *Harvard Business Review on Customer Relationship Management*. Cambridge, MA: Harvard Business School Press, 2002.

Cycle counting

Using an **ABC classification**, an organization may choose to use cycle counting to prioritize the stocktaking of items in the company's inventory. Items which fall into the 'A' category are counted more often than the others. This is undertaken as a means by which the inventory count, or balance, can be made as accurate as possible. Items which fall into the 'C' category, however, will not be counted very often, but will be picked up in an annual inventory count. By ensuring that the important items in the inventory are counted on a regular basis, the organization seeks to eliminate the possibility of running out of stock. The system also allows the organization to make an on-the-spot assessment immediately prior to placing a new order, or, indeed, just after a new order has arrived. Normally a cycle count will take place after a specified number of transactions have been completed.

Brooks, Roger B. and Wilson, Larry W., *Inventory Record Accuracy: Unleashing the Power of Cycle Counting*. Chichester: John Wiley, 1992.

Cycle time

The cycle time is the length of time required to complete a given product from the start time to the moment it rolls off the production line. In other words, it is the total completion time, less any start-up times. Cycle time can be complex to calculate when products require a large number of assembly activities, largely as a result of the fact that each component has a different starting time. The easiest way to work out the cycle time is to examine the inventory turnover ratio. If the inventory or stock turnover is 6 turns in a 12-month period, then the cycle time is 2 months.

Gaynor, Gerard H., *Exploiting Cycle Time in Technology Management*. New York: McGraw-Hill Education, 1992.

Cyclical factors

Not only can cyclical factors affect demand and employment, but they also have a major influence on the level of productivity. Cyclical factors are either predicted or unexpected changes in demand, which can be caused by a wide variety of different influences. Often there is no underlying reason why a cyclical factor may affect demand, yet they are often caused by short-term concerns, particularly on behalf of consumers, in relation to the threat of inflation, recession or unemployment. The knock-on effect of consumers' reluctance to purchase at the levels or along the same trends as they had done in the past can have an enormous impact along the **supply chain**. This is one of the many causes of the **bullwhip effect**. There is a tendency for a cyclical factor to have a permanent impact on the productivity of a given industrial sector. A drop in demand from consumers leads to lower orders being placed by retailers, which in turn prompts distributors to reduce their levels of stock and reorders. The manufacturer is then faced with the prospect of either cutting back on production in order to match the reduced demand, which could mean a reduction in the workforce, or continuing to produce at the current levels, taking the attendant risk that they will be unable to sell the excess stock. Should the manufacturers decide to cut back on production, then naturally this impacts on their suppliers, and their suppliers' suppliers, and so on. All along the supply chain, organizations may be reducing their levels of production and their levels of employment, which in turn, as employees move out of the job market, simply compounds the impact of the cyclical factor.

Cyclical factors are not always negative; they can be positive in terms of increased demand, which reverses or is contrary to the example given above.

Decomposition

Decomposition involves the isolation of **cyclical factors**, or seasonal trends, or other random events which may manifest themselves in **time-series** data used in **forecasting**.

Decoupling

The concept of decoupling implies that even in cases of continuous production, if an organization ensures that it has sufficient stock, or inventory, and that **buffering** has been set up between each stage of the production, all the processes on that production line can operate independently of one another.

Delayed differentiation

Delayed differentiation involves the partial completion of a product; at a predetermined point, or stage, in the production, the production is stopped until such a time as the manufacturer has received confirmation as to the precise specifications required by the customer. Typically, part-finished goods will be constructed and stored, on the basis that the fundamentals of the product remain constant. The partly finished products are then taken from stock and completed according to the customers' specific preferences.

Delphi technique

The Delphi technique is a means by which qualitative forecasting can be achieved through defining a problem by interviewing a panel of experts. The process requires depth interviews aimed at ascertaining the views of individuals such as managers, sales personnel and other participants, whose views are then aggregated in order to achieve a forecast. The collective view of these experts is considered to be more objective and tends to be used for forecasting long-term changes.

Sahakian, Curtis E., *The Delphi Method*. New York: Corporate Partnering Institute, 1997.

Demand

Put simply, demand is a measure of customer requirements in terms of either sales or production over a given period of time.

Demand filter

Essentially, a demand filter operates in a very similar way to a **control limit** in as much as it seeks to generate a report to warn the organization that there has been a substantial deviation from the forecast. Normally the demand filter alerts the organization if the forecast error has exceeded, plus or minus, three standard deviations.

Deming, William Edwards

William Edwards Deming was born in Sioux City, Iowa, on 14 October 1900. In 1921, he graduated in electrical engineering. In 1925, he received an MSc at the University of Colorado, and in 1928, a PhD from Yale. Deming is perhaps best known for his work in Japan, where from 1950 he instructed management and engineers in methods of managing quality.

Deming's 'fourteen points' aimed to identify key success drivers derived from industry leaders. The fourteen points are designed to be applicable to any situation and any type of business. They are therefore applicable to both manufacturing and service-based industries. The fourteen points are listed in Table 10.

Table 10 Deming's fourteen points

Deming point	Description and implications
1	Create constancy of purpose towards improvement of product and service, with three aims: to become, stay in business, and provide employment.
2	Recognize that the business is operating in a new age (as indeed it always is to this day), so management needs to be aware of these challenges and adopt a policy of leading change.
3	Eliminate the policy of inspection in order to achieve quality. Build quality into the product from the earliest stages in order to eliminate the need to carry out inspections.

⇒

Table 10 Deming's fourteen points (*continued*)

Deming point	Description and implications
4	Instead of making outsourcing and supplier decisions purely on the basis of price, aim to minimize total costs. This can be achieved by forging a long-term relationship based on loyalty and trust between one or a few suppliers.
5	If the production and the service levels are improved, productivity and quality will follow and also reduce overall costs.
6	Introduce on-the-job training as a means to increase productivity, job satisfaction and quality.
7	Introduce leadership by ensuring that anyone in a supervisory or management position focuses on assisting the workforce to do their jobs more effectively.
8	Ensure that there is no fear in the organization, as this does not assist the workforce in performing effectively, as they are concerned about their jobs and how they are treated by the management.
9	Encourage cross-departmental cooperation by breaking down barriers; all areas should work as a team in order to see problems before they occur.
10	Eliminate demands for zero defects as the causes of defects are often beyond the power of the employees. Zero defect demands are empty statements if not supported by the management in terms of ensuring that the workforce has materials of sufficient quality. Zero defect demands simply lead to adversarial relationships.
11	Eliminate work standards such as quotas, and substitute effective leadership. Eliminate concepts such as management by objectives, numbers or numerical goals, and replace these with effective leadership.
12	Eliminate the use of quotas, in relation to the performance of hourly paid workers as this robs them of any hope of being able to display craftsmanship. Substitute the concept of quality rather than numbers. Equally, eliminate annual or merit ratings on the basis of productivity and substitute rewards for sustained quality.
13	Ensure that the entire workforce has an opportunity to improve their knowledge, skills and education.
14	Ensure that the entire workforce is involved in transforming the business; transformation is not a management responsibility or interest alone.

These fourteen points have achieved a level of reverence commensurate to the Ten Commandments; their corollaries are Deming's 'seven deadly sins':

1 Lack of constancy of purpose.
2 Emphasis on short-term profits.
3 Personal review systems.
4 Mobility of management.
5 Use of visible figures only for management.
6 Excessive medical costs.
7 Excessive costs of liability.

These rules together are used in what is called a '**plan, do, check and act**' **(PDCA)** cycle.

Deming, W. Edwards, *Out of the Crisis: Quality, Productivity and Competitive Position*. Cambridge: Cambridge University Press, 1982; 2nd edn 1986.

The W. Edwards Deming Institute: www.deming.org/

Dependent demand

Dependent demand is calculated or determined by the interdependence or interrelationships of different products. The demand for product A may be determined by the demand for product B. For example, the demand for blank DVDs is governed by the demand for and subsequent sales of DVRs. To an extent the relationship between the two products should make the demand for the secondary product more predictable, but in many cases the secondary product is a consumable, such as ink cartridges for a printer, and the scale of use, rather than the sales of the printer itself, will determine the demand. Internally, the demand for a particular part or component will be in direct relation to the demand for the products into which those parts and components are inserted. In this respect, an organization purchasing or manufacturing its own components and parts need not be concerned with forecasting demand for them as this is already clear from the demand for the finished product.

See also **bill of materials** *and* **independent demand**.

Dependent demand inventory

A manufacturing organization may have a number of products, components or parts which are associated with **dependent demand**. Normally it is relatively straightforward for the organization to assess the demand for these products with regard to internal use. It is less easy to assess demand as far as external customers are concerned. In the majority of cases the demand needs to be planned rather than forecasted. The dependent demand inventory therefore not only seeks to identify items which are susceptible to dependent demand, but also aims to put in place planned reorders and specified stock levels in order to accommodate this planned use or demand, as opposed to simply ordering on the basis of a forecast.

Dependent variable

A dependent variable is the variable on a graph or forecast which needs to be predicted or estimated. It is usually plotted on the *Y* axis of a graph.

Depreciation

Depreciation is a systematic reduction of the acquisition costs of fixed assets, such as machinery, over the period during which those assets are of benefit to the organization. Depreciation is, in effect, a paper-based accountancy exercise which seeks to take account of the fact that the value of fixed assets gradually decreases over time and that those attendant losses should be written off against the expense accounts of the organization.

In the US this process is known as amortization, which is the systematic reduction of the value of primarily intangible assets such as goodwill or intellectual property. The value of these intangible assets, such as a breakthrough in manufacturing processes, reduces in value over a period of time as it is either replaced or copied by other competitors.

Design capacity

An organization's design capacity is the theoretical maximum output of their production operations. In reality, few organizations, at least in the early stages, are able to reach this design capacity, as it requires all factors which may affect operations to be in place. Design capacity can therefore be described as simply a paper-based capacity figure which gives an indication of optimum output under ideal conditions.

Design for assembly (DFA)

Design for assembly (DFA) is a means by which the design process is guided in order to ensure that the physical assembly of a product can be undertaken at a low cost. It also aims to reduce the assembly time and increase labour productivity, whilst ensuring that quality standards are maintained.

Molloy, O., Warman, E. A. and Tilley, S., *Design for Manufacturing and Assembly: Concepts, Architectures and Implementation*. New York: Kluwer Academic Publishers, 1998.

Design for disassembly (DFD)

At its most basic, DFD aims to simplify repairs to a product or the need to disassemble products for possible remanufacture. In other words, DFD attempts to facilitate the re-use or recycling of a product and its component parts once it has reached the end of its useful life. It is widely believed that in time DFD may be one of the major solutions to the enormous generation of waste caused by the disposal of products. Taken to its ultimate extreme, all products which have a DFD philosophy will be able to be reprocessed in some manner, thus obviating the need to burn, bury or otherwise dispose of obsolete or broken goods.

Lambert, A. J. D., *Disassembly Techniques for Remanufacturing: Cost Analysis, Design, Sequencing and Modelling*. Boca Raton, FL: CRC Press, 2003.

Design for manufacturing and assembly (DFMA)

See **design for assembly (DFA)**.

Design for operations

Design for operations aims to examine a manufacturing organization's ability to produce and successfully deliver a particular product or service according to a schedule. In other words, this is an attempt by the organization, and possibly the customer, to make a judgement as to the manufacturer's ability or suitability to supply certain products or services.

D

Design for recycling/environment

See **design for disassembly (DFD)**.

Desired output rate

When manufacturing organizations calculate or estimate the actual demand for their products over a given period of time, it is usually the case that they will attempt to assign an ideal daily output rate, in order to fulfil this demand. This daily output rate, or desired output rate, when summed over the relevant period, should be equal to or in excess of the actual demand for the products.

Deskilling

Deskilling is the process by which **division of labour** and technological development may lead to a reduction of the scope of an employee's specialized tasks. Work becomes fragmented and employees lose the integrated skills and knowledge associated with a craftsperson. Deskilling has been seen as a negative impact of technology, where a process or machine can perform a task better than the human hand.

Harry Braverman wrote a Marxist critique of capitalism and in particular the organization of work under 'antagonistic' social relations. He was concerned with the loss of craft skills in the organization of work. He was one of the first theorists to define the term as 'deskilling', which he described as being the effective separation of mental work and manual work. Deskilling is closely associated with scientific management and is seen as a means by which management can closely control the labour process in the sense that it removes the skills, knowledge and science of the labour process and transfers these to management. An additional concern is that it can mean that manual and mental workers feel diametrically opposed to one another.

Braverman went on to suggest that deskilling leads to decomposition (the dispersal of the labour process across numerous sites and time) and that, as such, deskilling increases the opportunities for management to exploit labour and reduce the capacity of workers to resist their control.

Both **Frederick Taylor** and Henry Ford were deeply involved in early attempts to deskill and initiate decomposition. As scientific management practitioners they attempted to transform the organization of work to improve profitability, and to reduce craft skills' control of work. The terms **Fordism** and Taylorism are closely associated with the use of the **assembly line**. Fordism itself attempts to harmonize the dual desires of **mass production** and mass consumption.

Deskilling therefore involves the following:

1. the maximum decomposition of the labour process as a series of work tasks across time and space;
2. the separation of direct and indirect labour;
3. the minimization of skill in any work task;
4. the creation of standardized products;
5. the use of specialized machine tools (as opposed to general purpose machine tools);

6 the use of the assembly line and methods of continuous production (at a pace set by management and not by the workforce).

Braverman, Harry, *Labor and Monopoly Capitalism: The Degradation of Work in the Twentieth Century*. New York: Monthly Review Press, 1999.

Taylor, Frederick Winslow, *The Principles of Scientific Management*. New York: Dover Publications, 1998 (reprint).

See also **Fordism** *and* **Taylor, Frederick Winslow**.

Deterministic control model

Ideally, this form of inventory control aims to be far more accurate than some other forms, as it seeks to incorporate any variables or parameters which may affect the overall demand for stock. The model assumes a specific demand for stock items and the associated costs involved, as well as assuming constant replenishment lead times.

Deterministic time estimate

The concept behind setting deterministic time estimates is the assumption that all relevant influences or variables have been taken into account in assessing all of the factors which may affect the total processing time for a given number of products. The deterministic time estimate will incorporate known **lead times** related to supply, setting up, actual processing and the finishing of goods prior to their despatch. The estimates will be based on average, rather than optimum production or process conditions.

Dies

Dies are essentially either software or hardware that is inserted into a general purpose manufacturing machine to instruct it to produce a particular part, with a unique specification. This process is also known as tooling, and may include a combination of tools and dies, such as moulds, templates, stamps or, in publishing, camera-ready copy.

Dimensions of quality

Dimensions of quality are simply the criteria by which quality is measured. The dimensions of quality need to have tangible operational measures and may include the reliability, durability, reputation or performance of the product which is being produced. Further measures may include the degree to which failures or defects are reported over a given period of time after the sale has been completed.

Direct labour

Direct labour is either the proportion of employees who are required to be intimately involved in the manufacture of a product, or the standard number of direct hours required to manufacture a given component or product.

Direct materials purchasing (DMP)

Direct materials purchasing (DMP) involves the contractual arrangement between a supplier and a manufacturer. The supplier undertakes to provide a given amount of a product, part or component at a specified price and quality over a given period of time. The DMP will not necessarily state the exact schedules of deliveries. None the less, an agreement is made as to the schedule, but the major consideration is that by the end of the particular fixed time the supplier will have delivered the given number of items as specified. The supplier and the manufacturer are tied in terms of price and quality agreements throughout the contract. In most cases this is a mutually beneficial arrangement as the supplier is assured of an agreed number of sales over a period of time, and the manufacturer can rely on the supplier ensuring that the full contract is honoured.

Disaggregation

Disaggregation is a technique which breaks down the **aggregate planning** into specific product areas. In other words, once aggregate planning has been carried out, and medium-range capacity planning considerations have been addressed, each of the elements which make up that overall aggregate plan are then examined in order to ascertain whether there may be any conflict issues, particularly those arising out of changeovers in the manufacture of different products, or the availability of materials and components.

Diseconomies of scale

Diseconomies of scale are said to be the point at which a manufacturing process simply becomes too large and the normal rule of **economies of scale** no longer applies. In certain cases, as capacity continues to increase, the manufacturing organization may encounter the problem of average unit costs increasing, rather than falling. There are usually three reasons for this:

- The different processes within the manufacturing procedures may have already reached their optimum **capacity** and so are unable to produce any more products, thus causing difficulties for other processes which are capable of a higher rate of production. This means that various parts of the production process are literally starved of parts and components by these **bottlenecks**.
- As the organization grows, there are attendant difficulties related to the coordination of activities. To support the production process there is an attendant increase in administration and a proliferation of bureaucratic procedures which may inhibit the production process itself, whilst adding indirect costs to each unit of production.
- Under the assumption that the capacity levels of the organization could, up to a point, be supplied by other organizations within a viable geographical area, as production increases the manufacturing organization may need to cast their net wider in order to secure sufficient supply. They may also need to make compromises as to the **lead times**, **quality costs** and delivery costs of these supplies from the additional suppliers. All of these issues will add costs overall, which in turn are applied to each unit of production.

Diseconomies of scale, therefore, occur as a mixture of internal and external diseconomies.

Disintermediation

Disintermediation occurs when an organization in a **supply chain** is replaced by an alternative means by which the product or service passes down the supply chain to the end-user. Typically, this would involve a manufacturer's decision not to sell products or services through distributors and the retail trade, but to sell direct, possibly via a website. Alternatively, a distributor could be cut out of the supply chain, or disintermediated from it, by the manufacturers supplying retailers themselves.

Distinctive competencies

The term 'distinctive competency' is usually used to describe any specific specialisms or advantages which a manufacturing organization may possess. It is these distinct competencies or abilities that mark the organization as having a competitive edge in a specific aspect of its operations.

Distribution

Distribution is the physical movement of products and services from the producer to the end-user and often involves the transfer of ownership through intermediaries between the producer and the end-user. A distribution channel ends when an individual or a business buys a product or service without the intention of immediate resale.

Part of the distribution channel consists of organizations such as storage and transport companies and banks. They are integral parts of the distribution process, but they are outside of it in the sense that they never take ownership of the product or service; they merely aid the channel.

A business faces several different options when setting up the distribution system for its products and services. The key determinants of how this distribution channel is organized usually depend on the following:

- A determination of the role of the distribution and how it will help achieve the marketing objectives.
- The selection of the type of channel, and decisions as to whether intermediaries are required.
- An assessment of the intensity of the distribution, which allows the business to calculate how many intermediaries will be needed at each level and in each area.
- The choosing of specific channel members which most closely match criteria set by the business.

Distribution centre (DC)

A distribution centre is a warehousing facility which accepts inbound shipments of products and then breaks up those shipments, combining them with other inbound shipments for onward distribution.

A distribution centre may also operate as a warehouse rather than as a centre which only holds the products for a limited time before making an outbound shipment.

Distribution requirements planning (DRPI)

DRP is a system by which each warehouse which is holding stock can relay its future stock requirements to the source from which the stock is derived. Clearly, in the case of organizations which have a complex network of distribution, each level of the network systematically passes on information, including the aggregated figures from those they supply themselves, until it reaches the ultimate source of the products. The manufacturer is normally at the end of this process and, using information based on the stock requirement levels of each part and stage of the distribution system, or network, can create a **master production schedule (MPS)**.

Oden, Howard W., Langenwalter, Gary and Lucier, Raymond, *Handbook of Material and Capacity Requirements Planning*. New York: McGraw-Hill Education, 1992.

Distribution resource planning (DRPII)

DRPII is essentially an extension of **material requirements planning** as it incorporates resources which are contained within the distribution system.

Division of labour

The term 'division of labour' refers to rigid and prescriptive allocation of work responsibilities. Formerly, skilled employees were allocated specific job roles and because of the complexity of their work, it was difficult to assign individuals who did not have the same degree of skill to those particular roles. Equally, the skilled individuals were keen to avoid any moves by the management to deskill their work and thus undermine their position. Division of labour therefore became a system by which different employees within a manufacturing organization could be identified and compensated in different ways. As the process of **multi-skilling** has swept manufacturing, coupled with the introduction of more complex technology, many of these former divisions have either disappeared or become blurred over time. None the less, division of labour can still be typified as instances where specific groups or teams of employees are allocated specific roles, and where only these individuals carry out that work.

See also **deskilling**.

Double exponential smoothing

Double exponential smoothing is also known as 'trend adjusted exponential smoothing', and is used to eliminate potential errors in single exponential smoothing. Typically, the forecaster would use **exponential smoothing**, applied to the raw data, and then use secondary exponential smoothing of the predictions which have been derived from that process.

Drum buffer rope (DBR)

DBR is a **theory of constraints (TOC)** which is, in effect, a production control system. The drum refers to a signal which signifies that a **bottleneck** in the manufacturing process has completed the production of a unit. The rope, as a result of the drum, is then pulled into production to make or provide resources for the bottleneck. The buffer is the queue of work completed by the rest of the production line, waiting for the attention of the bottleneck. The buffer is essential in order to ensure that the bottleneck is always kept busy and in full supply. DBR recognizes that it is the bottleneck in a production system which effectively manages or constrains the amount of products which can be processed on that line. In other words, the bottleneck is a valve and although this valve can only open to a limited degree, it still needs to have the steam behind it in order to make it work. Therefore, the rest of the production process needs to be geared to ensuring that the bottleneck is fully supplied and that operations before and after the bottleneck are in step with the bottleneck. If the bottleneck is not identified and fully supplied, then the business runs the risk of increasing the **work in progress** and **cycle time**.

Dummy activity

Dummy activities are encountered on a **critical path** or network diagram. They are displayed as dotted lines and are inserted into the network diagram in order to suggest the correct logic, which would otherwise lead to a complicated or untidy diagram. Dummy activities consume no time or resources, as such, but are incorporated into the diagrams in order to illustrate all of the stages involved. Many dummy activities are eliminated from the diagram should it be considered that they are not dependent issues. Note that dummy activities are only used on **activity-on-arrow** charts.

Earliest due date (EDD)

When a manufacturing company organizes its production processes according to the required delivery dates of the customer, it will investigate the earliest due date (EDD). In other words, the manufacturing schedule will be determined by the products which are required first, or which have the earliest due date.

Early finish (EF)

The early finish, or earliest finish (EF) date for an activity is determined by the activity's **early start** and its duration. Therefore:

EF is equal to earliest start (ES) + duration (D).

Early start (ES)

Early start, or earliest start (ES), refers to the best estimate as to when an activity or a process can begin. It assumes that all of the preceding activities which lead up to that event will have been fulfilled. In other words, the **latest finish** of a preceding activity becomes the ES of the next activity.

Early supplier involvement (ESI)

Early supplier involvement recognizes that a manufacturer's suppliers may well have **core competencies** which are superior to their own. Therefore ESI is the practice of involving suppliers at the earliest possible stage in the design of new products and how they will be processed. ESI should eliminate delays in the development and not only increase quality, but also reduce production and subsequent service costs.

E-business

The term 'e-business', or electronic business, was probably coined by IBM in 1997. It used the term as part of a major advertising campaign. In effect, e-business is the process of conducting business using elements of the internet. E-business is a more generic term than **e-commerce** because it transcends the acts of buying and selling, to mean the collaboration with business partners and the servicing of customers. In effect, e-business is a fusion of business processes, applications and organizational structures. The vast majority of businesses are now incorporating e-business as part of their overall planning procedures. Typically, in manufacturing for example, the internet can be used to buy parts, components and supplies. Provided the organization is satisfied with the quality of products (which would certainly entail the receiving of samples), the global implications for supply are enormous. It is perfectly feasible for a manufacturing organization to now access, interrogate and evaluate organizations remotely in ways in which it would have been impossible to do so in the past. The convenience and availability of suppliers, notwithstanding the attendant delivery costs, may continue to revolutionize the supply and fulfilment functions of manufacturing industry.

E-commerce

'E-commerce', or electronic commerce, is a term specifically used to describe the buying and selling of products and services via the internet. In many respects the term has been superseded by **e-business**, as the latter description is taken to encompass more aspects of trade using the internet. In effect, e-commerce is a paperless exchange of information via emails, bulletin boards, the electronic transfer of funds and fax transmissions. These tools allow online buying and selling in a wide variety of consumer and industrial sectors.

Economic order interval (EOI)

When an organization has a fixed order interval system, the intervals between orders aim to reduce, or keep to a minimum, the total inventory costs. Using EOI principles, the organization will examine the relative advantages and disadvantages of the costs of holding stock in the inventory against the costs of placing an order.

Economic order quantity (EOQ)

EOQ aims to identify the optimum size of an order which will minimize the cost of holding that stock, as well as the cost of ordering the stock from a supplier. The formula for calculating the economic order quantity is:

$$\sqrt{\frac{2SA}{ic}}$$

where A = annual demand; S = order cost; i = carrying charge or warehousing costs; and c = unit cost

In reality, businesses rarely bother to calculate the economic order quantity, as the tendency is always to order expensive items more frequently in smaller quantities. EOQ is, however, useful in helping the organization understand that in trying to minimize the costs associated with placing orders with suppliers, this has to be measured against the organization's immediate demands for that product.

Economic production quantity model (EPQ)

The EPQ model is based on the same assumptions as the **economic order quantity (EOQ)** model, with one notable exception in that it assumes a finite replenishment rate. The assumptions are that demand is known and constant, also that the costs of stock-holding, ordering and purchasing are known and constant.

The final assumptions are that no quantity discounts are available or apply to the situation and that replenishment occurs over a period of time. The chart drawn to represent this can be typified in the graph in Figure 14.

The terms used in the graph and in the following equations are

t_P production period = Q/P
t_R time from beginning of one production period to another
D daily demand rate
P daily production rate
A annual demand
S set-up cost for production
H unit annual holding cost
V total annual variable cost
Q production lot size

E

The average inventory can be calculated using the following formula:

$$\textit{average inventory} = \frac{Q(P-D)}{2P} = \frac{Q}{2} - \frac{QD}{2P} = \left(1 - \frac{D}{P}\right)\frac{Q}{2}$$

The next step is to calculate the variable cost per unit (which is the set-up cost plus the stock-holding costs):

$$V = S\frac{A}{Q} + H\left(1 - \frac{D}{P}\right)\frac{Q}{2}.$$

V is differentiated to Q and the optimum lot size (Q_0):

$$\frac{dV}{dQ} = -S\frac{A}{Q^2} + \frac{H}{2}\left(1 - \frac{D}{P}\right) = 0$$

This then provides the following formula:

$$Q_0 = \sqrt{\frac{2SA}{H\left(1 - \frac{D}{P}\right)}}$$

This allows the calculation of the optimum number of production runs in a given year by using the following formula:

$$N_0 = A/Q_0.$$

Therefore, the EPQ is dependent upon the following:

- the set-up costs;
- the annual demand;
- the stock-holding costs;
- the daily demand;
- the daily production rate.

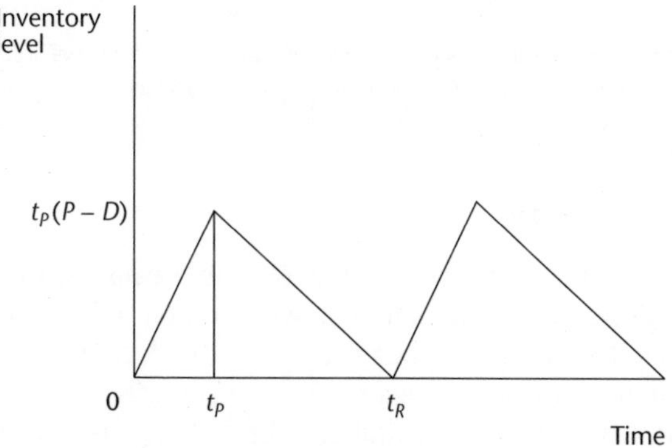

Figure 14 Chart showing EPQ assumptions

Economies of scale

Strictly speaking, the term 'economies of scale' is an economics related issue. However, it has considerable implications for operations management and production. The basic concept revolves around the fact that a business needs to build up a critical mass. In other words, it needs to be large enough to be able to enjoy the benefits associated with larger-scale production. Once a business has reached a point where it is a large trading entity, it can enjoy many of the benefits associated with large-scale production or distribution. In other words, as the size and scope of the business increases, the generally held view is that the unit costs are driven down. The corollary is that having achieved economies of scale, a greater amount of funds are available to further improve the market position and efficiency of the business.

Jackson, Dudley, *Profitability, Mechanization and Economies of Scale*. Aldershot, Hants: Ashgate Publishing, 1998.

Economy of scope

'Economy of scope' is an economics term which puts forward the proposition that a business will enjoy a lower unit cost as it increases the variety of products it offers. Rather than receiving benefits associated with the basic form of **economies of scale**, the business derives advantages from the synergies (similarities) of the production of similar products. The unit costs are driven down by the fact that several products share the same resources, and a number of the same components may be used to produce this variety of products, which have **commonality**.

Ashton, John Kevin, *Cost Efficiency, Economies of Scale and Economies of Scope in the Retail Banking Sector*. Bournemouth: Bournemouth University School of Finance and Law, 1998.

Effective capacity

Effective capacity can be differentiated from **design capacity** in as much as it describes the actual achievable output of a manufacturing organization. The design capacity refers to the optimum output given optimum circumstances. However, effective capacity is a more realistic measure as it takes into account any operational issues which may affect the output as experienced by the organization.

Efficiency

Efficiency can be assessed by an organization comparing the average time taken to carry out a particular process on a production line against a standard processing time. In other words, if the performance of a particular process takes a standard time of 30 minutes per production unit and the current production time is actually 25 minutes, then the efficiency of that part of the process is 30/25 = 1.2, which is normally expressed as a percentage, in which case this would be 120%.

Coelli, Tim., Prasada Rao, D. S. and Battese, George E., *Introduction to Efficiency and Productivity Analysis*. New York: Kluwer Academic Publishers, 1997.
Wheelwright, Steven C. and Clark, Kim B., *Revolutionizing Product Development: Quantum Leaps in Speed, Efficiency and Quality*. New York: Free Press, 1992.

Efficient/effective consumer response (ECR)

Effectively ECR is a means by which **just-in-time systems (JIT)** are gradually being applied to the retail food trade. The hope is that by using **electronic point of sale (EPOS)** and **electronic data interchange (EDI)**, inefficiencies, imbalances of stock, and nil stock situations can be avoided. This means that an ECR system needs to be applied to the whole of the **supply chain**, aiming to eliminate inefficiencies and waste along the length of it.

Martin, André J., *Infopartnering: The Ultimate Strategy for Achieving Efficient Customer Response*. Chichester: John Wiley, 1995.

Electricity at Work Regulations 1989 (UK)

These regulations require employers to ensure that all electrical systems are safe and regularly maintained. The Electricity at Work Regulations 1989 are, in practice, an update of the old Factory Act Electricity Regulations of various years, brought together under the **Health and Safety at Work Act 1974**.

www.hmso.gov.uk/si/si1989/Uksi_19890635_en_1.htm

Electronic data interchange (EDI)

Electronic data interchange (EDI) is applied to the transfer of business documents between computers. In essence, EDI is the paperless movement in electronic form (often automated) between or within businesses to reduce the need for administrative documents. EDI has revolutionized the way in which businesses conduct their trading activities, by allowing a fast, efficient and accurate means of electronically exchanging business transactions. Traditional documents are converted into a structured, machine-readable format so that a remote computer can receive and process data from another business or from a computer in the same business.

Typically, documents will relate to purchasing, sales, inventory management, accounts received and accounts payable. EDI offers a

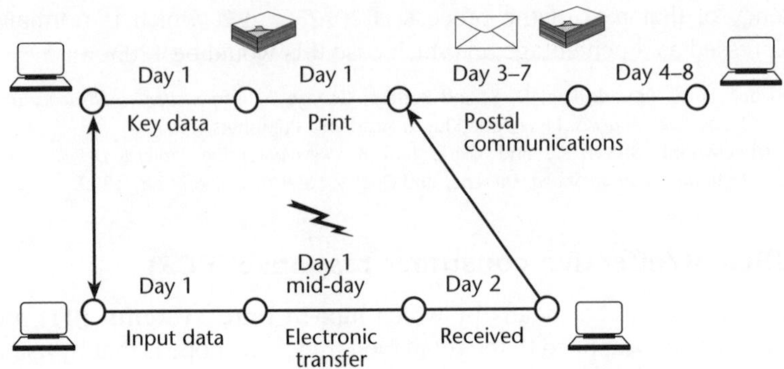

Figure 15 Advantages of electronic data interchange

faster trading cycle with greater speed and accuracy between the ordering and invoicing systems (see Figure 15). EDI has also assisted businesses in adopting **just-in-time system (JIT)** techniques, cutting the time between an order and delivery, often a key determinant in winning or losing a contract. EDI also enables businesses to reduce their stock levels, improve their cash flow, increase security and reduce errors. Automated confirmations of delivery are integral, and recent developments allow the system to be extensively used by customers electronically via the internet.

Busby, Michael, *Demystifying EDI*. Plano, TX: Wordware Publishing, 2000.

Electronic point of sale (EPOS)

EPOS or Electronic Point of Sale is data which is captured electronically when a sale is made. The system relies on the presence of a bar code and an appropriate bar-code reader. When the sale is made the salesperson scans the bar code, or in some cases, the shoppers do it themselves by using a portable reader. The bar code itself contains information including an identification of the item sold, the price and the store location. When coupled with a customer loyalty card, EPOS is able to match the purchases to the individual customers, thus enabling the business to target special promotions in line with the customers' buying habits.

E

The other major purpose of EPOS is to send the information to a computer which is linked to the purchasing facilities of the business. Having registered the fact that a product has been sold, the EPOS system, in conjunction with purchasing software, generates a reorder once a minimum order level has been reached. In this way a business can be assured that it has largely accounted for the stock which has left the shelves and that a process has been put in place in order to restock.

Brook, James, *Payment Systems: Examples and Explanations* (Examples & Explanations Series). New York: Panel Publishing, 2001.

E-manufacturing

E-manufacturing is a result of the rapid growth of internet-based and related systems. The application of open, flexible and reconfigurable systems to enhance existing manufacturing practices as well as the creation of new business models and processes are typical examples of the trend towards e-manufacturing.

As can be seen in Figures 16 and 17, e-manufacturing relies on a fundamental change in the ways in which information is handled, how

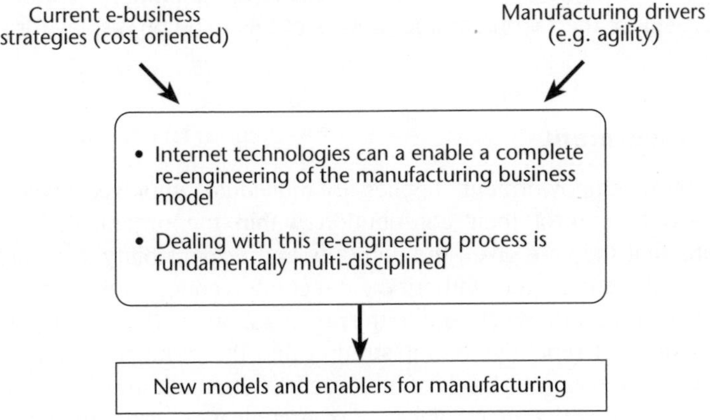

Figure 16 The use of e-manufacturing

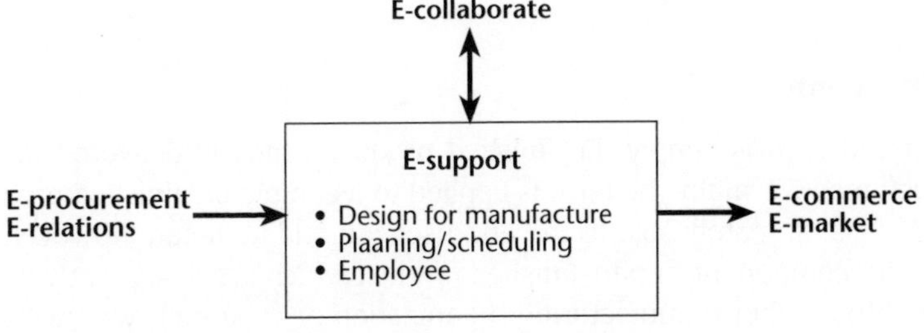

Figure 17 A fully integrated e-manufacturing system

decisions are made and, above all, how materials are handled. The systems are designed to be flexible, open, reconfigurable, scaleable and extendable. The focus is, therefore, on the quality and manner in which the communications and data-management system are configured.

Given that business has become, essentially, a global entity, the organization will seek to move towards a fully integrated system in which **mass customization** of products is the norm and the quality of the service support is often as important as the product itself. The essential concept of e-manufacturing extends beyond our understanding of e-business as new models and enablers for manufacturing are gradually being developed.

Employers' Liability (Compulsory Insurance) Regulations 1969 (UK)

These regulations require employers to have necessary insurance in the event of their employees having an accident or suffering from ill health as a result of their work, and for details of this to be on display for staff to see.

Empowerment

The term 'empowerment' applies to individual employees who are allowed to control their contribution within the organization. This means that they are given the authority and responsibility to complete tasks and attain targets without the direct intervention of management. The benefits of empowerment to the organization are that it reduces the importance of repetitive administration and the number of managers required at the various levels of the structure. Streamlining management levels increases the effectiveness of communication. From the employees' point of view, empowerment increases their creativity and initiative, as well as their commitment to the organization, by allowing them to work with autonomy.

End item

An end item is simply the finished product which is delivered to the customer. Normally the term is applied to a completely finished product which is ultimately sold to the end-user. An end item can, however, be a part, component or part-finished product which is subsequently delivered to another manufacturing organization or customer, who will use those end items in their own production process.

Engineer to order (ETO)

Engineer to order is often known as 'design to order', and refers to situations where businesses undertake engineering of products and their subsequent manufacture in line with specific instructions or requirements of customers. ETO is considerably more complex than most other forms of manufacture, as each product has to be designed to the customer's exact specification. Therefore, the business needs to be able to give the customer an accurate assessment of the delivery time, which incorporates all the **lead times** associated with engineering, procurement, manufacture, assembly, packing and shipping. Although the manufacturer may have many of the key components required by the customer to be incorporated in their specific design, it may be necessary for them to obtain additional items specifically for that manufacturing project.

Organizations which offer ETO to their customers need to have a fully integrated system, which incorporates close cooperation between the designers, the engineers, the buyers, the production team and any other associated area of the business. Although each specific project may be significantly different from those which the business has already experienced, customers will expect relatively accurate indications of the stages through which their products will be developed and manufactured, as it may be a requirement of the customer to be involved in the progress and inspection of the products. It should be made clear that ETO only applies to organizations which actually design, engineer, manufacture and then fulfil the customer's specification.

Enterprise resources planning (ERP)

ERP is an integrated software system which is often used by manufacturers. It incorporates accounts, payroll and **manufacturing resources planning**, as well as other related systems.

Gunn, Tom, *In the Age of Realtime Enterprise: Managing for Sustained Performance with Enterprise Resource Planning*. New London, NH: Oliver Wight Publications, 1994.

Shtub, Avraham, *Enterprise Resource Planning (ERP): The Dynamics of Operations Management*. New York: Kluwer Academic Publishers, 1999.

E

Environmental scanning

Environmental scanning is the process of monitoring and detecting external changes in the environment. In essence, environmental scanning can be seen as a way of identifying new, unexpected, major and minor possible impacts on a business. Environmental scanning, however, needs to be systematic for two main reasons. First, indiscriminate collection of information is somewhat random and it may not be possible to distinguish the relevant from the irrelevant. Secondly, it provides early warnings for managers of changing external conditions in a measured and paced manner. The key objectives of environmental scanning are:

- to detect scientific, technical, economic, social and political trends and events of importance;
- to define the potential threats, or opportunities for changes, implied by those trends and events;
- to promote future thinking in both management and staff;
- to alert the management of trends which are converging, diverging, speeding up, slowing down or interacting in some manner.

At the heart of environmental scanning is the notion that decision-makers need to be aware of the environment in which they operate. In this respect environmental scanning provides the business with strategic intelligence which can help frame its organizational strategies (see Figure 18). Environmental scanning should help a business to forecast in the light of the expectation of change.

Halliman, Charles, *Business Intelligence using Smart Techniques: Environmental Scanning using Text Mining and Competitor Analysis using Scenarios and Manual Simulation*. Houston, TX: Information Uncover, 2001.

Morrison, J. L., 'Environmental Scanning', in M. A. Whitely, J. D. Porter and R. H. Fenske (eds), *A Primer for New Institutional Researchers*. Tallahassee, FL: Association for Institutional Research, 1992, pp. 86–99.

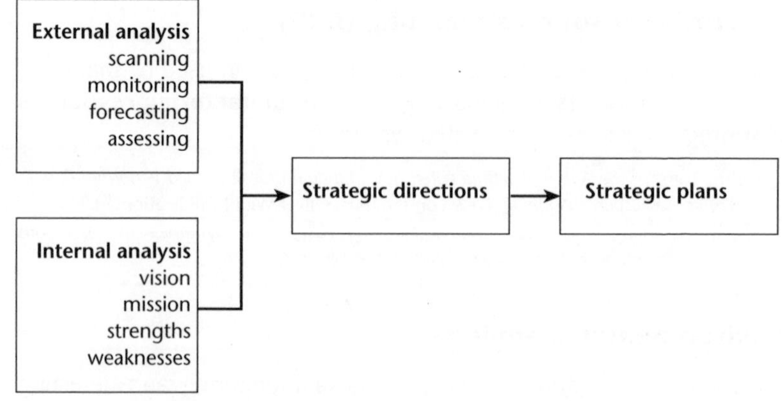

Figure 18 The role of external analysis in strategic planning

Source: After Morrison (1992).

E

E-procurement

E-procurement is the process of obtaining supplies via the internet. Usually a software system is incorporated into the purchasing operation, which handles specifications, authorization and the acquisition of products and services. E-procurement can involve the customer requesting supplies that conform to specific specifications, deliveries, price ranges and other factors, and requesting that suppliers quote to fulfil the order.

Ergonomics

The term 'ergonomics' relates to the study of the design of equipment and the working procedures and environment in which it is used, in order to promote employee well-being and organizational efficiency and effectiveness. Ergonomic design can trace its history back to the Second World War, when tank designers acknowledged the fact that a human being should be considered in the design of tanks, guns and planes. Now it is active in the use of computers and their related equipment, such as tables and chairs and screen design, but ergonomics now also incorporates the human being in designing much of the commonly found equipment and machinery on the production floor, providing the user with the ability to:

- obtain a stimulus in the use of machinery – by incorporating instruments, flashing lights and buzzers so that the tedium is removed to a degree;
- perceive, through touch, smell, sight and sound, whether there is a problem that needs addressing;
- make a decision about what action to take if there is a problem;
- respond, by operating controls on the machinery or by communicating with others.

Ergonomics also takes into account the working environment of the employee and addresses issues such as:

- suitability and level of lighting;
- noise levels;
- suitability of heating and ventilation systems.

Ergonomics seeks to address both the capabilities and the limitations of the human body, aiming to reduce the cumulative impact of motions or forces which may be applied to it.

Wilson, John R. and Corlett, E. Nigel (eds), *Evaluation of Human Work: A Practical Ergonomics Methodology*. London: Taylor & Francis, 1995.

Error

The term 'error' is applied to forecasting and describes the difference between the actual value and the forecasted value depicted on the forecast chart.

Error proofing

See ***poka-yoke.***

Event

An event refers to the starting and finishing times of activities which are displayed as nodes on an **activity-on-arrow (AOA)** or an **activity-on-node (AON)** diagram.

Excess cost

Inevitably, when an organization purchases a range of parts or components which are to be allocated to a particular production process, there will be a mismatch in the number of those items required. Excess cost, therefore, refers to any items which had been earmarked for use in a production process, but were, in fact, unused or were accidentally overstocked in order to provide a **buffering** of items in the event of a series of defects being identified. The excess cost is equal to the unrecovered costs of those items which are left in the inventory once the production process has been completed.

Exponential smoothing

Exponential smoothing is a weighted moving-average forecasting method in which the weight applied to old data decreases exponentially with age.

Using this method, the following assumptions are made:

- $D(t)$ is the demand observed in period t.
- $S(t)$ is the forecast computed after observing $D(t)$.
- α is the smoothing constant.

Therefore $S(t) = \alpha \times D(t) + (1 - \alpha) \times S(t - 1)$.

There can be extensions made to include trend, seasonality, and estimation of demand variability.

E

External factors

Manufacturing organizations do not, of course, operate in a vacuum and, as such, there are issues which have a direct impact upon the **capacity** and the output of their manufacturing processes. External factors are usually taken to mean events or issues which arise outside the actual industrial sector itself and therefore do not normally incorporate the availability of supply, labour, or demand. External factors tend to revolve around government legislation, such as health and safety issues, which may require the organization to amend or rethink the way in which it processes products. Equally, external factors can include **trade union** action or agreements with unions as to how their members will be deployed and the conditions under which they work within the facility.

Facilities factors

The term 'facilities factors' is a generic one used to describe the location, design and layout of a manufacturing facility, which have a direct impact on that facility's **capacity**.

Facilities-based/field-based services

Facilities-based services and field-based services are alternative ways in which to describe different production processes and the interrelationship of those processes with customers. Facility-based production requires the customers to bring their products which require processing to the place of manufacture. Field-based service is a more flexible and often smaller operation, where production takes place within the customer's own environment.

Factor rating

Commonly, factor ratings are used either in the evaluation of the location of a manufacturing facility, or in the positioning of equipment and machinery within a facility. A factor rating, which incorporates relevant advantages and disadvantages derived from both quantitative and qualitative information, will seek to identify the prime, or most suitable, location for either the facility or the production units within the facility.

Fail-safe

Theoretically, most products have an element within the design which should make it impossible for either a customer, or an employee, to misuse them or incorrectly carry out an operation with regard to them. The fail-safe should not only protect the user in relevant cases, but should also ensure that the product is not rendered defective, or does not cease to operate, as a result of the users' actions.

Failure mode and effects analysis (FMEA)

FMEA looks at the likelihood of failure occurring at a given point in a process and the significance of that failure. FMEA was a tool designed by NASA which attempted to square the problem of dealing with the concepts that failure was not an option and that in many cases perfect construction did not necessarily mean maximum utility. FMEA, therefore, tries to predict failures and plan preventative measures. It estimates the costs of those failures and the ability of systems to respond to them. Effectively FMEA can be defined as a bottom–up method of analysing a manufacturing process, with the purpose of identifying and evaluating the potential for failure. Systems will be studied in order to identify the ways in which the processes can be modified in order to increase reliability and reduce failures to a minimum. In some cases, FMEA is also known as 'design failure mode and effects analysis' (DFMEA). In actual fact, both FMEA and DFMEA have a significant commonality with ***poka-yoke***.

Failure rate curve

A failure rate curve is a curve which plots a machine's probability of failure over a specified interval of time. The assumption is that the curve begins at a point when the machine has not yet failed. If the failure has an exponential distribution, then the business can assume that the failure rate curve is constant.

See also **Croston's forecasting method.**

Fault tree analysis

Generally, a fault tree analysis is not dissimilar to a **cause-and-effect diagram**. It is a graphical representation of the minor faults, or mistakes, which have led to the failure of a process or a system. In identifying and analysing these minor issues, it is possible to see how they contributed towards that failure. Individually each fault should be comparatively easy to rectify and the organization will henceforth be aware that should one of these faults occur, it may well trigger subsequent faults which may, in turn, lead to the complete failure of the process once again.

Faxban

Effectively faxban is a form of ***kanban*** **system**. It is a modification of *kanban* in as much as it uses faxed forms to identify demand, rather than the more traditional use of cards or squares in a standard *kanban* system.

Gross, John M. and McInnis, Kenneth R., *'Kanban' Made Simple: Demystifying and Applying Toyota's Legendary Manufacturing Process*. New York: Amacom, 2003.

FCFS

See **first come first served.**

Fill rate

There are essentially two different forms of fill rate, one which relates to specific units and the other relating to orders as a whole.

The 'unit fill rate' is the percentage of units that can be immediately supplied from stock.

The associated term is the 'line fill rate', which is the percentage of lines on a given purchase order that can be filled directly from stock.

In addition to these there is a third associated term, the 'order fill rate', which is the percentage of orders that can be completely fulfilled from immediate stock.

The most difficult of the three fill rates to satisfy is the order fill rate, as it is contingent upon the organization's ability to fulfil both the unit fill rate and the line fill rate.

Final assembly scheduling (FAS)

The final assembly schedule (FAS) is, as the term implies, related to the last part of the manufacturing process which sees the product completed. At this stage all of the necessary processes will have already been undertaken in order for the product to have arrived at the FAS. The FAS itself is designed to ensure that the product conforms with the specific customer orders, where appropriate, and that all quality issues have been addressed. The FAS is, in effect, bolted onto the end of the **manufacturing resource planning (MRP)**.

Finders, grinders and minders

The trio of terms 'finders', 'grinders' and 'minders' refer to the three most common areas of work and job roles associated with manufacturing. 'Finders' are effectively salespersons and those who deal with customers. They are called finders as their responsibility is to generate orders for the manufacturing organization. 'Grinders' are the individuals who are directly involved in the manufacturing process. Literally they are the ones who grind out the products and services which the finders offer to their customers. The grinders are managed by the 'minders', who not only deal with day-to-day management situations, but are also inextricably involved in the framing of future projects and new product developments.

Finished goods

Finished goods are simply those products which have been fully processed and completed and are awaiting sale. Finished goods include goods which have already been allocated to a specific customer order and those made in anticipation of a customer order, or those which are simply placed into stock for future orders.

Finite capacity scheduling/loading

Finite capacity scheduling or finite loading is a pragmatic approach to the sequencing of activities. It recognizes that any schedule needs to ensure that no single resource is expected to operate beyond its **capacity** constraints. In other words, in framing a schedule or a sequence of activities, there may be a temptation to overload a certain part of that schedule in order to ensure that the project is completed by a defined date. The schedule needs to take into account that there may be other activities which require equal priority, or that it is not feasible to assume that a particular part of the schedule can be completed in less time than is normally the case.

Plenert, Gerhard and Kirchmier, Bill, *Finite Capacity Scheduling: Management, Selection and Implementation*. Chichester: John Wiley, 2000.

Finite population source

Many manufacturing organizations will be cognizant of the fact that the products which they can process, or the systems and services which they offer, only have a limited number of potential customers. This limited number of customers is referred to as a finite population source, and is used to define the overall size of the potential market.

See also **infinite population source**.

F

Fire Precautions Act 1971; Fire Precautions (Factories, Offices, Shops and Railway Premises) Order 1989; Fire Precautions (Workplace) Regulations 1997; Fire Precautions (Workplace) (Amendment) Regulations 1999 (UK)

This series of Acts and subsequent amendments and additions require employers to have a valid fire certificate, specifically in the case of hotels and boarding houses, and of factories, offices, shops or railway premises. In the second case a certificate is needed if more than 20 employees are working in the building or more than 10 employees are working on a floor other than the ground floor.

www.hmso.gov.uk/si/si1989/Uksi_19890079_en_1.htm
http://194.128.65.3/si/si1997/97184001.htm
www.hmso.gov.uk/si/si1999/19991877.htm

First come first served (FCFS)

FCFS is an alternative approach which can be differentiated from **earliest due date (EDD)** as it deals with orders strictly on the basis of when they were received. In other words, rather than considering the earliest due date, the business schedules work according to the order in which customers confirmed their orders.

First in, first out (FIFO)

'First in, first out' is used in both stock valuation and stock rotation. When FIFO is applied to stock valuation an assumption is made that the oldest stock will be consumed first, and sets the oldest relevant price as the value of that stock. When FIFO is applied to stock rotation it is used to ensure that the oldest stock is sold first, or consumed first, in order to make sure that the business is not left with stock which may become obsolete, or in the case of perishable items, out of date.

See also **last in, first out (LIFO)**.

F

Fishbone diagram

See **cause-and-effect diagram** *and* **Ishikawa diagram**.

Five Ss

See **5s** (see p. 264).

Five Ws, Two Hs

See **5W2H approach** (see p. 264).

Fixed cost

Fixed costs incorporate all the costs attached to a manufacturing process which do not change, regardless of the volume of production. Typically, fixed costs can be related to overheads, such as the rent of the premises, lease payments on equipment, or other predictable costs which remain static.

Fixed order quantity model (Q model)

The Q model is a rigid inventory management system where ordering is triggered by the inventory dropping to a predetermined and specified level. Only when the inventory has fallen to this level does the organization reorder.

Fixed-position layout

Because of the size and complexity of the equipment and machinery associated with the manufacturing process, it may be necessary or desirable for an organization to permanently determine the exact location of those items. With the fixed-position layout of the equipment, and with associated areas set aside for parts and components which will be fed into the process, and storage areas for finished goods, the employees are deployed along the static process as and when required.

Fixed storage location system

A fixed storage location system is an orderly and closely managed means by which all stock is placed in a defined position within the warehouse. Typically, each storage area, down to the shelf, has an inventory number and product identification code. In theory, when items related to the inventory code or product identification are required, they should be located in that space.

Fixed time period model (P model)

See **periodic (inventory) review system.**

F

Fixtures

The word 'fixtures' is used to describe tools and components which can be literally fixed to general purpose machines. They are tools which are located close to the general purpose machines and can be fitted into place, or exchanged with another tool, in order to carry out a particular job.

Flexible manufacturing system (FMS)

Theoretically, a flexible manufacturing system is an integrated group of machines which have the capacity to carry out automated handling between them. In other words, they share an integrated information system which automatically passes part-finished products between the machines for the next stage of the process to be carried out.

Gunasekaran, A., *Agile Manufacturing: The 21st Century Competitive Strategy*. Oxford: Pergamon, 2001.

Kidd, P. T. and Karwowski, W. (eds), *Advances in Agile Manufacturing: Integrating Technology, Organization and People*. Amsterdam: IOS Press, 1994.

Flexibility

Flexibility is a measure of an organization's ability to change. From a manufacturing perspective, there are four variants which can measure the flexibility of the organization. These are:

- *Volume flexibility* – which demonstrates the organization's ability to remain profitable whilst increasing or decreasing its production rate. An integral part of this is to address issues related to the **aggregate planning**.
- *Mix flexibility* – this is a measure of how able the organization is to introduce or extend the range of products, parts or components which it produces. The measure requires the organization to remain profitable, yet to be able to produce a mix of different products within the same facility.
- *Customization flexibility* – effectively this is a measure of the organization's preparedness to **respond to order** and still retain profits. Alternatively, this measure of flexibility can be typified as being the organization's ability to engage in **mass customization**.
- *New product development flexibility* – given the other imperatives of continuing production and retaining profitability, this measurement indicates the ability of the organization to swiftly develop new products and put them into production.

Float

Float is stock, including **work in progress**, which is in excess of the immediate requirements for it.

See also **slack**.

Flow process chart

A flow process chart is a diagrammatic representation of the individual parts of a process operation and the tasks which are carried out by employees during those processes. An example is shown in Figure 19.

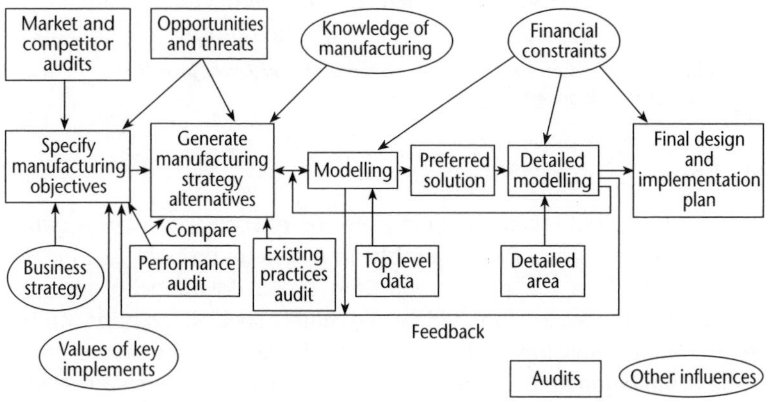

Figure 19 A flow process chart

Flow shop scheduling

As the term implies, flow shop scheduling is the way in which an organization chooses to arrange the scheduling of its **flow systems**.

See also **flow system**.

Flow system

The term 'flow system' refers to manufacturing processes which utilize standardized equipment and activities as integral parts of their production process. Typically, flow systems are high-volume or high-output production lines which produce products with very little or no variation, as the organization supplies customers with standard parts, components or products, which require very little variation.

Focused factory

The term 'focused factory' implies a close synergy between the manufacturing organization and its market. The focused factory is often typified by the installation of automated manufacturing processes, the use of **manufacturing resource planning (MRP)** and **just-in-time systems** of delivery of supplies. In reality, of course, many manufacturing organizations have elements of their production facility which can be described as focused factories, as they seek to continue to provide a high volume of product to a market which has little variance, either in requirements or in demand. In this situation these parts of a factory, which may be a **plant within a plant**, are relatively untouched by developments or realignments of other processes within the rest of the production facility.

Kotha, S., 'From Mass Production to Mass Customization: The Case of National Industrial Bicycle Company of Japan', *European Management Journal*, vol. 14, no. 5 (October 1995), pp. 442–50.

Fordism

The term 'Fordism' takes its name from Henry Ford (1863–1947), who, although not inventing the **assembly line** system, brought this means of production into the public eye. Ford broke down the production process into hundreds of individualized, highly specialized parts, creating a complex division of labour in which individual workers could specialize in being able to complete a specified task, or series of related tasks, in a much shorter period than had been the case before the production line system was introduced. In effect, Ford rationalized the production system, whilst simultaneously **deskilling** his workforce.

Alongside the division of tasks and deskilling, Ford introduced higher wages than the industry norm to encourage the employees and partially compensate them for the fact that they would now be working as part of a three-shift system, allowing the plant to run 24 hours a day. It was a measure of the effectiveness of this introduction that the price of a model T Ford fell from $950 in 1908 to $290 in 1927, yet the turnover of the business increased significantly over the same period.

Ford, however, did not wish to proceed beyond the process of deskilling to introduce full automation of his factory. He still believed that employees were essential in being able to create quality products. Fordism remains at the heart of much of the **mass production** standards of products to this day.

Matthews, Richard A., *Fordism, Flexibility and Regional Productivity Growth*. New York: Garland Publications, 1997.

See also **Taylorism**.

Forecasting

There are a number of associated terms related to forecasting, but forecasting itself is an attempt to predict the future of a variable. Businesses will attempt to forecast the demand for their products or services in order to plan both their stock and manufacturing requirements. The accuracy of a forecast very much depends upon the reliability of the data upon which the forecast has been based and, indeed, the length of time into the future which the forecast is expected to encompass. Generally a manufacturing organization will seek to forecast demand slightly in excess of its average manufacturing **lead time**. The further into the future a forecast is projected, the more chance there is of a significant error, as variables become far more unpredictable as a result of other, unknown variables having an influence upon them.

Forrester effect

See **bullwhip effect.**

Forward buy

Periodically there may be situations or inferences which lead a manufacturing organization to believe that there may soon be a price increase related to the parts, components or products which they purchase from their suppliers. In order to anticipate and counteract the detrimental effects of these price increases on their margins and profitability, manufacturers may initiate orders ahead of their needs. Unfortunately this anticipation or forward buying policy may well hasten the price increase, as it will inevitably catch suppliers unaware and reduce the overall supply of those items, thus justifying a price increase on the basis of supply and demand. In the worst case, it may well initiate a **bullwhip effect**.

Forward scheduling/loading

Essentially, forward loading or scheduling is the exact opposite of **backward scheduling** in as much as the scheduling of a particular project begins with the start date. The schedule is then continued, looking at relevant activities which will be required at various stages along the schedule, ensuring that capacity constraints are not violated. Once this scheduling has been completed, the organization has a very definite and accurate indication of the completion date.

Freeze window

Having established the schedule for a particular production, process or project, an organization will set a freeze window, which alerts all those involved to the fact that there will be no further amendments to the schedule, and that the time allocated to that process or project is now fixed.

Front office

See **back office/front office.**

Gantt chart

The Gantt chart was developed as a production control tool by Henry L. Gantt in 1917. Gantt was a US engineer and social scientist and developed this type of horizontal bar chart, which is now commonly used to illustrate many different types of schedule.

Gantt charts are also used in project management. They provide a graphical illustration of a schedule, which assists the planning, coordination and tracking of each task within an overall project. Gantt charts can be simplistic horizontal bar charts, drawn on graph paper, or, as is more common, can be created using proprietary software, such as Microsoft Project or Excel.

Geographical information system (GIS)

A geographical information system is a software tool which is generally used primarily by a distribution centre or an organization wishing to assess the delivery cost component of its order costs. The GIS will collect, store and display demographic data or locations of suppliers and customers. It can be used to determine the best routes for deliveries, as well as options to collect, or request that freight carriers pick up additional supplies from other suppliers *en route* to the manufacturing facility.

Gross material requirements

The term 'gross material requirements' is an alternative means by which an organization may describe the total expected demand for a given part, component or product over a given time period.

Group technology

Group technology is most closely associated with the organization of production processes. Group technology adopts the assumption that economies, in terms of both employee compensation and savings related to the movement of materials, can be achieved if similar parts or components are processed in the same location. In these cases similar parts and components are organized into families and their production takes place using appropriate machinery in specialized work cells.

GUS classification

In order to assist an organization in its flow and stock controls, it may often be the case that products, parts and components are classified or categorized in one of three areas. GUS is an acronym for 'General, Unique or Specific' products. Typically, general products would include those required in a wide variety of different manufacturing processes. Unique products or items are those which are only associated with a particular range of associated processes. Specific products or items are those which are exclusively used in particular processes and are usually bought in according to the requirements of a specific customer order.

Hazmat

Hazmat is an acronym which means 'hazardous material'. There are associated environmental and health and safety regulations and legislation attached to the handling and processing of Hazmat.

See also **Control of Substances Hazardous to Health (COSHH)** *and* **Health and Safety at Work Act 1974.**

Health and Safety at Work Act 1974 (HASAWA)

The HASAWA places a duty on employers to ensure the health, safety and welfare at work of all their employees (as far as is practicable). The Health and Safety Executive and local authorities enforce HASAWA and there are criminal sanctions for breaches or failure to comply.

In addition to this legal responsibility, employers also have an implied responsibility to take reasonable steps as far as they are able, to ensure the health and safety of their employees is not put at risk. Employers are required to assess the levels of risk against the costs associated with the elimination of those risks in order to make a judgement as to whether they have taken all reasonable steps. Usually the employer's responsibility is only to his or her own employees and premises; however, the responsibility can be extended in some circumstances.

www.hse.gov.uk

Health and Safety Information for Employees Regulations 1989 (UK)

These regulations require employers to display a poster informing their employees of what they should know about health and safety.

www.hmso.gov.uk/si/si1989/Uksi_19890682_en_1.htm

Health and Safety (Safety Signs and Signals) Regulations 1996 (UK)

These regulations came into effect following a European Union Directive. They require employers to provide safety signs where there is a risk which has not been avoided or controlled by other means. The safety signs are aimed at reducing the risks, by such means as the regulation of traffic, the marking of dangerous substances or areas, and incorporating fire safety signs, including directions to exits.

www.hmso.gov.uk/si/si1996/Uksi_19960341_en_1.htm

Hedge

Hedge or hedging is, to all intents and purposes, an inventory **buffer** which is used by an organization to ensure that it has sufficient materials in stock at all times. The term is applied to this in the sense that the organizations are hedging their bets. In effect they are being ultra careful in the knowledge that future shortages may occur or that the prices associated with the materials in question may rise at some point in the future.

Heijunka

Heijunka was a term coined by Taiichi Ohno, and in effect it means attempting to ensure that the production rate remains as constant as possible. Ohno typified it as being production levelization, or smoothing. The Japanese word itself means 'to make flat and level'. The concept recognizes that customer demand is not level, so in order to compensate for this, periodic changes in the product being manufactured on a given line are made. *Heijunka* is most closely associated with the **Toyota production system (TPS)**, which involves the manufacture of small batches of several different models over a short period of time. Although this requires a great deal of flexibility in changing over from one product to another, it means that there are available stocks of finished products which can immediately satisfy the often unpredictable customer demand. It also means that the business does not build up large stocks of one particular product, which it subsequently discovers is in lower demand than other products which have lower stock levels.

Ohno, Taiichi, *Toyota Production System: Beyond Large-Scale Production*. New York: Productivity Press, 1988.

High involvement work practices

Pil and MacDuffie studied motor vehicle assembly plants to test a series of factors which affect what they termed 'high involvement work practices' (HIWPs). The practices include **job rotation**, use of teams and suggestion schemes. They considered that HIWP were more difficult to change than normal human resource policies because the work practices are more integral to the core business processes and coordination requirements of the organization.

Pil and MacDuffie discovered the following:

- Plants are more likely to increase their use of high involvement work practices when they already have implemented complementary human resources management practices.
- Higher levels of managerial tenure have a positive association with greater increase in the use of HIWPs, suggesting that longer-term relationships provide a possible basis for greater trust.
- Actions which reduce employee trust, such as management layoffs, production-worker layoffs and early retirement programmes, have no statistically significant association with the introduction of HIWPs.

Pil and MacDuffie found that businesses in developing countries use HIWPs and not automation. They tend to use training, performance-based pay, more selective recruitment and hiring than an investment in automated processes.

Pil, F. K. and MacDuffie, J. P., 'Organizational and Environmental Factors Influencing the Use and Diffusion of High Involvement Work Practices', in P. Cappelli, *Employment Practices and Business Strategy*. Oxford: Oxford University Press, 1999, pp. 81–106.

High-volume systems

The term 'high-volume systems' refers to either manufacturing organizations or their production systems which use standardized equipment and processes in order to produce products or services with little variation.

H

Holding cost

See **carrying charge/cost**.

Horizontal loading

Horizontal loading is a process-scheduling technique which seeks to give the highest priority to immediately required jobs. Each work centre associated with the production of a particular job is instructed to give it the highest priority. After that job has been completed, the job with the next highest priority moves to the top of the ladder.

Human factors

Human factors are the various employee-related issues which directly impinge upon or influence the manufacturing process. Typically, human factors would incorporate the employees' experience, skills, training and flexibility.

Hungarian method

The Hungarian method is a means by which an organization seeks to assign specific jobs on a one-to-one basis. Particular machines or employees which are most ideally suited to the particular job are allocated the work on the basis that they will be the most cost-effective method of production.

Independent demand

'Independent demand' is a term used to describe a demand for various parts, components or products which is not influenced by the demand for other items.

See also **dependent demand.**

Indirect labour

The term 'indirect labour' encompasses all employees whose work aims to support those directly involved in the production process. Indirect labour would therefore include warehousing staff, and those carrying out inspection, maintenance, machine set-up and product testing. The normal rule of thumb is that the level of indirect labour should not exceed the level of those involved in **direct labour** activities and that wherever possible indirect labour tasks become part of the overall function of workers directly employed on the production process. This is usually achieved by **job enlargement**.

Industrial action

Industrial action is often the result of lack of agreement in dispute resolution. Industrial action can take a number of different forms, all of which will have been the centre of discussions between **trade union** members, their representatives and the management of the organization. If, after a series of negotiation discussions, there is no resolution to the issue, then trade union representatives have the following options to present to their members:

- Withdrawing cooperation with management by ending negotiation and assistance in future dispute resolution and the compilation of agreements until the industrial action issue has been resolved.
- Insisting on formal rights – this means that the trade union representative would bring to the attention of the management every issue that arises, however trivial. Normally such trivial incidences would have been dealt with in a less formal manner.

- Withdrawing of willingness to work **overtime** – this means that employees would not be prepared to work additional hours to those stipulated as their normal working hours. This form of industrial action can have serious implications for an organization that relies on employee cooperation to meet production output targets.
- Working a 'go-slow' – this means that employees will continue to adhere to the requirements of their contract of employment, but will not carry out any additional duties, nor respond to urgent requirements or rush jobs as they may emerge.
- Withdrawal of labour – in effect this is strike action, when either a trade union calls for an *unofficial strike*, which could be for short periods of time until the dispute is finally resolved, or in some cases an *official strike* is called, usually when the dispute has remained unresolved for a length of time or a collective agreement is thought to have been broken by the employer.

Industrial relations

The term 'industrial relations' has largely negative connotations since it is often preceded by the words 'poor' or 'bad'. As a general term, 'industrial relations' refers to the ongoing dialogue or relationship between employers and employees, which may, or may not, involve aspects of collective bargaining, discussions regarding working conditions, rewards, job structures and a variety of other human resource topics. Industrial relations also implies an underlying conflict between those who own and control industry and those who provide the labour in order to fuel it. In most countries industrial relations have had periods during which the relationship between employers and employees (largely represented by **trade unions**) has been extremely poor, confrontational and irreconcilable on the basis that their objectives are mutually exclusive.

The term 'industrial relations' is also interchangeable in many respects with the term 'labour relations', which again refers to the ongoing attitudes of employers and employees towards one another, and their ability or willingness to cooperate on various matters. There is an underlying suspicion for both parties that decisions and stances are taken without regard to the other's desires.

Industrial union

An industrial union is a **trade union** which recruits members from only one industry. Notably, however, an industrial union is a vertical union in the sense that it recruits members from all grades, either manual or non-manual, within that industry. There are very few industrial unions left in existence as over the past quarter of a century many unions which had formerly been industrial unions have merged or amalgamated with one another in order to improve their bargaining strength and ensure their continued existence. Membership of an industrial union became extremely fragmented during this period and many of the unions opted for horizontal recruitment, thus making them general unions.

Infinite loading

Infinite loading is a technique which assigns work to a particular area, cell or production process on the basis of the amount of parts, components or products required over a given time. It is known as infinite loading as the technique does not take **capacity** considerations into account.

Infinite population source

'Infinite population source' refers to situations where the actual number of customers has a close relationship with the production capacity of the manufacturing organization. This may be achieved in one of two ways. Either the manufacturing company adapts its **capacity** to feed the customer **demand** at a steady rate, or the demand for the product is higher than the capacity and the manufacturing organization gradually seeks to supply that demand over a period of time.

Information velocity

Information velocity is a measure of the speed at which collaborative information is passed from one point in the **supply chain** to another. Increasingly, the reliance on data received by a partner in the supply chain has become a vital part of the decision-making process. Information is shared as its dissemination is mutually beneficial. Therefore the information velocity along a supply chain should be as fast and as clear as possible.

Input/output control

Input/output control involves the management and the association of inputs and outputs. In other words, the general rule is that inputs which are sent into a particular work centre or process should not exceed the ability of that unit to create output. If input exceeds output, then there is a **bottleneck** at that work centre which could have a detrimental effect upon the rest of the production process.

Inspection

As the term naturally implies, this is the process of checking individual parts or batches of parts which have been completed, in order to ensure that they meet specifications and exacting quality standards. Inspection will tend to be undertaken either by the individual operators themselves (also known as a source inspection), by the next individual in the process (known as a successive inspection) or at the last step of the process (known as a final inspection). Inspections tend to take place prior to the product being released for despatch to the customer. It is also common for inspections to take place before the parts reach a **bottleneck** in the production process. This ensures that the capacity of the bottleneck is not wasted by spending time on parts which are faulty. In the past it was common practice to carry out inspections on parts or components when they arrived from a supplier, in order to ensure that they met the quality standards. This has largely been eliminated by a supplier certification, which guarantees the level of quality. Given the fact that the suppliers would invariably be carrying out their own inspections during the production process, it is only one single step forward for the supplier and the customer who is using the components to agree on a quality standard to obviate the need for an inspection on delivery.

Schraft, R. D. and Melchior, K. W., *Automated Inspection and Product Control.* Heidelberg: Springer Verlag, 1992.

I

Integrated product development (IPD)

Integrated product development (IPD) has a great deal in common with **concurrent engineering** as it aims to use a cross-functional team to ensure that the steps needed to design and manufacture a product will ultimately satisfy customer needs. The process should ensure that less development time is actually spent on a product, as product ideas will not proceed any distance along the process if they do not enjoy the full support of the cross-functional team. This also means that there will be fewer changes in the immediate period before manufacture, as the majority of potential problems will already have been ironed out by the combined expertise of the team. It is also believed that IPD can ensure, therefore, that products reach the market much faster and with a higher level of quality than could be expected if the product was developed in a more traditional or conventional manner.

Brethauer, Dale, *New Product Development and Delivery: Ensuring Successful Products through Integrated Process Management*. New York: Amacom, 2002.

Interchangeable parts

Interchangeable parts are often standardized parts and components. The theory is that any part of a batch of these identical parts would serve the same purpose as another in a more complex product being processed on the production line.

Intermediate volume systems

'Intermediate volume system' is a generic term which is used to describe a manufacturing organization that is neither a **job shop** nor a high-volume production facility. An intermediate volume system tends to be a flexible manufacturing base which seeks to adapt to customer requirements rather than pushing higher capacity levels through the system.

Internal failure costs

Internal failure costs are expenses incurred by the production of faulty or defective products which have not been picked up in the normal inspection process during manufacturing. At the simplest level, internal failure costs can be taken to mean the cost of failures which are discovered before they reach the customer. More often these internal failures have reached a customer, who then discovers the defect. The products would have been counted as finished and sold goods, but must now be reduced in value and replaced as they are substandard.

Inventory position

The inventory position of a product, part or component is equal to the number of those items which are immediately available, plus those which are expected to be delivered in the very near future. From this combined total it is necessary to deduct those items which are still in stock, but have already been allocated to the production of a product or products to fulfil an existing order from a customer.

Inventory turnover

Inventory turnover, or stock turnover, is equal to the cost of goods sold, divided by the average investment in the inventory. Or, in other words, the cost of goods sold, divided by stock. The inventory turnover is the inverse of **cycle time**. Normally the inventory turnover increases in proportion to demand

Inventory velocity

Inventory velocity can be measured in one of two ways. It refers either to the speed at which items enter a manufacturing organization, are then processed and subsequently sold on to a customer, or to the general movement of parts, components or products within a **supply chain**. Manufacturing organizations will seek to ensure that the inventory velocity is as fast as is practicable, as the higher the speed, the shorter the time between paying for parts and components and receiving payments for the finished products.

Ishikawa diagram

The Ishikawa, or fishbone, diagram was created by Kaoru Ishikawa and is, to all intents and purposes, a cause-and-effect graphic representation. The diagram is designed to identify all the possible causes which lead to a specific effect (see Figure 20). In this respect the Ishikawa diagram is also referred to as being either a **cause-and-effect diagram**, or root-cause analysis.

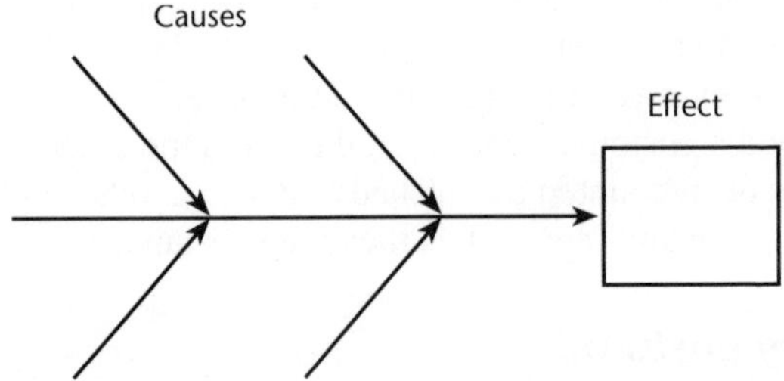

Figure 20 An Ishikawa diagram

An Ishikawa diagram is a graphic tool which is often used as a means to note the progress and content of a brainstorming session aimed at attempting to identify the causes of a problem.

The Ishikawa diagram is named after the inventor of the tool, Kaoru Ishikawa (1969). It is called a fishbone diagram because its shape resembles a fish skeleton. The name of the basic problem is entered at the right of the diagram at the end of the main 'bone'. The causes of the problem are then drawn as bones off the main backbone.

Typically, four 'M's' are used as a starting point, namely Materials, Machines, Manpower and Methods, although different categories can be used if needed. The main point of the exercise is to have between three and six main categories, which cover all of the possible influences.

Brainstorming allows the addition of causes to the main bones of the diagram and more specific causes to bones on the bones. The subdivision of the problems continues for as long as there are identified problems which can be subdivided.

Usually, the diagram has four or five levels and when the fishbone has been completed, the individuals involved will be able to view a full picture of all of the possibilities related to the root cause of the problem.

Ishikawa, Kaoru, *Guide to Quality Control*. Tokyo: Asian Productivity Organization, 1986.

See also **cause-and-effect diagram.**

ISO9000

This is a certification standard which was created by the International Organization for Standardizations (1987). ISO9000 plays a major part in establishing the documentation standards for global manufacturers. The standards are recognized in many countries around the world and the ISO standards can be summarized as being an externally driven methodology which aims to persuade organizations to 'document what you do – and do what you document'.

As far as many countries are concerned, the ISO standards are seen as only seeking to bar them from markets (notably Europe), whilst others see the system as being a **benchmarking** process by which overseas business can aspire to match the best standards of the leading European and North American organizations.

The latest versions of the ISO9000 importantly focus on ongoing improvements rather than striving for a specified goal and then remaining there.

ISO14001

ISO14001 are certification standards created by the International Organization for Standardizations and are related to environmental impacts of business. The standards require organizations to have an environmental management system as a driver to formulate a policy (and objectives) on their environmental impacts. The standards also require the organizations to take into account any relevant legislative requirements derived from countries and/or areas in which they operate.

The certification is reliant on the organization effectively controlling the environmental aspects over which it can reasonably be expected to have a degree of control.

Jidoka

Jidoka is a Japanese term which is used to describe the practice of designing processes, and empowering workers, to close down the production process when abnormal incidents or conditions occur.

The literal translation of the word is 'automation with a human touch (mind)'. The underlying philosophy is that a defective product or component should not proceed from one work station or processing unit to the next, even if it is a question of quality rather than of it being defective.

The main goal is quality and, therefore, both the machinery and the employees can stop the process if a quality-related problem is picked up. Primarily, the machinery itself determines whether the process needs to be stopped, taking some of the onus from the employees to spot those defects.

Jidoka is also used when workers encounter a problem at their work station, as they are responsible for correcting the problem and if they cannot solve the issue, then they are authorized to stop the line. Practically, *jidoka* is implemented by a signal which communicates the immediate status of the machine.

The prime objectives of *jidoka* are:

- to ensure quality 100% of the time;
- to prevent equipment breakdowns;
- to use manpower efficiently.

www.nummi.com/tps.html

JIT II

JIT II extends the **just-in-time system** by having a representative of the supplier working at a customer's location. This presence is designed to facilitate product design and coordination activities.

Originally, 'JIT II' was a term and concept developed by Lance Dixon at Bose Corporation. In essence, JIT II is a version of **vendor managed inventory**, coupled with the early and immediate supplier involvement in problems and opportunities as well as the physical relocation of supplier personnel.

See **just-in-time system (JIT).**

Job design

The implementation of a system of job design can assist an organization in increasing employee motivation. An organization that carries out job analysis during the process of job design aims to improve its employees' job satisfaction and ultimately their performance. Job design does not, however, simply involve motivation, but has some added determining factors which may restrict or limit the job. These are:

- technology;
- the cost of providing essential equipment or materials;
- resistance from current employees or their representatives;
- the organizational structure of the business.

If a job has significantly changed, then an organization might choose to amend the job by using **job enrichment**, **job enlargement** or **job rotation** and accordingly amend the employees' job descriptions, rather than go through the costly and time-consuming process of a new job design.

Wall, Toby and Parker, Sharon, *Job and Work Design: Organizing Work to Promote Well-Being and Effectiveness*. London: Sage Publications, 1998.

Job enlargement

As an alternative to designing a new job, an organization might decide to redesign the parameters of an existing job to incorporate additional required tasks. Job enlargement involves an employee having to expand into carrying out additional, but similar activities. Although it is often hoped that this enlargement of tasks will lead to a higher level of job satisfaction and motivation, it has to be remembered that once the enlarged job has been orientated, then there is a risk that this job, too, will become boring. An organization would need to ensure that this job enlargement process does not simply incorporate into a tedious job yet another set of equally tedious tasks. However, it has been concluded that the job enlargement process does give employees a greater degree of job satisfaction and that their performance was improved as a result of the process as compared to those who remained in restricted job roles. From an organizational point of view, however, the job enlargement process can be a costly exercise, with few guaranteed benefits.

Job enrichment

Job enrichment is, effectively, another form of **job enlargement**, but one in which the employee often finds a higher degree of job satisfaction and motivation. The closest type of job enrichment to job enlargement is known as 'horizontal job enrichment', which involves the incorporation of similar tasks into the job for the employee. This has proved not to be as satisfactory as the more successful form of job enrichment, known as 'vertical job enrichment'.

Vertical job enrichment involves an individual employee being given the opportunity to see the task in hand through to its completion. This allows the employee to become involved in related, but not necessarily similar tasks, allowing a higher degree of motivation. Research has identified that this type of job enrichment has both short-term and longer-term effects. After approximately three months the employees' performance levels have been shown to decrease, possibly as a result of the difficulties they have been facing in taking on board the added considerations in their enriched role. However, after approximately six months these employees show an improvement on their original performance levels, possibly because they have had the time to develop a confidence in what they are doing.

Peters, Tom, *Projects 50: Or, 50 Ways to Transform Every Task into a Project that Matters.* New York: Alfred A. Knopf, 1999.

Savall, Henri, *Work and People: An Economic Evaluation of Job-enrichment.* Oxford: Oxford University Press, 1981.

Job evaluation

An organization can undertake a process of job evaluation in a number of different ways, the three most common being:

- by placing the different jobs in ranking order so that the value of each job can be identified;
- by grading the job from the job specification point of view;
- by giving each job a points rating, again from the job specification point of view.

The considerations of each of these job evaluation methods are given in Table 11.

The job evaluation process is carried out by the human resources department, in collaboration with functional managers, in order to ensure that the pay structure matches the demands and conditions of jobs. The process looks in detail at:

- the tasks involved in each job;
- the responsibilities and obligations of each of the post holders;
- the skills used in each job;
- the knowledge required for each job;
- the initiative required by each of the post holders;
- the ability of each individual post holder to cope with stress;
- the organization's requirements to plan for the future;
- the organization's need to control employees;
- the overall coordination of the organization's environment.

Table 11 Methods of job evaluation

Job evaluation method	Considerations
Ranking	A committee will often be established to rank different jobs according to their worth to the organization. This is an inexpensive and speedy process for smaller organizations to use, provided they have a sensible pay structure in place. Larger organizations may have difficulties using this method as experience has proved that issues regarding pay inequality have been the outcome.
Grading	Normally this process uses data taken from the job descriptions, with the job requiring the lowest degree of skills or the highest level of supervision being the starting point. Jobs are then graded from this starting point according to the skills, knowledge and responsibility involved. This is a straightforward way of carrying out the job evaluation process, although there are significant numbers of routine jobs that are difficult to categorize in this way, particularly again in larger organizations.
Points rating	This is possibly the most popular way of carrying out job evaluation. Several factors contribute to the measurement of the job, including the skills and degree of effort required, the responsibilities undertaken and the working conditions within which the job is undertaken. These basic starting points are often expanded on by creating subdivisions within each factor, with a number of points being allocated for each. Where one particular skill or level of expertise is imperative to a job, the score is doubled, trebled or quadrupled to reflect its importance.

Having established a need for the job evaluation process and categorized each job using the most suitable method, the organization would place a monetary value on each of the jobs. They would do this to ensure that:

- the pay administration process is as uncomplicated as possible;
- internal rates of pay can be harmonized;
- each of the jobs receives a reasonable rate of pay;
- each of the post holders can see the possibility of promotion to a higher job grade.

Quaid, Maeve, *Job Evaluation: The Myth of Equitable Assessment*. Toronto: University of Toronto Press, 1996.

Job rotation

Job rotation is a way of extending or enlarging the tasks carried out by employees. It involves the training, or retraining, of employees so that they are capable of exchanging jobs with one another, often on a regular and predetermined basis. Job rotation can often lead to increased job satisfaction because employees feel that they have a fuller picture of related jobs and feel more involved in the organization as a whole. The employees also feel more versatile and consider that the scheme gives them a wider variety of tasks, as well as eliminating the need for them to carry out difficult or disliked tasks regularly, as it means they only have to confront these tasks on an infrequent basis.

The main benefits of introducing a job rotation system, for an organization, are that there is constant cover for periods of holiday or sickness. Individual employees can, however, feel that they are constantly on the move and not given sufficient time for the development of specific skills, particularly if the process is carried out during times of high demand, when they often consider they have left a job with too many loose ends still undone. Additionally, levels of competence have to be reasonably parallel; otherwise individual employees could find themselves completing the bulk of the tasks involved in a job whilst the next employee finds little to do.

The question of motivation through job rotation is a questionable one as often employees are motivated at the introduction of the system, but once they have grasped the aspects of the new tasks involved, they find little reason to continue to strive. The job rotation scheme is an ideal system to be put in place by an organization employing large numbers of unskilled or semi-skilled workers.

Job shop

A job shop is a factory (or part of a factory) which has a number of general purpose machines, and multi-skilled employees who have the capacity to process orders for customers.

Job shops are the embodiment of the **make-to-order** process as they offer fixed planned **lead-times**, usually with a complex queuing system and employ highly skilled employees who cannot only process the orders but also take an active role in estimating the necessary lead times and fixing them into the schedules for the machines and associated labour.

See also **job shop scheduling.**

Job shop scheduling

'Job shop scheduling' refers to the process of creating a sequence with associated times, for queued jobs or orders which are being, or are about to be, processed by a **job shop**.

See **job shop.**

Johnson's Rule

Johnson's Rule is a technique that can be used to minimize the completion time for a group of jobs that are to be processed on two machines or at two successive work centres.

In order for the technique to be used, several conditions must be satisfied:

1 Job time (including set-up and processing) must be known and must be constant for each job at each work centre.
2 Job times should be independent of the job sequence.
3 All jobs should follow the same two-set-up work sequence.
4 Job priorities cannot be employed.

Johnson's Rule involves four steps:

1 All jobs are listed, as well as the processing time of each machine.
2 The job with the shortest processing time is listed and if the shortest time is with the first machine or work centre, the job is scheduled first. If the shortest time is with the second machine or work centre, then the job is scheduled at the end.
3 Once the job is scheduled, move to step 4.
4 Steps 2 and 3 are repeated for the remaining jobs, working towards the centre of the sequence.

Judgemental forecast

A judgemental forecast is a forecasting technique which is based on qualitative rather than quantitative data. Rather than estimating future demand or trends on the basis of historical data, a judgemental forecast is calculated from the experience or personal opinions of qualified experts. Typically the **Delphi technique** will be employed in order to collect and assess the relevant opinions.

Just-in-time system (JIT)

JIT is a philosophy which was developed in Japan, emphasiszing the importance of deliveries in relation to small **lot sizing**. The philosophy stresses the importance of set-up cost reduction, small lot sizes, pull systems, level production and importantly, the elimination of waste (***muda***).

JIT is designed to allow the achievement of high-volume production, whilst ensuring that minimal inventories of raw materials, **work in progress** and finished goods are held by the business. Parts arrive at the manufacturing plant from suppliers just in time to be placed into the manufacturing process and, as the products are processed along the line, they arrive at the next work station just in time, thereby moving through the whole system very quickly.

JIT relies on the management ensuring that manufacturing waste is kept to a minimum and that nothing is made or brought onto the premises that is not immediately required. JIT requires precision, as the right part needs to be in the right place at the right time. Waste is described as being the results from any activity that adds cost without adding value (which includes moving and storing).

JIT is also known as **lean production** or stockless production and the theory is that it should improve the profits and the returns on investment by the following means:

- reducing inventory levels;
- increasing the inventory turnover rate;
- improving product quality;
- reducing production and delivery lead times;
- reducing other costs (machine set-ups and equipment breakdown).

JIT also recognizes the fact that any under-utilized capacity can be used to build up a small stock of products or components (buffer inventories) in order to ensure that in the event of a problem the production process will not be interrupted.

JIT is primarily used in manufacturing processes which are repetitive in nature and where the same products and components are used and produced in relatively high volumes. Once the flow has been set up, there should be a steady and even flow of materials, components and finished products passing through the facility. Each work station is linked in a similar way to an **assembly line** (although the exact layout may be a jobbing or batch process layout). The goal is to eliminate all queuing and to achieve the ideal lot size per unit of production.

Delbridge, Rick, *Life on the Line in Contemporary Manufacturing: The Workplace Experience of Lean Production and the 'Japanese' Model.* Oxford: Oxford University Press, 2000.

Gross, John M. and McInnis, Kenneth R., *Kanban Made Simple: Demystifying and Applying Toyota's Legendary Manufacturing Process.* New York: Amacom, 2003.

Kaizen

Kaizen is a Japanese term which describes the adoption of the concept of aspiring towards gradual, but orderly, continuous improvement. The *kaizen* business strategy seeks to involve individuals from across the organization at any level of the organization.

The goal is for people to work together in order to achieve improvements without having to make large capital investments. Each change or improvement collectively complements and moves the process onwards. *Kaizen* requires a culture of sustained continuous improvement, whilst focusing on the elimination of waste in all areas, systems and processes of the organization. Above all, the cooperation and involvement of all the employees is vital to the overall success of the philosophy.

www.kaizen-institute.com/kzn.htm

Colenso, Michael, *Kaizen Strategies for Successful Organizational Change: Enabling Evolution and Revolution in the Organization* (Kaizen Strategies). Harlow, Essex: Financial Times/Prentice-Hall, 1999.

Imai, Masaaki, *Gemba Kaizen (Collaborating for Change)*. San Francisco, CA: Berrett-Koehler Publishers, 2002.

Kanban system

Kanban is a Japanese word which means 'signal'; in effect this is exactly what the system does, by sending a signal to employees to perform a particular action related to the process or work station in which they are involved. The system works on the following set of rules:

- An empty container gives a factory worker permission to work to fill the box.
- If a worker does not have an empty box to fill, the worker is blocked from doing any more work and is reassigned somewhere else where their work is needed.
- The *kanban* control system uses a signalling device to regulate JIT flows.

- The cards or containers make up the *kanban* pull system.
- The authority to produce or supply additional parts comes from downstream operations.
- A *kanban* is a card that is attached to a storage and transport container. It identifies the part number and container capacity, along with other information.
- A *kanban* system is a pull system, in which the *kanban* is used to pull parts to the next production stage when they are needed.

The *kanban* system differs from an **MRP** or schedule-based system as these are push systems. They have a detailed production schedule for each part to be used in order to push parts to the next production stage on schedule. *Kanban* is more flexible as it does not rely on the forecasting of customer demand in order to estimate the production lead times.

The *kanban* system requires the full embracing of **just-in-time (JIT)** production philosophy, particularly with regard to rapid set-up times and small **lot-sizing**.

See also **faxban**.

David, J. L. *Kanban: Just in Time at Toyota*. New York: Productivity Press, 1989.
Gross, John M. and McInnis, Kenneth R., *Kanban Made Simple: Demystifying and Applying Toyota's Legendary Manufacturing Process*. New York: Amacom, 2003.

Keiretsu

Keiretsu was formerly a unique Japanese type of corporate organization, but increasingly other countries have been moving towards this form of organizational typology.

The key aspect of a *keiretsu* is that a group or a family of affiliated trans-national organizations operate together (both vertically and horizontally) in an integrated manner. Importantly, the *keiretsu* has its own trading entities and banks, thereby allowing it to control each part of the economic chain in a major industrial or service-based sector.

Therefore, not only can a *keiretsu* research and develop a technology and products, but it can also plan the production, secure the finance, cover the insurance implications and then find the resources (wherever they are) in order to process them. The purpose of the exercise is to maintain control and production in Japan, where they will be turned into finished products, packaged and then distributed across the world.

Keiretsu use the **just-in-time system** and specific forms of **supply chain management**.

- They apply pressure to suppliers to reduce prices.
- They encourage supplier involvement in ***kaizen***.

- They involve suppliers at the earliest stage of the development of new products, in as much as they ask for comment on designs and do not merely supply the designs prior to the commencement of production.
- They commit suppliers to the notion that they will only supply quality parts and components.
- They use a two-vendor policy, a means of ensuring that suppliers remain competitive as they risk losing a portion or all of their contracts to the better supplier.
- They encourage suppliers to use just-in-time.
- They use a monthly master schedule using ***kanban*** as a signal for the adjustment of this schedule.
- They are committed to a levelled production.

Burt, David, *American Keiretsu: A Strategic Weapon for Global Competitiveness*. Chicago, IL: Irwin Professional, 1993

Miyashita, Kenichi and Russell, David, *Keiretsu: Inside the Hidden Japanese Conglomerates*. New York: McGraw-Hill Education, 1993.

Knowledge management

Knowledge management can be seen as one of the key factors of organizational development. Knowledge management recognizes that information and ability are among the most valuable assets an organization possesses. In the past, organizations have not been able to quantify or recognize this aspect as being one of their prime assets, as it is intangible. Knowledge is not just information or data, it needs to have a meaning and a purpose, and in human resources this means the ability to apply and use information. In other words, knowledge management is all about people being able to use information. There is no compelling definition of the term 'knowledge management'; and it has been variously described as intellectual capital or property, amongst a variety of other different attempts to explain its purpose and worth.

The key concern for human resources management is the retaining of individuals who are able to impart knowledge as an essential function of their relationship with the business. This knowledge management is a complex process, but includes questions as to how to share knowledge, how to find it, how to use it and how to convert it or transfer it from one individual to another.

Davenport, Thomas H. and Prusak, Laurence, *Working Knowledge: How Organizations Manage What They Know*. Cambridge, MA: Harvard Business School Press, 2000.

von Krogh, Georg, Ichijo, Kazua and Nonaka, Ikujiro, *Enabling Knowledge Creation*. Oxford: Oxford University Press, 2000.

K

Knowledge-based pay systems

Knowledge-based pay systems award employees on the basis of their knowledge and skills. In effect, there are three different ways of assessing and rewarding the overall knowledge or skills levels of employees:

- Horizontal skills – which reflect the variety of tasks the employee is capable of performing.
- Vertical skills – which reflect the management tasks the employee currently undertakes or may be capable of performing.
- Depth skills – which reflect the overall quality and productivity results displayed by the employee.

Lawler III, Edward E., *Rewarding Excellence: Pay Strategies for the New Economy*. New York: Jossey Bass Wiley, 2000.

Labour flexibility

Labour flexibility is a measure of a business's ability to change the jobs or nature of the jobs carried out by its employees. Labour flexibility depends on employee attitudes, specifically their resistance to change. It may also be restricted by a **trade union** or by employees' representative's view of how their members should be employed. One of the other key factors is the ability of the workers to engage in **multi-skilling**.

Labour-intensive

'Labour-intensive' describes workplace situations where the processes involved in either producing or managing the production of a particular product require a higher than usual level of staffing.

Lag

'Lag' refers to the difference between forecasted values and actual values. Lag is normally expressed in terms of time, rather than units sold or the value of those units.

Last in, first out (LIFO)

LIFO is an inventory policy in which the last item added to an organization's inventory is the first one to be used. It is of interest for tax purposes in that in a time of rising raw-material prices, taxable profits are postponed.

See also **first in, first out (FIFO)**.

Latest finish (LF)

Simply, latest finish (LF) refers to the latest time an activity can be completed without adversely affecting the overall production process or the project.

Latest start (LS)

A latest start schedule seeks to list activities by their latest start times. This date for the activity is determined by the activity's latest finish date and its duration. In other words,

latest start date (LS) = latest finish (LF) – duration (D).

Lead time

There are a number of definitions related to lead time. The term 'lead time' refers to the length of time that an organization takes to produce a product or a component. The planned lead time is a time parameter which is used in a planning and control system to determine the start date for an order.

The planned lead time for a manufacturing order is the sum of the planned lead times for all of the necessary activities in the assembly of that order. For a single operational step, this typically includes:

- the queue time before the production process begins;
- the set-up time for the machine for production;
- the run time to process the order;
- the post-production waiting time for the product to continue to the next stage.

From a customer perspective, the promised customer lead time is the length of time the customer can expect to wait for the product, and refers to the planned difference between order placement and order receipt.

All lead times have random variables – means, modes, medians, standard deviations, minimums, maximums, etc. Therefore, it is important that organizations are clear about when to use the term 'lead time'.

See also **lead-time syndrome.**

L

Lead-time syndrome

The lead-time syndrome is a perverse cycle whereby a supplier's planned lead times continually increase in length. The cycle is as follows:

- A manufacturer could increase their planned lead time for a number of different reasons, including holiday periods, an increase in demand for a particular product, or equipment failure.
- If customers discover the manufacturer is increasing lead times, they may increase their order quantity to compensate.

- The manufacturer sees the larger order quantity from the customer (or a number of customers) and makes the assumption that demand has increased, and consequently they increase their lead times to cover this.

So the cycle continues. The solution to lead-time syndrome is for customers to ensure that they are communicating their true demand to suppliers so that these organizations are able to forecast production requirements. Lead-time syndrome can have a knock-on effect throughout the **supply chain**.

See also **bullwhip effect**.

Lead-time variability

In many cases there are reasons why an accurate **lead time** cannot be calculated with any degree of certainty. In the majority of cases an estimate of the lead time is made and the lead time variability is measured by the standard deviation from that lead-time estimate. Lead-time variability is usually measured in the number of days for which the actual lead time has manifested itself compared with the estimate.

Lean production/manufacturing

Lean production/manufacturing is an approach based on the **Toyota production system**. An organization takes a number of steps to assist in ensuring that manufacturing activities focus on five key concepts:

- value centred on customer needs by creating activities as and when customers demand them;
- value creation – which occurs along a series of steps and is known as the value stream; this is achieved through a closely synchronized flow of the organization's activities;
- continually making improvements within the production process in order to maintain customer service and strive for perfection;
- waste reduction;
- engagement of personnel.

Central to an organization adopting the lean production/manufacturing approach is the question of waste reduction and a high level of engagement of all company personnel in implementing and improving the manufacturing process.

The benefits available to an organization adopting the lean production/manufacturing process are high. It is claimed that organizations have achieved benefits amounting to an 80% reduction in **cycle time**, a 50% reduction in **lead times**, a 50% reduction in the levels of their **inventory**, and an increase in customer response rates, as well as an increase in quality.

Lean Enterprise Institute: www.lean.org/

Learning curve

A learning curve shows the relationship between an individual's performance and the amount of time they spend learning, but can also be interpreted as an individual's level of ability or motivation. Very often the individual will reach a stage known as the *learning plateau*, where little progress is seen to be made (see Figure 21). However, this tends to be a temporary stage, sometimes due to lack of motivation, but also likely to be as a result of the need to refresh or revise what has been learned so far, before further progress can be achieved.

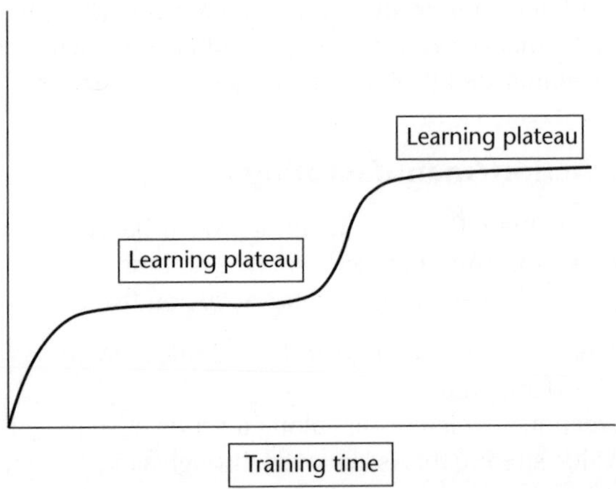

Figure 21 The learning curve.

The rate of learning very much depends on the difficulty of the task involved and often a learning plateau is reached on more than one occasion.

Learning organization

An exact definition of the term 'learning organization' is somewhat problematic since there are a number of different categories of learning organization. The essential encompassing concept is that organizations learn from external stimuli and, as a result, alter or amend their internal framework to match those opportunities. This requires a re-evaluation of goals and, in extreme circumstances, a change in organizational culture, organizational structure and the patterns of work in order to take advantage of new opportunities.

With regard to learning, the main recognized categories of organizations are:

- The knowing organization – which tends to be businesses in a static or mature market.
- The understanding and thinking organization – which is prepared to adapt its culture and structure within certain parameters.
- The learning organization – which accepts change as being both necessary and desirable. These are ultimately the businesses which drive their competitors to mimic them.

Clearly, the human resources operating in a learning organization, of whatever type, have to be far more adaptable and flexible, as well as effective and efficient, in driving changes within the organization. It has been recognized that there are two stages of evolution in a learning organization, of which human resources are an integral part. The first is known as a single-loop or adaptive learning organization, where new techniques and ideas are assimilated. The second type of learning organization is known as a double-loop or generative learning organization. In this case the business continually evaluates its goals and objectives, as well as its organizational culture, to suit any emerging external opportunities. Both forms of learning organization offer considerable challenges to human resources, who have to quickly learn that they are in an ever-shifting and adaptive organization.

Chawla, Sarita, *Learning Organizations: Developing Cultures for Tomorrow's Workplace*. New York: Productivity Press, 1995.

Kline, Peter and Saunders, Bernhard, *Ten Steps to a Learning Organization*. Arlington, VA: Great Ocean Publishers, 1998.

L

Level

See **load levelling**.

Level capacity strategy

A level capacity strategy is a management stance taken by an organization which seeks to maintain a steady rate of output. The management assumes that a specified level of output can be maintained over a given period of time. It then seeks to identify methods by which it can cope with or accommodate variations in demand by deploying extra resources, such as operating additional shifts, offering **overtime** or perhaps **outsourcing** part of the production process (this strategy is also known as **chase demand**).

Levelled production

In essence, levelled production is not dissimilar to **level capacity strategy** as it seeks to evenly allocate work across the entire manufacturing facility by days and weeks. The underlying concept seeks to ensure that resources, including machinery and employees, are used to the optimum effect and are neither overworked nor under-utilized.

Life cycle

The product life cycle is a widely accepted model which describes the stages a product or service, or indeed a category, passes through from its introduction to its final removal from the market. The model suggests that the introduction stage, or the launch, of the product, during which the product sells in small numbers and marketing activities are expensive, is superseded, if successful, by three other stages (see Figures 22 and 23). The growth stage is characterized by higher sales, greater profitability, but crucially, more competition. At the maturity stage, providing a product has managed to survive, stable sales and a higher level of profitability are enjoyed. The final stage, known as the decline stage,

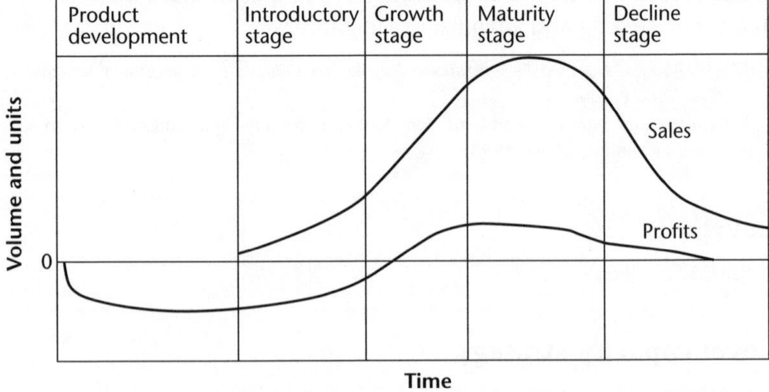

Figure 22 The standard product life cycle graph showing the phases of the life cycle and the association between profits and sales over the cycle

L

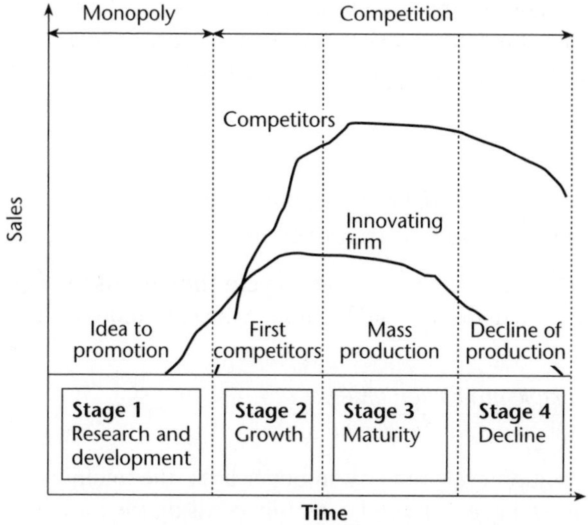

Figure 23 This is a more complex view of the product life cycle, which illustrates the dangers often faced by product innovators in developing new product ideas only to lose the potential of sales as a result of the actions of competitors

shows that the product is finally declining in terms of demand and associated profits. Optionally, it is possible to insert a further stage between maturity and decline, denoting a period of the product's life cycle when competition has reached a level which makes it difficult to sustain the original product. Indeed, it may be the case that the product is already growing stale. This saturation period marks a slight downturn, which can be adjusted by a relaunch or a repackaging of the product, otherwise it will begin its inevitable slip into the decline stage.

Shaw, John J., *Product Lifecycles and Product Management*. Westport, CT: Greenwood Press, 1989.

Line balancing

Once a product line, product or cellular layout has been developed, work is then divided among the process areas or work stations. Dividing the tasks evenly results in what is known as a balanced line.

A perfectly balanced line has zero balance delay, which means no waiting time at any work station. When products or processes change, line rebalancing becomes necessary. Line balancing analysis requires determining the number of work stations or number of assemblers (or both). This requires the establishment of a specified demand rate and data on time standards, work methods, and process flow.

Line balancing analysis uses the following formula:

$$d = \frac{nc - 3t}{nc}$$

where d = balance delay; n = number of work stations; c = station cycle time; $3t$ = total work content time for one unit

In order to balance a line, the station **cycle time** needs to be established (which will yield the per shift output which is required to meet the demand):

$$c = \frac{\textit{available production time per day}}{\textit{required output per day (in units)}}$$

Using the station cycle time as an upper limit, the minimum number of stations (n) which are needed is calculated using the formula:

$$n = \frac{\textit{total work content}}{\textit{cycle time}} = \frac{3t}{c}$$

The first work station is assigned elements, one at a time, until the sum of the times needed for the element equals the cycle time, or until no feasible elements remain under the precedence restrictions. This process is then repeated for the second and third work stations, and so on, until all of the work elements have been assigned to a station.

A calculation can then be made of the balance delay, based on minimum station cycle time. If the figure is unsatisfactory, the process technology can then be altered to allow more flexibility in balancing the line.

Scholl, Armin, *Balancing and Sequencing of Assembly Lines* (Contributions to Management Science). Berlin: Physica-Verlag, 2000.

Linear regression

Linear regression is a statistical methodology which attempts to fit a line across a series of historical data points, in order to minimize the errors. Linear regression is used to find the relationship between two or more variables.

When attempting to fit a linear model to a set of data it must first be determined whether there is a relationship between the variables being considered. It should not be implied that one variable necessarily causes the other, but there may be some association between the two variables.

A scatter diagram is often used to determine the degree of relationship between the two variables; if this proves to be inconclusive, then there is often little point in trying to fit a linear regression model to the data as it will not prove to be of any value. In this respect, a useful numerical measure of association between two variables is the correlation coefficient (a value between -1 and 1), which indicates the strength of the association between the data for the two variables. The linear regression line has the following equation:

$$Y = a + bX + e$$

where Y = the dependent variable, a = the intercept, b = the slope or regression coefficient, X = the independent variable, and e = the error term.

Little's flow equation

In 1961, Professor John D. C. Little carried out some research, the conclusions of which proved that there was a relationship between the average time in the system, the average arrival rate and the average number of units within the system. Little's flow equation states that:

average inventory level = average throughput rate × average time in system

See also **queuing theory.**

Load chart

A load chart is a particular type of **Gantt chart**. It is used by manufacturing industries to indicate the idle time and loading of particular machines, work centres and departments. The load chart should provide the management with a single-source overview of where work is being carried out, where there may be problems, with particular parts of the process being under pressure, and where machines or employees are located that could be redeployed elsewhere.

Load levelling

In framing a schedule for either a project or a production process, the organization will wish to attempt to have an even workload in terms of its use of resources, including employees and machinery, over the time span of that process. Within parameters the organization would seek to avoid overloading particular areas, either in the demand for parts and components, or through excessive workloads in the case of employees and machinery. They will also be aware that increasing the rate at which products are completed will have implications with regard to supplies and to the distribution and storage of the completed products at the end of the production line.

Load report

A load report may be generated either by the production department or by a specific work station. The load report compares both known and expected capacity requirements with the projected availability of **capacity**. The load report should then indicate where there may be a problem caused by excess demand, which is outstripping projected capacity, as well as indicating which areas of production may be under-utilized.

Loading, sequencing and scheduling

In planning and controlling the volume and timing of operations, there are three necessary activities: loading, sequencing and scheduling, as shown in Table 12.

Table 12 Loading, sequencing and scheduling

Operation	Description
Loading	This dictates the amount of work which is allocated to each part of the operation.
Sequencing	This determines the order in which work is tackled within the operation.
Scheduling	This determines the detailed timetable of activity. It can be performed either on a backward or a forward basis.

Scheduling can also be classified as push or pull scheduling. The former is a centralized system in which planning and control decisions are issued to work centres. The work centres are then required to perform their task and send their parts to the next work station. Pull scheduling, on the other hand, assumes that demand is set by requests from another work centre.

Locational cost–profit–volume analysis

Locational cost–profit–volume analysis is a statistical technique which is used to evaluate location options. The graphical assumptions are that fixed costs will remain constant over a range of probable output and that variable costs are linear. The required level of output can then be estimated (usually one product is considered). The total cost lines for each alternative location are plotted onto the same graph, using the familiar fixed costs (FC) + variable cost (VC) × quantity of output (Q), to calculate the total cost.

Logistics

Logistics incorporates the planning and control of all materials and products across the entire production and **supply chain** system. Logistics is, in effect, a managerial function which deals with the flow of materials – including purchasing, shipping and distribution issues – before, during and after the completion of the finished product.

Lot sizing (order size, batch size)

The term 'lot sizing' or, as it is also commonly known, order sizing or batch sizing refers basically to the quantity that is ordered. Organizations use these terms in different circumstances. When dealing with suppliers, the term 'order sizing' is used, but when dealing with internal manufacturing orders, then the terms 'lot sizing' or 'batch sizing' are more typically used.

Lot splitting

Lot splitting is a manufacturing concept which relates to the splitting, at some stage of the production process, of a final order size into smaller lots. In other words, if a customer orders 100 units and the production of these units involves two stages of manufacture, the organization would lot-split after the first stage of production of the first 10 units. This sub-lot of 10 units is despatched to the second stage of production. The advantage to an organization is that the lot splitting may allow the order to be taken through the production process in less time. The disadvantage, however, is the increase in administration costs during the tracking of the different sub-lots.

See also **just-in-time system (JIT).**

Lot-for-lot ordering

Lot-for-lot ordering is an aspect of **material requirements planning (MRP)** in which attempts are made to match incoming orders, or the timing of incoming orders, with exact net requirements on the production line.

Maintenance, repairs and operations (MRO)

'MRO' is an inventory-based term which is used to highlight the need for the organization to purchase materials or components in order to carry out routine maintenance and repairs. The materials and components will not be associated with the organization's assembly of products for sale to customers, but will be used internally on the organization's machinery and equipment.

Make to order (MTO)

Make to order (MTO) is a process that allows an organization to produce its products in response to a customer order. In other words, the organization does not keep any finished products on its inventory. Make to order allows the organization to process products that are unique to the customers' requirements, but it is also possible to use the MTO process for the production of standard products.

See also **respond to order (RTO)**.

Make to stock (MTS)

Make to stock (MTS) is a process that concentrates on standard products to be stored in an organization's inventory. The use of MTS allows the swift delivery of products to a customer.

See also **service level**.

Make versus buy

For many manufacturing organizations this is a fundamental decision. Given the premise that organizations should never outsource products or services for which they have a **core competence** the decision still remains as to the merits and demerits of **outsourcing** as opposed to producing parts or components in-house. Clearly, buying more parts and components in than the company actually produces itself does add to

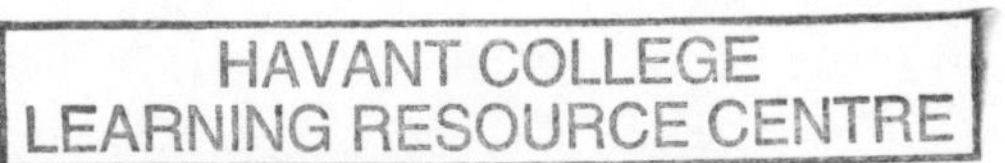

the overheads and complications arising out of inventory or stock control. It is generally the case that the more a manufacturer outsources, the more it has to outsource in order to continue operations, as it has reorganized its internal production routines to take into account the fact that it does not need to produce those parts or components.

Makespan

'Makespan' is an alternative term used to describe the total amount of time required to complete an associated group of jobs. The makespan is equal to the time between the start of the first job and the completion of the last job.

Management of Health and Safety at Work Regulations 1999 (UK)

These regulations require employers to carry out risk assessments and to make the arrangements to implement any necessary measures. Competent individuals should also be identified to pass information on to other employees and to carry out the necessary training.

These Regulations set out broad general duties which apply to almost all work activities aimed mainly at improving health and safety management and can be seen as a way of making more explicit what is required of employers under the Health and Safety at Work Act. They also introduce requirements contained in the European Health and Safety Framework Directive into British law.

www.hmso.gov.uk/si/si1999/19993242.htm

Manual Handling Operations Regulations 1992 (UK)

These regulations cover the movement of objects in the workplace, either by hand or by force.

The Regulations do not set legal limits for weights that can be lifted; neither do they explicitly require training to be given in manual handling techniques. The Regulations do require, where reasonably practicable, that manual handling is eliminated. In cases where this is not possible, then a risk assessment must be carried out where there is a risk of injury due to the manual handling operation.

www.hmso.gov.uk/si/si1992/Uksi_19922793_en_1.htm

Manufacturing cell (MC)

See **cell manufacturing**.

Manufacturing decision areas

Hayes and Wheelwright devised ten manufacturing strategy decision areas as outlined in Table 13.

Table 13 Manufacturing decision areas

Decision areas	Scope
Capacity	Capacity flexibility, shift patterns, temporary subcontracting policies.
Facilities	The size, capacity, location and focus of manufacturing resource.
Production equipment	Degree of automation, technology choices, configuration of equipment into lines, cells, etc., maintenance policies, and the potential for developing new processes in-house.
Vertical integration	Strategic 'make versus buy', supplier policies, extent of dependence on suppliers.
Human resources policies	Recruitment, training and development, culture and management style.
Quality systems	Quality assurance and quality control policies and practice.
Production planning and control	Production and order, material control systems.
Performance measurement	Financial and non-financial performance management and linkages to recognition and reward systems.
Organization	Structure, accountabilities and responsibilities.
New product introduction	Design for manufacturer guidelines, introduction stages, organizational aspects, e.g., manufacturing role in concurrent engineering.

M

See also **capability and maturity (Hayes and Wheelwright's Four Stages)**.

Hayes, Robert H., and Wheelwright, Steven C., *Restoring Our Competitive Edge: Competing through Manufacturing*. New York: John Wiley, 1984.

Hayes, Robert H., Wheelwright, Steven C. and Clark, Kim B., *Dynamic Manufacturing*. New York: Free Press, 1988.

Manufacturing execution system (MES)

A manufacturing execution system (MES) provides an organization with information on its manufacturing operations from the time an order is started until it is completed within the factory.

A manufacturing execution system is dissimilar to **enterprise resource planning** or **materials requirements planning** systems as it does not plan order launch dates or order sizes. An MES focuses on collecting data and information regarding the detailed operations and production process after an order has been started.

The main functions of an MES include:

- resource allocation and status;
- data collection and acquisition;
- quality management;
- maintenance management;
- performance analysis;
- production scheduling;
- labour management;
- process management;
- product tracking;
- order despatch;
- document control. Some systems take document control a step further and include detailed work instructions, videos, and drawings for use on the production line.

Some of the benefits of using a MES include:

- the reduction of manufacturing **cycle time**;
- the reduction of time involved in data entry;
- the reduction of **work in progress (WIP)**;
- increased inventory turnover;
- the reduction of **lead times**;
- improved product quality due to a reduction in defects;
- the reduction in levels of loss of paperwork and blueprints;
- an improvement in customer service due to improved delivery times;
- a reduction in the need for staff training;
- an improvement in the organization's levels of cash flow and performance.

www.mesa.org

Manufacturing process comparisons

Although it is a complex task to differentiate and typify alternative forms of manufacturing processes, each different form of processing has a set of associated characteristics which are designed to match the requirements (and often the stage of development) of an organization. The key characteristics are typified in Table 14.

See also **assembly line; batch shop; continuous flow; job shop** *and* **project management.**

Manufacturing resource planning (MRPII)

Manufacturing resource planning (MRPII) is a method to effectively plan all the resources of a manufacturing company. It is a natural development of **material requirements planning (MRP)** but is broader in concept and application. MRPII links functions such as business planning, sales and operations planning, production scheduling, MRP, **capacity requirements planning** and support systems for both **capacity** and materials. An MRPII system is designed to make maximum utilization of the resources available to the business. The underlying principles of MRPII require the following.

- An aggregate sales and operations plan to create a framework for the master production schedule to be produced, including all major inputs from each functional area of the business.
- A **master production schedule**, the critical element of MRPII, which specifies what is to be made and when, fitting within the aggregate and financial plans and the capacity constraints. This schedule requires updating to take into account **lead times**.
- A materials resource plan, which gives a detailed listing of all the materials and resources required for each order.
- A capacity requirement plan, which analyses the processes helping to anticipate difficulties, thus allowing for short-term adjustments to the master production schedule.
- **Shop floor control (SFC)**, which maintains, evaluates and communicates data.

MRPII improves production timing, cuts inventories, improves customer service and staff productivity and allows the business to plan across all its operations. The system requires, however, the availability of accurate data and expertise in implementation and enforcement.

Wallace, Thomas F., *MRPII: Making it Happen: The Implementer's Guide to Success with Manufacturing Resource Planning*. New London, NH: Oliver Wight Publications, 1990.

Table 14 Characteristics of different manufacturing processes

	Project	Job shop	Large batch shop	Assembly line	Continuous process
Life-cycle phase		Startup	Growth	Maturation	Decline
Product volume	One of a kind	Very low	Low	High	Commodity
Product standardization	None	Very little	Low	Moderate–high	High
Important competitive dimension	Product characteristics	Product characteristics	Quality and availability	Price and dependability	Price
Equipment	Low cost, general purpose	General purpose	General purpose	High cost, specialized	Very high cost and very specialized
Supplier relationships	Very informal	Informal	Informal or formal	Formal	Very formal
Layout	Product design focus	Functional departments: process focused	Functional departments or mini flow lines	Product focused flow lines	Product focused with little flexibility

Mass customization

Mass customization is an increasing trend and of considerable importance to manufacturers. Mass customization involves the production of mass produced, standard products, with slight variations or customizations for particular market or customer segments. As the manufacturing process has developed technologically, and become more flexible, it is possible to produce these personalized products without having a detrimental effect on profit margins. Indeed, these customized products can often warrant a premium price, providing a margin in excess of what had previously been enjoyed by the manufacturer. Manufacturers have therefore realized that mass customization is a means by which they can improve their profitability without the attendant loss of production or productivity. A prime example of mass customization is the computer manufacturer and distributor Dell.

Gilmore, James H. and Pine, B. Joseph II (eds), *Markets of One: Creating Customer-unique Value through Mass Customization* (A Harvard Business Review Book). Cambridge, MA: Harvard Business School Press, 2000.

Mass production

Mass production refers to manufacturing processes which are engaged in the production of large volumes of standardized products. Mass production facilities are typified by having highly specialized equipment manned by low skilled or semi-skilled employees.

Master production schedule (MPS)

A master schedule indicates the desired quantity and timing of deliveries, whilst a master production schedule takes into account planned production, as well as on-hand inventory.

The master schedule has three major inputs:

- beginning inventory;
- forecasts for each period in the schedule;
- customer orders.

The outputs of the scheduling process include projected inventory, production requirements, and the amount of uncommitted inventory (**available-to-promise**).

The master production schedule is a time-phased plan which explicitly specifies how many of each product the business intends to build, and when. A fully integrated MPS programme combined with a **material requirements planning** programme will be able to calculate precisely how much raw materials, parts, components, or other supplies are required to make these products.

Gessner, Robert A., *Master Production Schedule Planning*. Melbourne: Krieger, 1993.

Material control/flow/release

Material control is a process which is inextricably linked to the **master production schedule**. The process seeks to manage the ordering, receiving and distribution of materials throughout the organization.

The term 'material flow' refers to the process of those materials within an operation or organization. Material release is a means by which organizations control the delivery of raw materials, parts or components from their suppliers. Working under the assumption that a purchase order has already been placed with the supplier, it may not necessarily be the case that the entire shipment is delivered in one lot. The suppliers may have been requested to store the materials on behalf of the manufacturer until such a time as they receive from the organization a materials release notification that they wish the materials to arrive at their facility by a particular date. The materials release will specify the parts and quantity of those parts required.

Material master record (MMR)

An MMR is a data record which contains all the basic information required to manage a material. A material master record contains data of a descriptive nature (e.g. size, dimension and weight) and data with a control function (e.g. material type and industry sector).

In addition to this data, which can be directly maintained by the business, MMR also contains data that is automatically updated by the software system (e.g. stock levels).

Material requirements planning (MRP)

Material requirements planning (MRP) is primarily concerned with the scheduling of activities and the management of inventories. The process begins by measuring or forecasting the potential customer demand. The demand is broken down into component parts which will be required against existing inventories and then seeks to schedule the parts needed against available **capacity**. A schedule is produced for all component parts (including those to be purchased if necessary). The process also identifies any expected shortages due to capacity limitations. The basic procedure is updated at regular intervals, during which demand is forecast and necessary adjustments are made in order to fulfil that demand. MRP requires considerable data capture both in order to accurately predict future demand, and for the full scheduling of all component parts required. MRP has the following inputs:

- **bill of materials (BOM)** (identifying the component parts of a final output product);
- **master production schedule (MPS)** (showing the quantity of each item required and when they are needed);
- opening inventory (showing available inventories of all materials);
- opening capacity (derived from the above information);
- **lead time** and **lot sizing** rules.

MRP has the following outputs:

- purchase requirements;
- manufacturing activity schedules;
- expected shortages;
- surplus components inventory;
- available free capacity.

Plossl, George W., *Orlicky's Material Requirements Planning*. New York: McGraw-Hill Education, 1994.

Materials management

Materials management involves the planning, organization and control of all aspects of inventory. This includes procurement, warehousing, **work-in-progress**, shipping, and distribution of finished goods.

Mayo, Elton

Elton Mayo was employed by the Hawthorne Works during the 1920s and 1930s to attempt to improve the electrical company's productivity. As a result of this work he developed a theory which has since become known as the Hawthorne Effect.

Initially Mayo adopted the scientific management theory of **F. W. Taylor**, in his attempt to discover what environmental features of the workplace were affecting productivity. He made amendments to the lighting, the heating and the availability of refreshments, then went on to make changes to the length of the work day and week. Each time he made a change the rate of productivity increased. Puzzled by his findings, Mayo reversed his actions by removing tea-breaks and reducing the level of lighting, but productivity continued to increase. Mayo's conclusion was that the changes had been made in consultation with the employees and that this factor had been the determining influence on productivity, together with the fact that the employees had a good working relationship with their supervisors.

Further research was then undertaken in another department of the organization. Two different groups of employees were working on complex equipment; one group considered that their status was high because of the complexity of the job role. The second group considered themselves to be lower in status and this resulted in a degree of competition between the two groups. Both groups had established their own sets of rules and code of behaviour and each had established the pace of work and degree of output. Individuals within the group who did not comply with these standards were put under pressure from the other members of the group.

Each group was given a target output for the day by the management of the organization. On some days these targets were exceeded but the groups would simply report that they had reached the target figures, and include the excess in the target figure for the following day. Mayo drew the following conclusions from this:

- The groups had been given a **benchmark**. Their benchmark had been the employer's output targets and they had been able to compare this with their own output totals.
- They had established for themselves a concept of a fair day's output and did not feel they needed to exceed these targets.

Mayo felt that lessons could be learned from this research in that a group's needs have to be in accord with organizational rules. Consultation was the key to achieving this, together with close monitoring of day-to-day organizational activities.

Mayo made three interesting discoveries from his research, which form the basis of this 'solidarity theory':

- Output and motivation improved when employees were being observed.
- Peer pressure contributed to the level of support by the individuals within the group.
- The group had strong feelings about what was possible and reasonable. This was as important to the group as their reaction to the demands of their managers.

Bratton, John and Gold, Jeffrey, *Human Resource Management: Theory and Practice*. Basingstoke: Palgrave Macmillan, 2003.

Mayo, Elton, *Social Problems of an Industrial Civilization*. London: Routledge, 1998 (reprint).

Mean absolute deviation (MAD)

MAD is a measure of forecast error, where the following formula is used:

$$MAD = \frac{1}{N} \sum_{i=1}^{N} fi \mid xi - \bar{x} \mid$$

where N = sample size; xi = sample values; $\bar{x}$ = mean; and fi = absolute frequency.

Measured day work

Measured day work is a remuneration system where pay is fixed at a higher rate than the normal hourly rate, provided an employee attains a certain level of performance or output. Other measured day work schemes require a specified output in return for a fixed daily wage. There are also more complex schemes which allow employees to step up to higher rates if they consistently perform at a particular level of output, which, theoretically, has no limit.

Methods analysis/study

Methods analysis is an integral part of **job design** as it should be seen as the precursor to any attempts to determine the exact nature of a job or a series of related tasks. Methods analysis involves investigation into the requirements of a job in order to identify new or more efficient ways of performing that job or series of tasks.

Microfactory

See **plant within a plant (PWP)**.

Micromotion study

In effect, micromotion study is a development of **motion study** as originally designed by Frank and Lillian Gilbreth. In many instances it is very difficult for an observer to note all of the motions involved in a particular task or activity. Therefore the solution is to capture on video the process as it is happening and then to watch the tape played back in slow motion in order to analyse the motions undertaken by the employee that were too quick to note while they were actually happening.

M

Minimum/maximum cycle time

Minimum and maximum **cycle times** are used to arrive at an estimation of the shortest possible and the longest times taken to complete a particular series of associated processes. The minimum cycle time is the time which is required by the longest task in the process, whilst the maximum cycle time is the sum of all of the tasks involved.

Mission statement

A mission statement essentially describes, as succinctly as possible, an organization's business vision. This would include the fundamental values and the essential purpose of the organization. It will also make allusions as to its future or its aims for the future, as mission statements tend to be a statement of where a businesses wishes to be rather than a description of where it is at the current time. In this respect, mission statements, although the fundamental ethos may remain the same, are subject to periodic change. A business may choose to incorporate within its mission statement a vision of how it wishes its employees and systems to respond, react to, and fulfil the needs of, its customers or clients. The organization will, therefore, seek to match these aspirations by instituting employee development programmes and associated training, in order to fulfil the espoused desires and commitments made in the mission statement.

Modular design (modularity)

Basically, modular design is a way of organizing a complex system as a series of components that can eventually be joined together to form a whole. Although this is a simple design strategy, the critical issue is the development of the individual components and their ultimate connection.

Modularity is a general system which describes the degree to which a system's components can be separated and recombined. Modularity also refers both to the tightness of the couplings used between the components and to the degree to which components can be mixed or matched. Since all systems are coupled to some degree, they are almost all modular to some extent.

Schilling, Melissa A., 'Toward a General Modular Systems Theory and its Application to Inter-firm Product Modularity', *Academy of Management Review*, vol. 25 (April 2000), p. 312.

Motion study

Motion study is the systematic study of the human motions used to perform an operation. The fundamental goal of the motion study is to attempt to identify and then eliminate unnecessary movements and thereby identify the best sequence of motions for maximum efficiency.

The concept evolved from the studies and writing of the Gilbreths, who began by investigating brick-laying in the early part of the twentieth century. The most common forms of motion study which are used tend to be:

- Motion study principles – guidelines for designing motion-efficient work. They are usually divided into three categories: principles for use of the body, principles for arrangement of the workplace, and principles for the design of tools and equipment.
- Analysis of **Therbligs**.
- **Micromotion study** – Frank and Lillian Gilbreth also introduced motion pictures for studying motions, known as micromotion study. The use of micromotion study focuses on repetitive activities, identifying minor improvements which can provide savings because of the number of times an operation is repeated.
- Charts – analysts often use charts as tools for analysing and recording motion studies; a *simo chart* can be used to study simultaneous motions of the hands.

Stewart, James R. and Meyers, Fred E., *Motion Time Study for Lean Manufacturing*. Englewood Cliffs, NJ: Prentice-Hall, 2002.

Moving average method

Moving average method is a simple statistical technique which is applied to situations where the data have no real discernible trend, seasonality implications or cyclic components.

A three-period moving average forecast would look at three periods of data and create an average of that data. The average is used as a forecast of the next period. Where the process continues, periods 1 to 3 provide the data for period 4, the forecast for period 5 is the average of periods 2 to 4, and so on. The reasoning behind the moving average is that the oldest data which was used to calculate the previous set of figures is now too old to be considered useful for the prediction of a period that is further into the future.

In formula appearance, the forecasting would appear with the following conventions:

- F_t is the forecast for period t (a forecast of period 4 would therefore be F_4).
- Y_t represents the historical data related to a given period (a set of data related to period 1 would be represented as Y_1).

In order to carry out the three-period forecast for period 4 as outlined above, the following formula would therefore be used:

$$F_4 = (Y_1 + Y_2 + Y_3) / 3.$$

To calculate the forecast for the next period (period 5), the formula would be amended to:

$$F_5 = (Y_2 + Y_3 + Y_4) / 3.$$

The process can be continued, dropping off the aged data at the beginning of each of the previous sequences. However, the further into the future the forecasts are being made; the more reliant the organization will be on data derived from averaging forecast data rather than historical data. The technique does not take into account trends (as indeed it is not used for this purpose), therefore the technique is really only useful for short-term forecasts for which there is accurate historical data upon which to base the computations.

MRP

See **material requirements planning.**

Muda

Muda is a Japanese word that translates as 'waste', 'useless' or 'futile', and the term refers to any activity carried out by an organization that does not add value. In other words, anything which the customer is not prepared to pay for.

The term *muda* was originally part of a trilogy:

- *mura* (imbalance/discrepancy).
- *muri* (overload/strain).
- *muda* (non-value-added/waste).

See also **3Mu** (see p. 264).

Management using **just-in-time systems (JIT)** regards items that are bought, but not being used, as waste, even if they are regarded as an asset of the organization, because they add no value to products which are known to be required by customers.

Over-production, waiting, conveyance, processing, inventory, motion, and correction can all contribute to *muda*, which can be found throughout an organization or its production process.

See also ***kaizen.***

Multiple-priority model

The multiple-priority model is a means by which manufacturers seek to schedule their work. The model is in essence a waiting system which categorizes customers. When a customer arrives or an order from a customer has been received, according to predetermined specifications, the customer is assigned to a category. Their order or requirements are then processed by priority category, rather than on a **first come, first served (FCFS)** basis.

Multi-skilling

The term 'multi-skilling' relates to incorporating a higher level of flexibility into job roles across the organization, usually in those activities requiring unskilled to skilled or technical expertise. This flexibility often crosses boundaries which have historically or traditionally been set, and it requires the willingness of employees if it is to succeed. The newly multi-skilled employees would also have to be prepared to work at their newly acquired skills and follow training or retraining programmes in order to do so. Commonly, trained employees will assist with the retraining of those going through the multi-skilling process.

There are some advantages and disadvantages to multi-skilling, including those shown in Table 15.

The introduction of multi-skilling can affect employees in more than their work situation and the effects may spill over into their domestic life, particularly if their extended role involves irregular work hours. However, employees could find that their job satisfaction is increased, as they are no longer so strictly supervised or controlled.

Muther grid

A Muther grid is a chart which displays the closeness ratings of work stations or departments, and is used as a means by which an organization determines where work centres should be located within the facility. In carrying out this task the organization recognizes that there are various criteria which could influence the location of the work centres. A Muther grid uses a six-point scale, as can be seen in Figure 24.

Table 15 An assessment of multi-skilling

Advantages	Disadvantages
An organization can introduce new equipment and working methods quickly.	Labour turnover can increase as employees become more skilled.
The employees improve their overall level of skills and knowledge.	The costs of training and retraining programmes can be high.
All of the organization's resources are used to their full potential.	Because individuals can move from one group to another, there could be resultant shortages in particular groups. This can affect the way the group performs in the longer term as there is always a risk that one member of the group or team will be missing.
The employees can contribute more effectively, and to their full potential, to meeting the organization's objectives.	Managers tend not to be involved in the multi-skilling process and often remain rigid in their views of the tasks they should perform.
	Employees do not always enjoy job satisfaction, particularly if they are not involved in tasks they were initially trained to do.

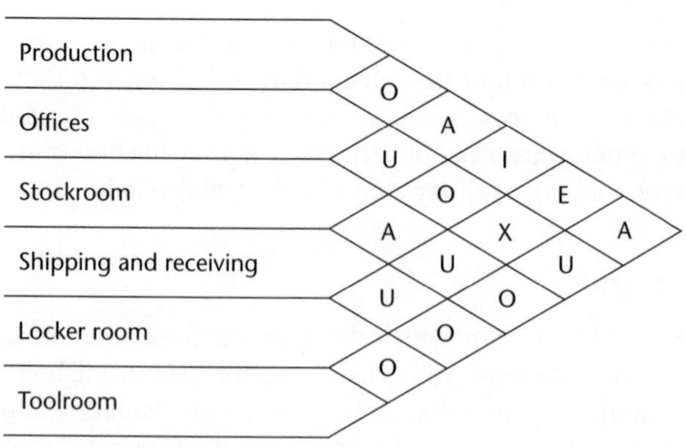

Figure 24 Example of a Muther grid

The chart uses the following lettering:

- A absolutely necessary
- E especially important
- I important
- O OK
- U unimportant
- X undesirable

The normal process involves the pairing of the As, then the separation of the Xs. The process then moves to dealing with the pairing of the Es and this continues until all the centres have been allocated.

In our example (Figure 24), the process identifies that it is absolutely necessary (A) to position production near the stockroom and the tool room, and to position the stockroom near shipping and receiving. It is considered especially important (E) to locate the locker room near production, and important (I) to locate shipping and receiving near production. The only identified undesirable (X) configuration refers to the relative location of the offices and the locker room.

Muther, Richard, *Systematic Layout Planning*. New York: Van Nostrand Reinhold, 1985.

Naive forecast

A naive forecast is a basic and simple forecasting technique which is often prone to assumptions being made with regard to one period of time being similar to others. Typically, a naive forecast will involve the assumption that a given future time will be the same as the current period, and that any variations, whether random or predicted, which have occurred during the current period will equally apply to the future one. A naive forecast may also suggest that differences between a past period and the present can be transposed to a future period of time.

Net material requirements

'Net material requirements' is a measure of the difference between the gross material requirements and the amount of those materials immediately to hand. The net material requirements therefore represent the actual amount of materials needed over a given period.

Net change system

A net change system is a continually updated **material requirements planning (MRP)** system. Every time a transaction involving movement of inventory occurs, it is immediately keyed in to the software. This means that the organization makes a note of both the availability of stock items and the requirements of those stock items as a real-time process.

Network (precedence) diagram

See **critical path.**

Noise at Work Regulations 1989 (UK)

These regulations require employers to ensure that their employees are protected from hearing damage as a result of their work. A new EU

Directive on the minimum health and safety requirements regarding exposure of workers to the risks arising from physical agents (noise), which repeals Directive 86/188/EEC, was adopted in early December 2002 and came into force on 15 February 2003.

www.hmso.gov.uk/si/si1989/Uksi_19891790_en_1.htm

Normal operating conditions

'Normal operating conditions' is a term which can be applied to various aspects of the production process, the organization itself or the parts, components or finished products it produces. Normal operating conditions are taken to be a standard or reasonable set of conditions against which a particular issue, process or product's reliability can be compared. The organization will tend to specify the normal operating conditions and seek to understand why there may be deviations from this reliability measure.

Normal time

'Normal time' is an industrial engineering term used in connection with observation for the purposes of time studies. There are three main steps involved in calculating normal time, and these are:

- The average time from a time study is collected.
- Each employee's average time is adjusted by a subjectively predetermined performance rating. The average of these times is called the normal time for the operation.
- The normal time is adjusted for allowances to compute the standard time.

Numerically controlled (NC) machines

See **computer numerical control (CNC).**

Observed time

Observed time may be calculated using a **motion study**, which is used to calculate the average time it takes to complete a given task. Observed time can be differentiated from **normal time** as this measure is not adjusted by a rating factor of the worker's performance and speed.

Occupational Safety and Health Act (OSH) 1970

The Occupational Safety and Health Act of 1970, requires US employers to provide workplaces free from serious recognized hazards and to comply with occupational safety and health standards.

www.dol.gov/dol/compliance/comp-osha.htm

Operating time

Traditionally, the operating time is the total number of hours or minutes available as production time during a day. The actual operating time is derived by calculating the average number of hours of production in a given day, less employee breaks and scheduled stops for maintenance, repair and inspection.

Operational factors

Operational factors are issues which directly affect the performance, **capacity** and output of a production facility. Generally these will include scheduled or unscheduled problems, including **bottlenecks**, failures in equipment, machinery breakdown or inadequate communication between different work stations or departments within the facility.

Operations management

Formerly, operations management was known as production management and was applied almost exclusively to the manufacturing sector.

For many organizations this term is still used rather than operations management. However, the management function related to manufacturing has broadened to incorporate many other aspects related to the **supply chain**. It has therefore become common to use the term 'operations management' to describe activities related both to manufacturing and increasingly to the service sector. At its heart, operations management deals with the design of products and services, the buying of components or services from suppliers, the processing of those products and services and the selling of the finished goods. Across all of these disparate areas of business, operations management can be seen as an overarching discipline which seeks to quantify and organize the whole process. None the less, there is still a considerable emphasis placed on issues directly related to manufacturing, stock control, and to a lesser extent, the management of the distribution systems. As Figure 25 illustrates, a large manufacturing organization will include aspects of operations management under a wide variety of different, but closely related managerial disciplines. Primarily, human resources, marketing, administration and finance and, of course, the research and development department of an organization, support and are mutually dependent upon the operations division.

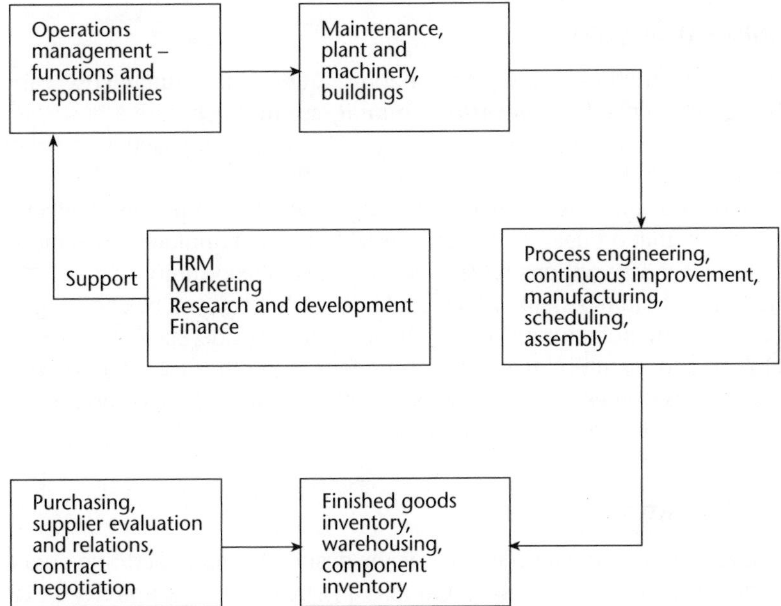

Figure 25 Operations management

O

Given the wide spread of different job roles and tasks within operations management, it is notoriously difficult to give a perfect definition of what an operations manager would actually do. Certainly he or she would be responsible for a wide range of different functions, but the functions themselves will often be determined by the nature of the business itself, whether it is a service-based industry or an organization primarily concerned with manufacturing.

Hill, Terry, *Operations Management: Strategic Context and Managerial Analysis*. Basingstoke: Palgrave Macmillan, 2000.

Operations strategy

Essentially an organization's operations strategy aims to deploy the organization's resources in order to gain a **competitive advantage**. The operations strategy is usually defined in very broad terms and invokes aspirations in respect of levels of service, quality, flexibility and cost control. In many cases an organization will identify a key objective which will give it a competitive advantage, but this may mean that other objectives may need to be sacrificed in order to achieve the primary goal.

Opportunity cost

Although, strictly speaking, an economics term, 'opportunity cost' can be equally applied to **operations management**. Each time a business chooses to pursue a particular form of manufacturing activity it has made that choice, having investigated all of the other options. Given the fact that it is unlikely, even with the largest production process budgets available, that a business can pursue all forms of manufacturing simultaneously, some options have to be discarded. Opportunity cost argues that the potential benefits which could have been enjoyed by choosing a particular manufacturing activity have to be considered if this is not chosen and an alternative action is preferred. In other words, opportunity cost examines the real cost of an action, taking into account a next best alternative that has been forgone.

Optimization

Optimization, as the term implies, is the desire of a manufacturing organization to ensure that its operations run at as close to **capacity** as is humanly possible. Given the fact that there are innumerable variables which could affect issues, such as the **capacity utilization rate**, most manufacturers take a pragmatic view as to the optimum levels of production. They will inevitably seek an average, which takes into account the possibilities of the production being interrupted by many factors both from within and beyond their control.

Optimistic time

Optimistic time is, as the term suggests, an estimate, given optimal conditions, of when a particular project or manufacturing process will be completed. The optimistic time is, invariably, the shortest time.

Order qualifiers/winner

In many respects these linked concepts can be likened to a supplier beauty contest. In effect, the purchasing organization identifies, using a series of screening criteria, potential suppliers whose products match the required specifications and other associated criteria, such as cost, **lead time** and delivery schedules. Those which are chosen as being potential suppliers are given the name 'order qualifier'. Once this process has been completed a secondary set of more stringent criteria are then used to differentiate like products offered by order qualifiers. The supplier who most closely matches these additional screening criteria will be the supplier who is awarded the order and becomes the order winner.

Slack, Nigel and Lewis, Mike, *Operations Strategy*. Harlow, Essex: Financial Times/Prentice-Hall, 2000.

Order releases

An order release is the authorization to place planned orders. The authorization will usually be triggered by **material requirements planning (MRP)** in conjunction with the **master production schedule (MPS)**. The authorization will trigger the ordering process, taking into account the supplier's **lead time**.

Ordering cost

Ordering cost is a measure of the actual costs of both ordering and receiving stock from a supplier. Ordering cost does not include the actual cost of the goods themselves, but incorporates all of the other costs associated with the order, including the cost of delivery and subsequent costs related to the storage of those parts or components.

Original equipment manufacturer (OEM)

An original equipment manufacturer is an organization which does not have any intermediaries between it and the end-user of the product. Many of the larger vehicle manufacturers are described as OEMs, although admittedly many have independent distributor networks between them and the customer. Increasingly, however, vehicle manufacturers and suppliers of other equipment, including computers, and machinery, have chosen to cut out parts of the **supply chain** below them for a number of reasons. Principally, of course, there is the question of profitability with larger margins, as margins do not have to take into account the profits required by distributors lower down the line. The establishment of a controlled distribution network, either owned or part-owned by the OEM, is an ideal compromise. It should be noted, however, that those companies which supply products and components to OEMs are not OEMs themselves, as the OEM is not an end-user.

Output-based (incentive) systems

Organizations tend to use one of two payment systems for compensating employees, either an output-based system or a time-based system.

Output-based (incentive) systems aim to compensate employees according to the amount of output they physically produce during a pay period. This means that their pay is directly related to their performance or productivity.

Time-based systems, which are also known as hourly or **measured day work** systems, base the compensation on the number of hours which an employee has worked during a specified pay period.

The key differences between the two systems are summarized in Table 16, which also addresses the advantages and disadvantages as far as the organization (management) are concerned.

O

There are, of course, a number of different variations in incentive plans, but many of them are related to a base rate of pay with additions. One of the simplest means of rewarding employees is a straight piece-work method that guarantees the employee a minimum payment which is not linked to output. The base rate is linked to an output standard, with employees who do not achieve this output standard still being paid the base rate. This is a means by which the employees can be protected against a lower output figure as a result of delays and breakdowns that were not their fault. Incentive payments are then paid to employees who manage to achieve output beyond the output standard (often called a bonus).

Table 16 Assessment of time-based and output-based systems

	Management	Employees
TIME-BASED SYSTEMS		
Advantages	There are stable labour costs.	There is stability in pay.
	It is easy to administer.	There is less pressure to produce compared to an output system.
	There is a stable level of output.	
Disadvantages	There is no incentive for workers to increase their output.	Any additional efforts made are not rewarded.
OUTPUT-BASED SYSTEMS		
Advantages	There is a lower cost per unit.	Additional efforts are rewarded.
	Output is greater.	More efforts are rewarded, so there is an opportunity to increase earnings.
Disadvantages	The computing of pay can be more complicated.	There may be fluctuations in earnings.
	There is a constant need to measure output.	There may be penalties for breakdowns which may result in loss of earnings.
	Quality may suffer.	
	It is difficult to incorporate wage increases.	
	Scheduling may prove problematic.	

There are a number of other ways in which incentive-based payments are described, amongst them those listed in Table 17.

Boyle, Daniel C., *Secrets of a Successful Employee Recognition System*. New York: Productivity Press, 1995.

O

Table 17 Incentive plans

Name of incentive plan	Description
Scanlon	Aims for a reduction in labour costs by offering employees a share in the savings made from any reduction in the costs.
Kaiser	Aims to reduce labour, material and supply costs by sharing the identified savings with employees.
Lincoln	A more complex plan, which incorporates elements of profit sharing, job enlargement and employee participation in the management decision making. Usually, employees are offered a package which includes a piece-work system, an annual bonus and the opportunity to acquire shares or stock in the business.
Kodak	With a base of higher than average pay, this system aims to provide the employees with an annual bonus linked to the profitability of the business. Employees are empowered to set goals and associated performance levels. The plan aims to fully involve the workforce and encourage them to set high performance goals, which can be exceeded in order to push the business into higher profitability and trigger the annual bonus payments.

Outsourcing

The term 'outsourcing' relates to the hiring of another organization, or its employees, in order to carry out a specific task or activity that would normally be carried out in-house. Examples of such activities are shipping/transportation, computing services or payroll accounting. The main advantages to an organization of outsourcing are:

- There are **economies of scale** because the outsourced organization also serves many other organizations.
- There is little likelihood of the outsourced organization gaining a competitive advantage.
- The outsourced organization is more likely to be conversant with current regulations or legislation regarding the task or activity if it is carrying out a similar activity for other organizations.

- The organization does not have to incur the expense of training its employees to carry out the outsourced work.

Overall equipment effectiveness (OEE)

Overall equipment effectiveness (OEE) is a key concept in **lean production** and is used extensively in **total preventive/productive maintenance (TPM)**. The formula for OEE is:

Availability rate × *performance rate* × *yield rate*

The *availability rate* is the operating or production time, less any stoppage time, divided by the total operating time. This calculation reflects the stoppage time due to shift changeover, equipment failure or problems, and loss of time through start-up of machinery and equipment. Therefore the formula is:

$$\frac{\textit{Production time} - \textit{stopping time}}{\textit{Total operating time}} = \textit{availability rate}$$

The *performance rate* is the total output divided by the potential output at a rated speed. This calculation reflects any speed losses due to machine idling, or minor stoppages which cause a reduced speed. Therefore the formula is:

$$\frac{\textit{Total output}}{\textit{Potential output at a rated speed}} = \textit{performance rate}$$

The *quality rate* is the level of particularly good bouts of output divided by the total output and the formula is:

$$\frac{\textit{Good output}}{\textit{Total output}} = \textit{quality rate}$$

There are six major losses that OEE takes into account:

- Breakdown losses – which reduce the quantity of products produced, as well as the levels of productivity, through machinery or equipment breakdowns.
- Set-up and adjustment losses – which are the result of defective units and the stoppage time needed to adjust machinery from the production of one product to another.
- Idling time and minor stoppage losses – which occur relatively frequently as a result of brief periods of machinery idleness occurring during minor product jamming.

- Reduced speed losses – which occur when machinery or equipment is operated to less than its full potential.
- Quality defects and rework – these losses are product-related and concern issues related to machinery malfunctions that cause product defectiveness.
- Start-up losses – these losses occur in the early production stages of a product when machinery has not reached its steady production level.

The major goal of an organization using OEE is to improve the effectiveness of its machinery and equipment. Since equipment effectiveness affects the production employees more than any other group within the organization, it is appropriate for them to be involved in tracking OEE and in planning and implementing equipment improvements, in order to reduce lost effectiveness. It is recommended that data about the equipment be collected on a daily basis.

Overtime

Overtime occurs when an employer requires or permits an employee to work extra hours over and above their normal working day or week. Under normal circumstances, the employer will provide premium pay for such overtime work.

In the US, under the terms of the Fair Labor Standards Act (FLSA), overtime payments must be one and a half times the normal pay for hours worked in excess of 40 hours in a week. Not all overtime necessarily means the payment of additional wages as often overtime work is traded for other time off from work (usually at the 1.5 times rate). Human resources departments would be responsible for the monitoring, recording and payment of any such overtime work carried out by an employee.

Pacing process

Ideally, a production line's pacing process should be in direct relation to **takt time**. In other words, the output of the production process should match actual demand. Normally, the pacing process is set by the last process on the production line, which gives the best impression of how many units have been produced and how this compares to the known demand. Signalling that the pace of the production line is in line with the takt time allows the rest of the production line to pace itself, following the lead of the last production process.

Pareto's Law/Pareto analysis

Vilfredo Pareto (1848–1923) was an Italian economist and sociologist, known more widely for his theory on mass and elite interaction as well as his application of mathematics to economic analysis.

While living in France in the early 1900s, Vilfredo Pareto studied the distribution of wealth in Milan. Pareto's conclusions were that 20 per cent of the people controlled 80 per cent of the wealth. Pareto's Law is also known as the '80–20 rule'. Its application is demonstrated in Figure 26.

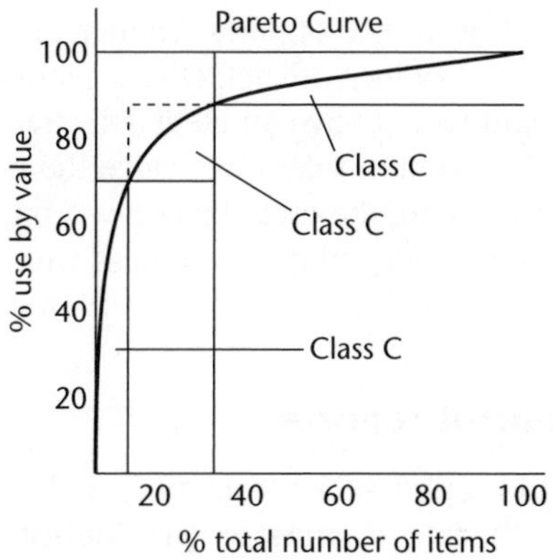

Figure 26 A demonstration of Pareto's Law

Pareto's Law can be considered in a number of organizational situations, including:

- Inventory/value distribution – where the majority of the value of the inventory is involved in a small number of items.
- Customer sales distributions – where a small number of customers give the organization the majority of its sales.
- Quality control – where the majority of the defects encountered can be attributed to a small number of problems.
- Human resources – where the organization considers the fact that the majority of the problems encountered can be attributed to a small number of employees.

See also **ABC classification**.

Part-period model

Organizations may choose to adopt a part-period model in order to balance the cost of holding inventory against the cost of setting up a process to use a specific part. The part-period refers to the holding of a particular part over a number of time periods in order to achieve this balance.

P-chart

A P-chart is essentially a quality control chart which aims to monitor the percentage of defective parts in a production process. Typically, a sample of the parts will be collected from the process according to a set schedule, which may define either the number of parts to be collected or that a set number of parts should be collected in each time period (probably each shift). The sample of parts are then analysed for defects and the percentage of parts which are defective is plotted onto a **control chart**. The control chart would have an ideal defective percentage line, with a minimum and maximum tolerance. Once the percentage defect result is plotted onto the chart, the organization will have a clear idea as to whether there are elements within the process which are causing an unacceptable number of defects.

Performance control reports

A performance control report seeks to identify and explain deviations from a production schedule or **master production schedule**. The performance control report will not only attempt to analyse these deviations but will also try to assess and quantify associated cost implications.

Performance management

Performance management can be seen as a systematic and data-oriented approach to managing employees, based on positive reinforcement as the primary driver to maximize their performance. Performance management assumes that there is a disparity between what an employee is currently achieving (on the basis that they have to do this work and perform to this standard) and the possibility that they desire to perform better (based on the assumption that they have desires to perform more effectively if given the opportunity and the encouragement). In many respects, the concept behind performance management is a recognition of this potential gap between actual performance and desired performance. This can be illustrated in the graph in Figure 27, which identifies the discretionary effort of an individual. This discretionary effort is applied according to circumstances and is variable; performance management seeks to identify the gap between 'having to' and 'wanting to', and to push the performance up to the 'want to' level.

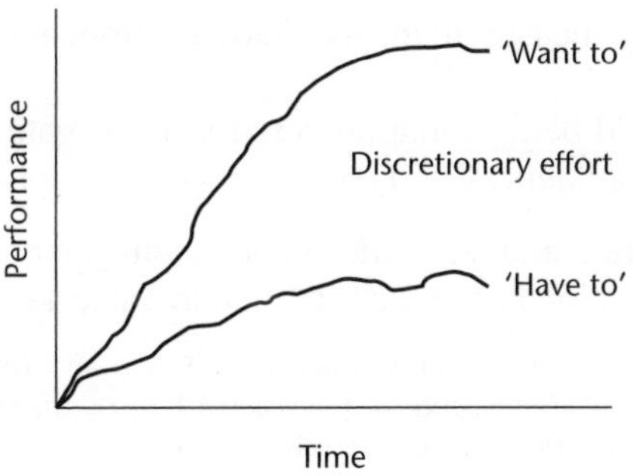

Figure 27 The potential performance gap

Source: www.p-management.com

Performance management has been used in its various forms since the mid-1970s and it is believed to be applicable to almost every area of a business. Its primary focus is, of course, employees. The first major step in implementing a performance management system is to move away from negative reinforcement of standards, which seeks to punish individuals for not performing to (often) unspoken levels of performance.

Performance management uses positive reinforcement to generate effort beyond what is normally (minimally) exhibited by the employees. In this way, the discretionary effort is encouraged and the organization as a whole can move towards a maximization of performance.

Kotter, John P. and Heskett, James L., *Corporate Culture and Performance*. New York: Free Press, 1992.

Porter, Michael, *The Competitive Advantage: Creating and Sustaining Superior Performance*. New York: Simon & Schuster, 1998.

Performance measures

Performance appraisals are the most common form of performance management, but the concept also incorporates employee feedback, development and compensation. Overwhelmingly, however, the majority of employees are dissatisfied with **performance management** systems (the Society of Human Resource Management quotes a 90% figure).

Framing an effective performance management system can be fraught with difficulties; however, the following aspects are seen to be integral in the creation of such a scheme:

- A clear definition and measurement of performance is vital.
- Content and measurement should derive from internal and external customers.
- There should be a formal process for investigating and correcting situational influences and constraints on performance.

Above all, accurate and fair performance management needs to assess employees in relation to the factors listed in Table 18.

Soltani, Ebrahim, Gennard, John, van der Meer, Robert and Williams, Terry, *Content Issues of HR-related Performance Measurement: A Total Quality Management Approach*. Paper given at the University of Strathclyde.

Performance rating

During periods of observation, or **motion study**, the individual analysing a specific job or series of tasks will make a judgement as to whether the individual worker or group of workers were performing to their optimum speed and efficiency. Using a comparative scale, the analyst will then seek to place that employee, or group of employees, on a rating scale. This job rating, or ranking, follows similar lines to job grading in that it requires managers to rank employees on their merit and capabilities of carrying out the set of activities involved in their job

Table 18 Requirements for performance management

Communication, coordination and support	Equipment and environment
Amount and relevance of training received.	Equipment and tools necessary to do the job.
Information, instructions, and specifications needed to do the job.	Process for obtaining and retaining raw materials, parts, supplies.
Coordination of work activities.	Dependability of equipment.
Cooperation, communication, and relations between co-workers.	Conditions in which job is performed.
Financial resources available and time allowed to produce quality and quantity of work.	

role. This form of performance appraisal does not identify any training or retraining and development needs but simply merits the employee, often for purposes of calculating pay increases or the future use of the employee within the organization. Performance rating is also used in the calculation of standard time.

Performance-related pay (PRP)

Performance-related pay (PRP) is used by employers to reward employees on an individual or a team basis. As a remuneration system, it is widely used, as it is perceived as a means by which incentives can be awarded to employees who are performing well without the requirement to progress them further up the pay scale.

In effect, it rewards individuals differently for carrying out the same job role and as such there is an inherent inequality in the system. It is therefore imperative that a transparent system is designed using the following criteria:

- Objectives need to be set and these need to be communicated to employees to ensure understanding.
- There should be some consideration of mitigating factors which may affect performance.

- The evaluation of performance needs to be translated into a form of performance rating.
- The link can therefore be made between the rating and the pay which will be awarded.
- There should be an in-built appeals procedure.

The framing of PRP schemes should also incorporate the following concepts:

- There should be a recognition that bias may creep into the performance assessment.
- In setting performance criteria, they should be quantitative rather than qualitative or subjective.
- There should be no differentials built in that might penalize women or minority groups.
- If the scheme is perceived to be unfair, then there is a likelihood that the system will fail.
- There should be no deployment of 'hidden criteria' to award pay.
- Whilst long service should be considered desirable, this should be rewarded in a different way from including it as a consideration in PRP.
- The distribution of appraisal ratings and PRP should be monitored by gender, ethnic group, job level and length of service.
- Managers and employees should have access to this monitoring data.
- Managers need regular training to update them on techniques of appraisal, objectives-setting and the elimination of bias in performance evaluations.
- Formal appeals should be outside the normal grievance procedures.
- Appeals should be monitored for obvious signs of bias.
- Comprehensive reviews of the payroll records need to be carried out.
- Employee attitude studies need to be carried out to assess the current levels of confidence in the system.
- These attitude studies need to be made available to all employees and managers.

Brown, Duncan, and Armstrong, Michael, *Paying for Contribution: New Performance-related Pay Strategies*. London: Kogan Page, 1998.

Chingos, Peter T., *Paying for Performance: A Guide to Compensation Management*. Chichester: John Wiley, 2002.

Performance standards

Performance standards are set in a number of different functions within an organization. The term could relate to the quantity or quality of work that individual employees produce during the course of their job, or alternatively could be used to assess an employee for appraisal or training purposes. In other words, they are the **benchmarks** against which standards are measured.

Typically, a performance standard would be set to measure the quantity of output, but it should be borne in mind that the quality of that output is also of prime importance. Assessment of standards of performance is easier to implement in a manual or production-output situation than in managerial or administrative jobs. Often this problem is overcome by selecting particular tasks within the variety completed as part of the job and ensuring their satisfactory completion. Imperative managerial targets can easily be monitored, like sales figures or customer contact numbers, but there is less scope for the setting of a performance standard for the whole job.

Performance tests

Employee performance tests are also known as 'job performance measures' (JPM). Usually performance tests are used during job application and recruitment exercises as part of the screening process. In the case of JPM, tests are carried out involving existing employees in order to assess their continued suitability for the post and to identify areas which may later require training and education. An identification of these areas may also help the human resources department to prioritize spending on training and education on the basis of a training needs analysis.

Cizek, Gregory L. (ed.), *Setting Performance Standards: Concepts, Methods, and Perspectives*. Hillsdale, NJ: Lawrence Erlbaum Associates, 2001.

P

Periodic (inventory) review system

Also known as a fixed-time-period model, or a P-model, this periodic inventory review system is used for planning independent inventories. The P, meaning 'period', implies that the system is triggered at a specific time, rather than by an event. In other words, orders are placed at predetermined times over the length of the project or production process. The system anticipates the demand for materials, components or parts, on the basis of presumed levels of production. Provided the production level does not exceed the estimates, then by using the P-model, the organization should always have sufficient stocks of necessary materials available. This does mean, however, that inevitably the organization will be over-stocked at times as the reorder periods are timed to occur before the new stock is actually required. This does prevent the organization from running out of stock, but it has storage implications.

Perpetual inventory system

A perpetual inventory system requires an ongoing count of the current inventory, either manually or by using a database which has been systematically updated as stock has been used or removed from storage.

Personal Protective Equipment at Work Regulations (PPR) 1992 (UK)

These regulations require employers to ensure that their employees have the appropriate protective clothing and equipment for their work. Personal Protective Equipment at Work Regulations (1992) form part of a series of health and safety regulations that implement European Directives. Personal protective equipment (PPE) is to be supplied wherever there are risks to health and safety that cannot be adequately controlled in other ways.

www.hmso.gov.uk/si/si1992/Uksi_19922966_en_1.htm

Pessimistic time

Simply, pessimistic time adopts the opposite stance to **optimistic time** in as much as, using a worst case scenario, an estimate is made of the time it will take to complete a project or a production process. Typically, pessimistic time will be the longest time that completion is likely to take.

PEST/PESTEL/SLEPT/STEEPLE

This concept originally began with just four criteria, with the acronym PEST (Political, Economic, Social and Technological). These forces are seen as being the principal external determinants of the environment in which a business operates. In later years the four forces became five under the acronym SLEPT (Social, Legal, Economic, Political and Technological). The concept has now extended to include seven forces, using the acronym STEEPLE (Social, Technological, Economic, Educational, Political, Legal and Environmental protection).

The purpose of the Five Forces, or its variants, is to examine or audit where threats originate and where opportunities can be found. In other words, the broader STEEPLE acronym applies to the macro-environment (factors outside the organization). The main areas of interest within each letter are listed in Table 19.

Table 19 The Seven Forces

Letter	Description
S	Social and cultural influences, including language, culture, attitudes and behaviour which affect future strategies and markets.
T	Technological and product innovation, which suggest how the market is developing as well as the future developments in research and arising opportunities.
E (E1)	Economics and market competition, which considers factors such as the business cycle, inflation, energy costs and investments, an assessment is made as to how they will affect the level of economic activity in each market.
E (E2)	Education, training and employment: primarily the trends in these areas which may impact upon the availability of trained labour as well as the potential demands of new generations and probable expectations.
P	Political influence, which focuses on current and proposed policies which will impact on the business and the workforce.
L	Legal aspects, which focus on current and proposed legislation; of equal importance is the business's adherence to current laws and regulations.
E (E3)	Environmental protection, which addresses the business's current and future impact on the environment, working on the basis that environmental protection will continue to be a major issue in restricting and amending the ways in which a business operates.

See also **environmental scanning.**

Porter, Michael, *Competitive Advantage*. New York: Free Press, 1985.

Piece work

Piece work means that employees are not paid for the hours they work; instead they are paid for the number of items produced. A worker should, theoretically, not get less than the minimum wage if paid on a piece-work basis.

Many factories pay staff a flat rate per hour plus 'piece' work (so much extra per piece of work), which allows experienced staff the opportunity to increase their wages.

Plan–Do–Check–Act (PDCA) cycle

The Plan–Do–Check–Act cycle, as illustrated in Figure 28, is the cycle of **continuous improvement**. The PDCA cycle is often referred to as the Deming wheel.

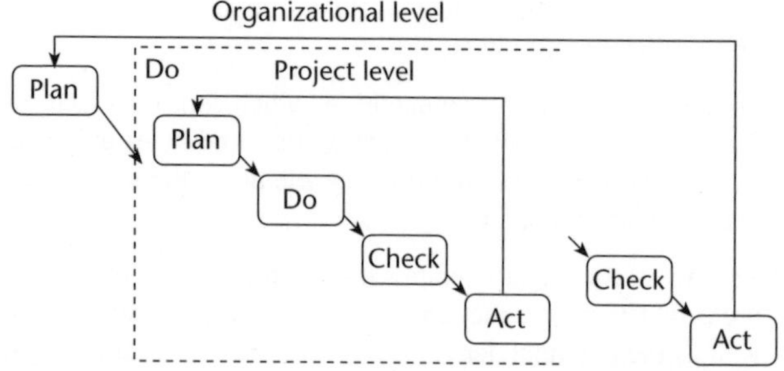

Figure 28 The PDCA cycle

See also **Deming, William Edwards.**

Plan–Do–Study–Act (PDSA) cycle

The plan–do–study–act (PDSA) cycle aims to provide an essential framework or structure for an organization to implement **continuous improvement**. The basis behind continuous improvement requires the organization to systematically address issues which have hitherto affected its ability to provide the level of production or service it desires. PDSA therefore allows the organization to create a framework to identify and investigate specific issues, which can then be actioned.

Planned orders

Planned orders are, in fact, a schedule which indicates the size and the timing of future orders. The schedule is an important indication as to when the manufacturing organization can confidently expect its inventories to be replenished and may well be an influence in deciding which of the orders currently under review, but not in the process, will be tackled first.

Planned-order receipt

'Planned-order receipt' is a term associated with the delivery of parts or components from a supplier. A planned-order receipt indicates the quantity of those items which are expected to be received by the beginning of the delivery period, as stated in the purchase order.

Planned-order release

Using a **material requirements planning (MRP)** system, a manufacturing organization will be aware of when it will require specific parts and components. The planned-order release signals to the suppliers that, taking into consideration their **lead time**, a pre-arranged order should now be initiated to ensure that it arrives with the manufacturing organization by the time that it is required for a production process.

Plant rate

Plant rate is taken to be the total value added by a production facility, divided by the total number of direct labour hours employed to produce that added value in a given year. Multiple-plant organizations can then make more meaningful comparisons between their different plants and note the ratios between the added value and the cost in labour hours. These are normally incorporated into the forthcoming yearly budgets.

Plant within a plant (PWP)

A plant within a plant is often referred to as a microfactory, but this is not the full description of exactly the purpose of a PWP, as indeed a microfactory can be a completely separate facility, located close to customers, which is set up to fulfil their immediate needs.

A plant within a plant is a manufacturing-process concept which sets aside specific areas of the facility, which are then dedicated to different modes of production, or specialisms in the production of parts, components or products. Each of these PWPs not only has its own location, but may also have its own integral management and control systems. PWPs will also adopt their own strategies and will cooperate with other PWPs, but will be primarily concerned with the **continuous improvement** of their own facility, rather than broadening out lessons learned to the rest of the facility. Clearly, where there are parallel production facilities under their own management and guidance, with **empowerment**, the production facility can quickly become an ideal **learning organization**.

Point of sale system (POS)

See **electronic point of sale (EPOS)**.

Poka-yoke

Poka means 'an inadvertent mistake' and *yoke* means 'avoid'. The term is Japanese and the most prominent and influential individual in developing the concept was Dr Shigeo Shingo, who was an industrial engineer with Matsushita. *Poka-yoke* forms the basis of **zero quality control (ZQC)**, which is a technique that aims to avoid and eliminate mistakes. The key issue is error avoidance and making processes as foolproof as possible. In other words, in manufacturing and in all aspects of office procedures, *poka-yoke* aims to identify the causes of errors and remove them, thus producing a **zero defects** situation. *Poka-yoke* recognizes that even minor mistakes, such as the incorrect processing of orders and invoices or inadequate routine maintenance, can have catastrophic consequences for a business. Although some basic systems, such as floppy disk drives or electrical plugs, have been fool-proofed in their design, many other devices require a *poka-yoke* approach in order to avoid and eliminate the most fundamental of errors.

Shimbun, Nikkan Kogyo (ed.), *Poka-Yoke: Improving Product Quality by Preventing Defects*. New York: Productivity Press, 1989.

Precedence diagram

More correctly, a precedence diagram should be referred to as a network precedence diagram, which is, in effect, an **activity-on-arrow (AOA)** or an **activity-on-node (AON)** style diagram. It incorporates the use of both arrows and nodes and shows the sequential relationships between the activities required to complete a project or a series of manufacturing processes.

P

Predecessor/successor

'Predecessor' and 'successor' are terms used to describe the activities in either **activity-on-arrow (AOA)** or **activity-on-node (AON)** diagrams. A predecessor is, at it suggests, an activity that precedes a node, and a successor is one that follows a node.

Predictive maintenance

The term 'predictive maintenance' refers to the practice of monitoring machinery with a measuring device that can anticipate and predict likely failure. The failure is often caused by vibration levels and the maintenance programme can be scheduled using feedback from the measuring device.

See also **preventive maintenance.**

Predictor variable

A predictor variable is usually plotted on the X axis of a graph and is a variable which is used to estimate values which may fluctuate over a given period of time over the production or project process.

Prevention costs

See **preventive maintenance.**

Preventive maintenance

The use of preventive, or preventative, maintenance involves an organization in the checking and/or repairing of machinery on a scheduled basis before failure occurs. The schedule is usually based on the organization's historical information on the length of time between similar failures for all of the organization's similar machinery. This checking is often performed by the machine operators.

Preventive maintenance eliminates the need for emergency maintenance, where the maintenance is done after the machine fails.

See also **predictive maintenance.**

Pricebreak

The term 'pricebreak' relates to the offering of quantity discounts to customers on a successive series of levels according to the number of items purchased. Manufacturing organizations will employ this technique in order to provide an incentive to customers to reduce the manufacturing organization's stock levels. This situation usually arises either when there has been an unexpected drop in the predicted demand for a product or service, or when the manufacturing organization has incorrectly estimated the level of demand and has set the production levels in excess of what was actually required by the market over that period of time.

Primary reports

Primary reports use **material requirements planning (MRP)** criteria and parameters to determine planned order schedules, **order releases** and any other changes to planned orders.

Priority rules

A priority rule, or a set of priority rules, is often established by a manufacturing organization as a specified set of instructions or imperatives which determine the order in which jobs will be processed.

Probabilistic inventory control model

A probabilistic inventory control model treats all variables and parameters as random variables. The model assumes that average demand over a period of time will remain constant and that it is possible to state the probable distribution of the demand, particularly in relation to **lead times** required by suppliers.

Process capability ratio

Process capability analysis can be performed without specification limits; process capability ratios incorporating specification limits can, however, be useful.

The most commonly used process capability ratio is known as the *Cp* index. This is defined as

$$C_p = \frac{USL - LSL}{6\sigma}$$

USL and *LSL* are, respectively, the upper and lower specification limits, and σ is the standard deviation of the process characteristic. The **six-sigma** spread of the process is the basic definition of process capability when the quality characteristic follows normal distribution. C_p therefore measures how well the process meets the specifications.

See also **six sigma**.

Process control

See **statistical process control (SPC)**.

P

Process factors

Process factors are usually taken to mean the quality characteristics of a product, or the quantity (capacity) capabilities of the production line, which have a direct impact on both the production line's performance and output.

Process improvement

See **continuous improvement.**

Process layout

The term 'process layout' refers to the grouping together of like machinery in respect of their function, as opposed to the requirements of a particular product or group of products. A process layout is appropriate for a **job shop**.

Process postponement

Process postponement involves the modification of the production and distribution process so that these functions are carried out at a later time and closer to when the customer requires the finished goods. Process postponement usually takes place as a result of the organization's desire to reduce the amount of finished goods using up valuable warehousing space, or to avoid having to make part deliveries of the product ahead of time in order to reduce the pressure on the stockholding facility.

Process velocity

Process velocity is also known as a throughput ratio, which is the measure of the time which it has taken to process a given number of products, compared with the amount of added value the process has contributed to the final value of those products.

Product design quality

Product design quality refers to the degree to which the design of a particular product contributes to its recognition as a high-quality product. Product design quality is often the responsibility of and input from the organization's groups of specialists in marketing, design, research and development, quality assurance, and production departments. They will attempt to integrate their ideas into the current production processes, but often there will need to be amendment and adaptation in order to incorporate product design quality.

In order to implement product design quality a series of blueprints, technical specifications, production requirements and analysis reports will be collated from those involved.

Product layout

Product layout is another approach to the way in which the grouping of machinery can be laid out on the production line. In direct contrast with **process layout**, product layout requires the physical configuration of the organization or its machinery to be designed according to the steps required in each process of completing a particular product or group of products.

Product life cycle

See **life cycle.**

Product process matrix

A product process matrix aims to illustrate the relationships between the characteristics and the volume of the products produced on a production line, with the structures of the production process itself.

Product/service factors

Product or service factors are issues which directly have an impact on the rate of output of a **production line**. They may be related either to the design of the production system itself, or to the degree of skill or specialization required to produce that product or service.

Production line

A production line is a standardized layout of equipment and of employees who process parts, components and products in a fixed sequence of related tasks.

See also **assembly line.**

Productivity

The word 'productivity' relates to the measure of output. It can be a measure of an individual, an organization, a machine, an industry or a country that is using its resources. Productivity can also be compared with other, similar activities carried out by other employees or other organizations over a given period of time. The formula for the measurement of productivity is:

Output/input = productivity

There are two measures of productivity; the total factor productivity is measured in monetary terms, whilst the partial factor productivity is measured in terms of individual inputs, with labour being the most common.

Project champion

A project champion (or champions), is an individual or individuals within an organization who promote and support the overall progress and successful completion of a project.

Project management

Project management involves the planning, organizing, controlling and directing of usually one-off activities. Typically, a team will be assigned to manage a specific project and will use the **Project (Program) Evaluation and Review Technique (PERT)** or critical path method (CPM) in order to structure the management of the activities related to the project.

Project (Program) Evaluation and Review Technique (PERT)

The Project (Program) Evaluation and Review Technique (PERT) is an approach for project planning originally developed by the US Navy for the Polaris project, which is essentially the same as the **critical path method**.

PERT initially considered each task to have three task-times estimates – the optimistic task time (a), most likely task time (m), and the pessimistic task time (b). The PERT technique estimates the mean task time using the following equation:

$$\frac{a + 4m + b}{6}$$

The formula for the variance of the task time is:

P

$$\frac{b - a^2}{36}$$

These equations were supposedly based on the 'beta distribution' but critics of this method suggest that the equations have little or no scientific basis. Beta distribution has a minimum and maximum value and is capable of assuming a wide variety of shapes.

Basically, the mean of the critical path time is estimated by adding together the means of the individual tasks along the critical path. In a similar way, the mean of the variance is estimated by adding together the variances of each of the tasks along the critical path. The project completion time is then estimated.

Because of the lack of confidence in this system, it is not a method used regularly throughout industry.

Projected on hand

'Projected on hand' is a term associated with inventory control management. Projected on hand is an estimation as to the amount of inventory that will be available at the beginning of each given time period.

Provision and Use of Work Equipment Regulations (PUWER) 1992 (UK)

These regulations aim to ensure that all equipment, including machinery, used by employees is safe and meets guaranteed minimum standards.

These Regulations tidied up the laws governing equipment used at work. They place general duties on employers and list minimum requirements for work equipment, to deal with selected hazards in all industry.

www.hmso.gov.uk/si/si1998/19982306.htm

Push and pull systems

Push and pull systems are at the very heart of both production and inventory control. The decision to adopt one or the other will have a dramatic impact on the way in which both of these crucial operations-management systems are handled. A push system puts the onus on the production facility to decide when, and how much of, a given product will be sent to the warehousing facilities, with the decision being based on forecasted demand and the current inventory position. In other words, it is the production facility which sets the pace and determines priorities from the point of view of the manufacturing process.

A pull system, however, uses exactly the opposite set of determinants as it is the warehouse which decides how much of a given product is required and when. In situations where the organization manufacturing the products does not maintain a buffer stock in a warehouse, the pull system may lead to certain customers not being able to have their orders fulfilled when they are required.

See also **constant work in progress (CONWIP)** *and* **just-in-time systems (JIT)**.

Quality at source

The concept of quality at source suggests that quality, as a separate issue, is not specifically inspected or investigated during the production process. Quality, using this philosophy, is an integral part of the overall process and employees who have a responsibility for a specific series of tasks, and hence a specific output, are those who monitor quality in practice, rather than it being considered as an abstract issue. In other words, quality at source means that quality begins with the first acts related to a process and continues throughout that and any subsequent processes, thus making quality an embedded concern for all.

Quality circles

A quality circle is a discussion group which meets on a regular basis to identify quality problems, investigate solutions and make recommendations as to the most suitable solution. The members of quality circles are employees and may include individuals with specific skills or expertise, such as engineers, quality inspectors or salespersons. Quality circles were first created in the 1950s in the Toyota motor company. In the 1980s this Japanese form of employee participation and consultation was adopted on a large scale in both Europe and the US. Quality circles aim to use untapped knowledge from the firm's employees, as well as providing them with the opportunity to show their knowledge and talents in terms of their problem-solving skills.

Quality control

Quality control essentially involves ensuring that a product or service conforms to predetermined specifications. In its most basic form, quality control is addressed in three major areas of the manufacturing process.

- *At the input stage* – where only the parts, components and partly finished products which conform to the given specifications are used or identified as being suitable for the production process.

- *During the production process itself* – when parts, components and other items are converted into finished products, all systems and control procedures need to be in place to continue to check that specifications are conformed to on a consistent basis.
- *At the output stage* – only products which are seen to conform to the specifications are allowed to exit the system and become available to customers.

The conclusion of this holistic system therefore incorporates input, process and output control. Typically, input control would incorporate an inspection of raw materials and of any subcontracted or purchased parts and a periodic review and rating of suppliers. During the process control, inspection is a key issue of **work in progress** and of the swift correction or rectification of problems, usually using **control charts**. At the output stage again inspections are crucial, as are **performance tests**.

Customers will provide a genuine assessment of the products being used as they were designed to be used. Therefore, interaction with customers and a swift response to any problems which they encounter are essential, the findings of which will then be passed down for action at the input and process stages.

Wild, Ray, *Essentials of Production and Operations Management: Text and Cases*. London: Cassell, 1995.

Quality cost

The fundamental ethos of quality cost is that it is the least expensive option to ensure the quality of the process and the materials used in that process, rather than dealing with quality-related costs as they arise, through having allowed substandard or defective elements to occur in the manufacturing process. Dealing with quality costs inevitably means that the manufacturing organization will seek to prevent, to measure and to deal with internal failures during the production process, thereby reducing the amount of failures or defects which slip through the system. Also, by implication, stringent quality measures must be imposed upon suppliers, as it may prove difficult or inappropriate for manufacturers to check quality issues concerning components and parts which are supplied to them.

It is not standard practice for a manufacturer to explicitly state the costs which have been incurred in ensuring quality, either internally or externally. Neither is it the case that manufacturers find it easy to identify costs saved as a result of these actions.

Quality framework

In the 1980s, David Garvin suggested that there were eight critical dimensions or categories of quality. He proposed that these should serve as a framework for strategic analysis. His theory is summarized in Table 20.

Table 20 Categories of quality

Dimension or category	Description	Implications
Performance	Performance refers to a product's primary operating characteristics. This requires measurable attributes (based on individual aspects of performance) so that brands can be ranked objectively.	Overall performance rankings are difficult to develop as often there are benefits that not every customer requires or finds important.
Features	Features are characteristics that supplement the basic functioning of the product.	It is difficult to differentiate between the primary performance characteristics and the secondary performance characteristics (or the features). It is important to use objective and measurable attributes as these translate into quality differences.
Reliability	This is the probability of a product malfunctioning or failing. Calculations need to be made as to the mean time to first failure, the mean time between failures, and the failure rate per unit of time.	Reliability is more relevant for durable goods than for products or services which are instantly consumed by the customer.
Conformance	This is the degree to which a product's design and operating characteristics meet established standards. Common measurements are factory defect rates and the incidence of service calls (i.e. after the product has been sold to the customer).	Conformance may not include other deviations from the established standards, which do not lead to product failure.

⇒

Table 20 Categories of quality (*continued*)

Dimension or category	Description	Implications
Durability	This is a measure of the life of a product, in other words the amount of use the customer gets from the product before it is worn out or has deteriorated.	Measurement should also include the time scale before the product breaks down and is replaced by the customer (rather than the customer having the product repaired).
Serviceability	This measures the speed, courtesy, competence, and ease of repair. Customers will be concerned about the fact that the product has failed, but will be equally concerned with the time that it takes for the business to deal with the problem. Measures would include the time to make a service call, response rate, repair rates and the time scales involved in successfully dealing with the service problem.	Even if the product requires repair or servicing the customers may not have an adverse image of the product. They may acquire an adverse impression if the level of service of the business is poor or does not match their expectations.
Aesthetics	Aesthetics is a subjective measure, but may include what a product looks like, how it sounds, tastes or smells. This is a reflection of the customer's own personal preferences.	This is a measure that may prove to be problematic as it will be impossible to please every customer.
Perceived quality	This is another subjective measure of quality and often based on incomplete knowledge or understanding of the product and its closest competitors. Customers will compare attributes as best as they can.	This will include various tangible and intangible aspects of the product. Advertising, for example, may have a disproportionate impact on the perceived quality as the claims may not be borne out in reality.

Garvin, David A., 'Competing on the Eight Dimensions of Quality', *Harvard Business Review*, November–December, 1987.

Quality function deployment (QFD)/House of Quality

Quality function deployment (QFD) is a means by which an organization can identify the key critical customer attributes and thereby establish linkage between these attributes and the design of the products or services it offers.

QFD requires the creation of a complex matrix which is used to put the information in order, so as to assist the organization in answering three key questions:

- What are the critical attributes, to our customers?
- What design parameters are crucial in the formulation of these attributes?
- What design parameters should be incorporated into new designs?

As a team, the designers, engineers and sales and marketing departments can work together in order to ascertain the critical attributes associated by customers with a particular product. The attributes are listed in the matrix diagram; a weighted value is then assigned to each of the attributes (with the full weighting equal to 100%).

The team identifies the crucial design parameters which drive system performance (in measurable terms and directly linked to attributes required by customers). The team then attempts to link each of the design parameters with the customer requirements (these indicate the direction and the strength of the relationship). Finally, the team members turn their attention to the customers' perceptions of the existing product (compared with that of the competitors), allowing the organization to identify any potential market threats or opportunities.

Wheelwright, S. C. and Clark, K. B., *Revolutionizing Product Development*. New York: Free Press, 1992.

Q

Quality of conformance

Having designed a new product and having identified its key attributes and performance standards, a manufacturer will be keen to ensure that once production has got under way, the product retains these characteristics. Quality of conformance is a means by which the manufacturer can consistently produce or deliver a product or service which conforms to these predetermined standards. The degree to which conformance has been achieved and continues to be achieved throughout the life cycle of the product or service is described as 'quality of conformance'.

Quality of design

As a necessary precursor to **quality of conformance**, quality of design seeks to establish the primary characteristics and attributes, as well as performance, of a given product or service. Quality of design is a measurement of that product or service's ability to match, or ideally to exceed, customers' demands and expectations.

Quality-based strategy

As the term suggests, quality-based strategy is an organization-wide approach that stresses quality issues across all phases of operations.

See also **total quality management (TQM).**

Quantity discount

The term 'quantity discount' relates to the discount that organizations often offer to customers when they order in larger quantities. The difference between the normal price and the reduced price is called a discount. There are two policies of quantity discount that are used commonly:

1 *The incremental units discount policy* – which allows the customer a lower price on the units ordered above a certain point. In other words, if the customer orders more than, say, 100 units, then the price for the units over 100 is lowered from, for example, £10 to £9.
2 *The all-units discount policy* – which offers a lower price on all units ordered. In other words, if the customer orders more than, say, 100 units, the price for all units ordered will be lowered from, for example, £10 to £9.

The order quantity required to obtain the discount will always be set by the organization, either at what is termed a breakpoint, where the price changes, or at a feasible **economic order quantity (EOQ)**.

Q

Queue discipline

Once organizations have established the precise procedures by which they will queue, or organize the order in which they deal with, customers' requirements, it is imperative, both for the customers themselves and for the employees involved in the processing of the jobs, to know that these systems will continue to be adhered to under the majority of circumstances. Although there are many ways of organizing queues, the following list identifies the most common methodologies:

- The most common type of queue discipline is **first in, first out (FIFO)**.
- **Shortest processing time (SPT)** involves the identification of the customer orders which need the shortest amount of machine and employee time.
- **Earliest due date (EDD)** orders the queue according to the time when the customer has specifically asked that the order be fulfilled.
- Shortest weighted service time (SWST) is similar to SPT, but weighted according to set criteria which determine the importance of the customer.
- Last come, first served (LCFS) may possibly base the queuing on the urgency of the customer order or the fact that the order may take little time to fulfil

Queuing theory

Queuing theory addresses how an organization deals with customers' orders and calls. Typically, queuing theory will attempt to estimate the average performance of the system by investigating various aspects of the time taken to deal with a customer's request. Investigations and estimations will be made of the mean time customers are in the queue before their request or order has been fulfilled. Similar calculations will be made regarding the number of customers in the queue and the number of individual products related to those orders which are in the queue. Queuing theory is useful in understanding the limitations or problems associated with **capacity**, but it does not necessarily take into account the mean arrival rates of the requests or orders, the changeover or set-up periods involved in switching from one customer's order to another, or, for that matter, service and maintenance issues.

See also **efficient/effective consumer response (ECR); Little's flow equation** *and* **utilization.**

Quick Market Response (QMR)

See **efficient/effective consumer response (ECR).**

Random storage location

It would appear that on first inspection, an orderly storage system in a warehouse, or in areas close to the production line, would be the most efficient and logical means of ensuring that the organization knows exactly where its inventory is being kept. However, in a practical sense, a rigidly determined set of storage locations is unlikely to be efficient in even the medium term. Parts and components, or indeed finished products, will constantly appear and disappear from the inventory. This will entail an almost constant movement of the stock, either to accommodate new items or to fill up the space when items have been deleted from the inventory. The most workable system, therefore, is a random storage system, as new items can be added to the inventory, old items can be removed and accommodation can be made with regard to differing stock levels (including increases and decreases), and the location of all these items can be clearly mapped.

A manufacturing organization or warehouse which uses a random storage system will generally allocate the first available space to incoming items or finished products which have come off the production line. They will be allocated a space commensurate with the size of the particular **batch**. Normally the most appropriately sized space will be allocated, provided that all of the stock will fit into that space and not leave much space unallocated within the location. This ensures that most of the items of a particular type are stored in the fewest possible locations and that the storage space itself is more efficiently used. The whole system breaks down, however, if the organization does not have an absolutely accurate item-location procedure which can identify where batches of a particular item are being stored and how much of each item is stored in each location. There should also be a system by which the normal use of the items is regulated. In other words, if the organization uses **first in, first out (FIFO)** or **last in, first out (LIFO)**, then the age of each batch of items also needs to be known.

Random variation

A random variation is taken to mean the residual variations which are still unaccounted for after all other factors have been taken into account.

Range chart

A range chart, or an R-chart, is a quality control diagram which aims to monitor and note the variations, or range, of processes. Normally a sample of parts is collected from the manufacturing process during a particular time period, or according to a specific schedule, and compared with the base specification. The variance between the specifications of these sample parts and the base specification are noted on the R-chart. Considerable variations may indicate that there are problems in the manufacturing process which are causing too great a degree of variance, or that the process is producing parts as predicted and desired.

Recycling

Recycling is alternatively known as re-engineering, de-manufacturing, reclamation and re-marketing and involves the various means by which products or components can be reused, either by the original manufacturer, or by an organization specifically set up to deal with this material. Recycling is an integral part of an increasing trend towards sustainable product design and sustainable manufacturing, as it not only accommodates demands that the lowest possible percentage of a product, once it has reached the end of its useful life, is then discarded, but also acknowledges that many parts or components of products can, in fact, have secondary value.

Re-engineering

See **recycling** *and* **business process re-engineering (BPE)**.

Regenerative system

'Regenerative system' is a term associated with **material requirements planning (MRP)**. Using an MRP, a regenerative system seeks to update its information on a regular basis in order to ensure that all possible requirements and implications are addressed.

Regression

Regression is a statistical technique used in forecasting. Regression involves the calculation or computing of a straight-line equation which illustrates the influences of causal variables on the dependent variable, whose values are the subject of the forecast.

Remanufacturing

See **reverse engineering** *and* **recycling**.

Reorder point (ROP)

At its simplest, the ROP is normally based on the average usage over a period of **lead time**, plus **safety stock**.

The reorder point system is a means by which independent demand items can be managed. A reorder is automatically triggered when the stock levels reach a certain (predetermined) level. In other words, amount Q is ordered whenever the inventory falls below ROP level. The process and necessary calculations are determined using the following formulae. First the reorder size and the number of orders per year are calculated:

$$Q = \sqrt{\frac{2DS}{Ic}} \qquad \text{and} \qquad N = \frac{D}{Q}\ .$$

Then calculations are made regarding the demand and the **lead times**:

$$s'_d = \sqrt{LT\ s^2_d + d^2\, s^2_{LT}}$$

It is then possible to work out the reorder point:

$$ROP = d \times LT + z\, s'_d$$

Finally, the total costs associated with the system of reordering:

$$TC = \frac{D}{Q}\, \mathrm{S} + IC\, \frac{Q}{2} + ICz\ s'_d + \frac{D}{Q}\, k\ s'_\mathrm{d}\ E_{(z)}$$

If P is not given, it is necessary to calculate Q and then repeat (a) and (b) until z does not change:

(a)

$$P = \frac{QIC}{Dk}$$

(b)

$$Q = \sqrt{\frac{2D\,[S + k\,s'dE(z)]}{IC}}$$

D = demand (annual)	LT = (average) lead time
S = order cost (cost/order)	s_d = standard deviation of demand
I = inventory carrying cost (% of value per unit time)	s_{LT} = standard deviation of lead time
	s'_d = standard deviation of demand during lead time
C = item value (cost per item)	
N = number of orders per year	ROP = reorder point
Q = order size	k = stock-out cost
TC = total cost during lead time	P = probability of being in-stock
d = demand rate	z = number of standard deviations

Repetitive manufacturing

Repetitive manufacturing (REM) is a form of manufacturing where various items with similar routings are made across the same process whenever production occurs.

Products may be made in separate batches or continuously, but production in a repetitive environment is not a function of speed or volume. REM is the production of discrete units in a high-volume concentration of available capacity using the fixed routings. Products may be standard or assembled from standard modules.

Table 21 serves as an illustration of the differences between a **job shop** and repetitive manufacturing.

Table 21 Job shop versus repetitive manufacturing

Attribute manufacturing	Job shop	Repetitive
Planning	Shop orders	Blanket schedule
Run length	Short	Long, continuous
Product	Custom or non-standard	Standardized
Material issues	Specific to jobs (orders)	Non-discrete flow issues
Job tracking	Discrete started/ complete jobs	Cumulative production
Material accountability	tight	Loose, accumulative

Reporting of Injuries, Diseases and Dangerous Occurrences Regulations (RIDDOR) 1992 (UK)

A revised version of these regulations came into force in 1996, requiring employers to notify the Health and Safety Executive of occupational injuries, diseases and dangerous events in the workplace.

www.hmso.gov.uk/si/si1995/Uksi_19953163_en_1.htm

Research and development (R&D)

New product development and the bright ideas associated with such an endeavour must be tempered with the practicalities of production. Whilst many good ideas appear to be workable on paper, the realities of the situation may mean that the product cannot be produced in a cost-effective and efficient manner.

An organization has to assess whether it is looking for a new product which its current production process is capable of producing. It would serve no purpose for an organization to develop an idea for a new product only to discover that the actual production process has to be carried out elsewhere, possibly by subcontractors or business partners. After all, one of the key considerations in developing new products, regardless of their design, is that the organization should make full use of its production facilities.

The design of new products is often changed gradually as the organization becomes aware that the actual design presents problems. This process, although not enjoyable for the designer, needs to be considered in terms of efficiency and overall benefit to the organization. Whether the design process is undertaken by the organization itself or by external organizations, the business must ensure that it carries out feasibility studies. These are undertaken at the earliest possible stage to ensure that resources are not wasted in the development of a new product design when there is no likelihood of that product being produced in a cost-effective way. This screening process needs to be rigorously enforced to make sure that the business does not invest funds in product designs that are impractical and will never come to fruition. The development of new products can be not only time consuming but expensive.

The desire to develop new products should be tempered by an awareness that many small businesses fail as a result of over-investing in new product development. However, the success of new products is central to the long-term success and growth of the organization. It should be noted that only a small percentage of new products are ever successful.

It is imperative for an organization to plan its new product development using the following steps:

- Allow an initial screening period in which an investigation is carried out to assess how the product fits in with current products and services.
- Investigate whether the new product could be produced using current production methods.
- Test the production process.
- Fully cost the production process.
- Carry out the necessary market research.
- Produce a test batch of new products and test market them.

Respond to order (RTO)

A general term created by Professor A. Hill and used to describe the different ways in which a business can respond to customer-led demand. His summary of the different ways of approaching this demand are summed up in Table 22.

Reverse engineering

Reverse engineering is a common process which involves the dismantling and minute examination of a competitor's product. An organization may be interested not only in discovering exactly how the competitor's product works, but also in how it was constructed. Typically, the process of dismantling competitors' products will seek to discover the order in which the product was processed, identify the possible sources of its components and make a judgement as to how cost-effective their production procedures were compared with those of the organization carrying out the reverse engineering process. The organization will be looking for specific strengths and weaknesses in the competitor's manufacturing processes, hoping to identify whether there are particular lessons to be learned with regard to different means of producing their own products.

Reverse logistics

Reverse logistics has both environmental and economic implications, as it involves the management of the return flow of products and components from customers. Clearly there are occasions when a distributor or customer will overstock and the manufacturer may be persuaded to take back this stock. In the majority of cases this stock will now no

Table 22 Business responses to customer demands

System	Concept	Inventory	Customer lead time	Examples
Make to stock	Standard finished products are stored in inventory,	Large finished goods inventory. Usually also has WIP and raw materials.	Only the delivery time from the finished goods to the customer	Medical devices, many consumer products, retailers.
Assemble to order	Standard modules are assembled in response to a customer order.	Inventory of modules. Usually also WIP and raw materials.	Only the assembly and deliver time.	Dell computers, picking an order from a distribution centre. Pack-to-order is a special case.
Make to order	Standard raw materials are transformed into a final product.	Usually inventories of raw materials. It is possible to implement with no inventory.	Fabrication, assembly, and delivery time. This could also include time to purchase raw materials.	Customized clothing, injection-molded parts. Print-to-order is a special case.
Engineer to order	A design is developed and produced for a particular customer need.	Potentially no inventory. Could have inventory standard modules and raw materials.	Design, fabrication, assembly, and delivery time.	Custom home construction.

Source: Adapted from Professor Arthur V. Hill, Carlson School of Management, University of Minnesota.

R

longer be current and therefore will not have the same value as current products.

There are various options in dealing with this type of material. Environmentally and for sound economic reasons, the manufacturer may seek to disassemble the items and re-use components if possible. Certainly some parts of the product may require safe disposal, particularly in the case of potentially hazardous elements of the product. Equally, some manufacturers encourage the return of worn-out products, which can then be recycled or refurbished. Additionally there is a need to deal with defective components, which may have had to be replaced on site or are now in the possession of the manufacturer after the product has been returned for repair or replacement. The manufacturer will recycle as many of these parts as possible, probably through repair. In any event, an investigation into the causes of the failure or the defect may well prove of value to the manufacturer.

Increasingly, manufacturers are also encouraging distributors and customers to return reusable components and packaging material, which can again be repaired, recycled, remanufactured or disposed of in a more systematic manner than would possibly have been the case had this function been left to the distributor or customer.

Robust design

The term 'robust design' relates to a component's strength, sturdiness and durability. A component that is said to be robust is hard to break or almost never breaks. Robust design can also be related to a component's versatility, or its application to a variety of different situations. In attempting to achieve robust design, an organization will aim to ensure that a component is designed in such a way that it will be variable in use but not cause an increase in the number of defective products produced.

See also **commonality**.

Rough cut capacity planning (RCCP)

RCCP seeks to verify whether an organization has sufficient **capacity** in order to meet the capacity requirements of the **master production schedule**. In effect, RCCP is a long-term planning tool which is used in order to balance the actual and required capacity of the organization.

The technique allows the organization to increase or decrease the quantities indicated on the master schedule, add or remove work shifts, institute overtime, outsource, or add and remove equipment and machinery. RCCP is, therefore, a gross-capacity planning technique which does not take into account scheduled receipts or stock in hand in its calculation of the capacity requirements; it is simply an estimation of the capacity required in order to meet the gross production needs.

RCCP can be used to effectively validate the master schedules by comparing them with critical resource needs prior to the formulation of a **material requirements plan (MRP)**. The result should be a realistic and, above all, achievable master schedule.

RCCP can be performed at two levels. The first is known as **routing**-based RCCP, where capacity is stated in terms of hours per week, per resource. Alternatively, rate-based RCCP can indicate the capacity by production line, by stating the production rate per week per line.

Routing

The term 'routing' has a number of definitions that can be applied to an organizational situation. The term is used to describe the process of deciding the sequence of stops to be made by an **automatic guided vehicle**. Routing can also be used to describe the journey a particular product or component will take along the production or **assembly line** during the production process. It is also used to describe the journey a document will take when it has to be read by a different number of individuals. In this case a routing slip will be attached to the document and as each relevant individual reads it, it is signed and passed on to the next person on the circulation list.

Run chart

A run chart is a means by which manufacturing organizations can track their results over a period of time. The run charts are used to analyse processes according to time or order, making them particularly useful in discovering patterns that occur over time. The process involved in setting up a run chart is summarized in Table 23.

R

Table 23 Setting up a run chart

Step	Process	Description
1	Gather data	To begin constructing a run chart, a process or an operation must be available which has measurable units. Measurements should be taken over a period of time, collected chronologically or sequentially. Run charts may start and end at any point and for the most useful results at least 25 samples should be taken.

Table 23 Setting up a run chart (*continued*)

Step	Process	Description
2	Organize data	Having placed the data in the chosen order, the data is then divided into two sets of values, x and y, value x representing time and value y representing the measurements taken.
3	Chart data	The y values are now plotted, using an appropriate scale.
4	Interpret data	The chart should now illustrate trends, patterns or other observations.

R

Safety capacity

Simply, safety capacity is a manufacturer's reserve capacity that is available in the case of a rush job or an emergency. As the term implies, safety capacity actually means the ability to produce extra stock rather than taking that stock from the inventory (which implies that the stock has already been produced).

Safety lead time

The use of safety lead time is often appropriate in the **material requirements planning (MRP)** process and relates to additional time above the normal lead time. The incorporation of safety lead time can help organizations to absorb any variability or uncertainty in their actual lead times.

Safety stock

Safety stock is the amount of an organization's inventory that it would carry to protect it against running out of components or materials needed during a **lead time**. Safety stock would be held to eliminate uncertainty either in the length of the lead time or the amount to be delivered, or resulting from an increase in demand or an unexpected timing of demand during a lead time.

Sales and operations planning (S&OP)

Sales and operations planning (S&OP) is a planning process during which key managers from the sales and production departments meet frequently to develop realistic plans and promise dates for the completion of new orders. Sales and operations planning attempts to balance market demand with resource capability.

The sales and operations planning process provides the organization with a way in which it can:

- identify and resolve conflicting objectives;
- develop a manufacturing/marketing contract;
- integrate all functions of the business;
- develop plans and schedules;
- evaluate current organizational performance.

The sales and operations plan takes into account projections made by the sales and marketing departments, the resources available from manufacturing or production, engineering, and purchasing and finance, and is directed towards meeting the objectives of the organization. This planning process is undertaken to ensure that the necessary resources are available at the right time.

Ling, Richard C. and Goddard, Walter E., *Orchestrating Success: Improve Control of the Business with Sales & Operations Planning*. Chichester: John Wiley & Sons, 1995.

Salvage value

The term 'salvage value' relates to the value of an item once it is has become obsolete and cannot be sold. Retailers and manufacturers who find themselves with obsolete products often find an organization specializing in salvage to buy the items on their inventory that have become obsolete. The salvage organization then sells on the parts, products or components at their normal book value.

Scatter diagram

A scatter diagram is a graph which illustrates the relationship between two variables. A scatter diagram literally shows a wide variety of different cross-referenced results, through which an organization can attempt to find a line of best fit which attempts to trace the most common pattern in the relationship between the two variables. The graph itself will show the degree and the direction of the relationship.

Schedule

Scheduling involves the organization of production in order to meet either actual or forecasted customer demand.

See also **master production schedule (MPS)**.

Schedule chart

A schedule chart is a variant form of **Gantt chart**. Typically, a schedule chart will show the progress of particular jobs and whether they are on schedule for completion at the assigned times.

Scheduled receipts

The term 'scheduled receipts' refers to orders which are expected to arrive from customers at the beginning of a particular period of time. Manufacturers will seek to be made aware of customers' future orders as a means by which they can forecast demand, and arrange their **capacity** and requirements in terms of parts and components from their suppliers. Having advance notice of the imminent arrival, or future arrival, of customers' orders, it is possible for the manufacturer to cut down the **lead time** when the order does finally arrive, by having all of the parts and components, manpower and machine capacity available to carry out the tasks.

Schematic models

The term 'schematic model' is a generic one which is used to describe a variety of different graphical representations of a product, a process or the internal workings of a complex piece of machinery. Typically, schematic models will include blueprints, diagrams and pictures.

Scrap factor

The scrap factor is the percentage of ruined components created during the operation of a process. The implication is that there was a failure in the process, either due to machine malfunction or caused by operator error, rather than that the process was inherently incapable of producing a fully conforming output.

General calculations have been made by various researchers which seem to suggest that a 10% scrap rate increases manufacturing **cycle time** by 40%, while at the same time creating a 50% increase in **work in progress**. This is caused by the uncertainties involved leading to overproduction and the creation of **safety stocks**.

Seasonal relative/factor

Seasonal factors are used as a more accurate means by which an organization can estimate demand in a given period. Typically, the organization will calculate the average demand across the year, giving a base line to work towards in each month. Many businesses experience fluctuations in demand as a result of seasonal influences. They will therefore calculate a weighting and apply it to specific months which match recognized fluctuations in demand. Therefore an organization which produces products for the Christmas period may weight the months preceding the critical months by a larger factor than months after the critical period has passed. For example, a business may weight October to December as 3.0, whilst they may weight January to March as 0.5. Using the average demand across the year, the factor is then applied to that average demand in order to calculate the required number of finished products to be ready by a particular month.

Seasonality

Many manufacturing organizations can detect and anticipate monthly fluctuations in demand. Patterns of demand will rise and fall over a given period in proportion to various phenomena, such as weather or fashions.

See also **cyclical factors.**

Self-directed teams

Self-directed teams are also known as self-managed teams and are designed to achieve the dual goals of higher-level teamwork and employee involvement.

The concept suggests that the employees, who are closer to the process and will have the best knowledge of it, are far better suited than management to make effective changes to improve that process. They are motivated by the fact that they have a vested interest and personal involvement in the changes and as a result tend to work harder to ensure that the desired results are achieved (a motivation that would be lacking if they had the changes imposed upon them by the management).

In order to be fully functional and effective, the self-directed teams need to be cognizant with quality issues, process improvement and, most importantly, teamwork.

Self-directed teams tend to offer the following benefits to an organization:

- Fewer managers are needed.
- Teams are responsive to problems.
- Teams have a personal stake in ensuring the process works.
- Teams need less time to implement improvements.

- Teamwork offers higher quality, higher productivity, and greater worker satisfaction.
- Teamwork leads to higher satisfaction, which in turn leads to less employee turnover and absenteeism, which in turn results in lower costs related to training and cover for absent employees.

Many businesses avoid self-directed teams as a result of pressure from middle managers who feel that their positions are threatened, as the teams take on some of their traditional functions.

Goldsmith, Joan and Cloke, Kenneth, *The End of Management and the Rise of Organizational Democracy*. New York: Jossey Bass Wiley, 2002.

Kraft, Rebecca J., *Utilizing Self-managing Teams*. New York: Garland Science, 1998.

Sequence-dependent set-up time

Sequence-dependent set-up time refers to the time it takes to change over from the production of one product to another. More precisely, the sequencing actually impacts on the set-up time. In other words, by managing the sequence so that the minimum number of activities are involved in switching across to the production of another product, it is possible to cut down on the sequence-dependent set-up time. The more that is involved in switching over from one product to another, the greater the sequence-dependent set-up time.

Service blueprint

A service blueprint in its most simplistic form is the **flow process chart** of the associated service processes related to a manufacturing process itself.

Service level

The term 'service level' is often misunderstood, as it can be used in a number of production and inventory-based situations. When considering a **make to stock (MTS)** process, the service level is the percentage of units, products or orders that are immediately available from the organization's stock or inventory.

When the term is used in connection with **respond to order (RTO)**, **assemble to order (ATO)**, **make to order (MTO)**, and **engineer to order ETO** systems, service level is usually measured in terms of on-time delivery. In other words, the on-time delivery is measured as the percentage of orders that are received by the customer either by the promised date or by the requested date. An organization can improve its on-time delivery averages by improving the safety of the level of promise it gives customers and by reducing its **lead times**.

SERVQUAL

SERVQUAL was created by Parasuraman, Zeithaml and Berry in the 1980s and is used consistently in industry, particularly by those in the service sector. It measures the difference between customers' expectations and their perceptions after they have undergone a customer service experience with the organization.

SERVQUAL assists an organization in obtaining feedback from customers on the following five dimensions of customer service:

- *Tangibles* – the organization's physical facilities, its equipment, and the appearance of its personnel.
- *Reliability* – the organization's ability to perform the promised service dependably and accurately.
- *Responsiveness* – the organization's and its employees' willingness to help customers and provide them with a prompt service.
- *Assurance* – the organization and its employees' levels of competence, courtesy, credibility and security.
- *Empathy* – the customer's ability to access the organization and its information, and its employees' ability to communicate with and understand the needs of its customers.

Despite criticism from some academics, SERVQUAL is used extensively in the service industry. One of the main criticisms is that service quality may not be a function of the gap between a customer's expectation and the actual service received, but that it is a function of the value that is delivered to the customer.

SERVQUAL was further developed by Parasuraman, Zeithaml and Berry in 1991 and their development work has been replicated by several researchers. Many have recommended that the scale be adapted to suit each particular service setting.

S

Parasuraman, A., Zeithaml, Valarie A. and Berry, Leonard L., 'A Conceptual Model of Service Quality and its Implications for Future Research', *Journal of Marketing*, vol. 49 (Fall 1985), pp. 41–50.

Set-up

Set-up involves the changing or fitting of tools to general purpose machinery in order to produce particular products. Manufacturing organizations will seek to reduce the set-up times by ensuring that necessary tools are immediately available and that the tools can be fixed or clamped to the machine with the minimum effort. Clearly a reduction in set-up times involves the systematic training and retraining of individuals to cope with different tools in different circumstances.

Set-up cost (change-over cost, order cost)

As the term implies, set-up cost relates to the marginal cost of a set-up. This generally includes the costs of the labour and the materials but fixed costs should not be included as a part of the set-up cost. The cost of a set-up at a **bottleneck** resource will also include the **opportunity costs** for the entire system. When the set-up costs are calculated at a non-bottleneck resource, then only the costs of the labour and materials should be included in the calculations.

Seven zeros

The seven zeros are an integral part of the **Toyota production system (TPS)**. The seven zeros are typified as:

- *Zero defects* – which involve the maintenance of **quality at source** in order to avoid delays due to defects.
- *Zero (excess)* ***lot size*** – in order to avoid delays in waiting for inventory.
- *Zero* ***set-ups*** – to reduce set-up time delays and allow for the processing of smaller lot sizes.
- *Zero breakdowns* – which means an efficient **preventive maintenance** programme.
- *Zero (excess) handling* – to ensure that parts and components are close to hand for the production process and that the movement of those items and of finished products is minimized.
- *Zero* ***lead time*** – to make solid arrangements with suppliers to ensure that parts and components are immediately available.
- *Zero surging* – to prevent parts of the production process being overloaded with **work in progress**.

S

SFC

See **shop floor control**.

Shift work

Shift work is a pattern of work in which one employee replaces another on the same job within a 24-hour period. Shift workers normally work in groups that make up a separate shift team. In some shift systems, each group of shift workers will regularly change its hours of work and rotate morning, afternoon, and night shifts.

The continuous shift-work system provides cover for 24 hours, 7 days a week. A non-continuous or discontinuous shift system provides cover for less than the total hours available in a week, typically a total of 5 × 24-hour periods in 7 days, or 12 hours out of 24.

Shift work is widespread throughout Europe, typically in industries in which equipment, services or manufacturing processes must continue on a 24-hour cycle. Examples of this type of industry range from newspaper production and public utilities, to hospitals and the emergency services. A development in more recent years has been the spread of shift working to industries such as tele-work and banking. The main reasons for developing a system of shift work are:

- Economic. Because the pace of change has quickened together with the rate at which machinery and equipment become obsolete, shift work enables employers to make maximum use of machinery and equipment to reduce production costs and increase output.
- Social. Changes in living and working patterns have created a demand for products and services outside the more traditional working hours. Retail outlets are now commonly open every day of the week and some are open 24-hours a day.

The **Working Time Regulations** (1998, 1999 and 2002) govern the hours people can work and prescribe special health provisions for night workers.

Shingo, Shigeo

Shigeo Shingo, a Japanese industrial engineer, was born on 8 January 1909 and was to distinguish himself as being one of the world's leading authorities on the improvement of manufacturing processes. He wrote regarding **just-in-time systems**, manufacturing methods and processes, particularly the **Toyota production system** as well as other related production systems.

In 1988, after Shingo received an honorary doctorate from Utah University, the Shingo Prize Model was developed to reward world-class models of manufacturing which incorporate Shingo's ideology. Shingo was the author of a number of key texts including *A Study of the Toyota Production System*; *Revolution in Manufacturing: The SMED System*; *Zero Quality Control: Source Inspection and the Poka-yoke System*; *The Sayings of Shigeo Shingo: Key Strategies for Plant Improvement*; *Non-Stock*

Production: The Shingo System for Continuous Improvement; and *The Shingo Production Management System: Improving Process Functions*.

He died on 12 November 1990.

The Shingo Prize website and information about Shingo can be found at www.shingo-prize.org/

See also **zero defects**.

Shop floor data collection (SFDC)

Shop floor data collection (SFDC) is the systematic means by which data from work centres and other areas directly involved in the production process can provide information to assist planning. Typically, information on the progress of orders, or the availability of parts and components, can be passed to this system, which should be able to pick up potential problems and deal with them before they become serious issues.

Shop floor control (SFC)

The term 'shop floor control', or 'production activity control', relates to all the activities carried out by an organization in order to monitor the process of moving an order through a production or **assembly line**, from the release of an order to its completion. SFC systems often involve information systems to communicate the status of shop floor orders and work stations.

A shop floor control system would enable an organization to:

- assign a priority for each shop floor order;
- monitor the quantity of **work in progress (WIP)**;
- communicate shop floor order information to the organization's administration department;
- provide output data for **capacity** control and **capacity requirements planning (CRP)** purposes;
- provide data for accounting purposes;
- measure levels of **efficiency**, **utilization**, and **productivity** in both labour and machinery.

Shortage cost

Shortage costs are those which are incurred by a manufacturing organization when it is unable to supply customers because of a **stock out**. Shortages clearly arise when demand exceeds the supply at a particular time. Shortage costs can be calculated purely in terms of lost sales which could not be converted into **back orders**, but the true cost of shortages may be far more complex to calculate as they may include the permanent loss of customers who have successfully sought an alternate product from a different supplier, or those who have decided not to stock that item because of its variable availability.

Shortest processing time (SPT)

SPT is a work-despatching technique which states that the highest priority is given to work with the shortest expected processing time. SPT is a static despatching rule and tends to ensure that the greatest number of jobs are despatched.

SPT, however, does not deal with jobs in relation to their real urgency, and jobs which have long processing times become increasingly late. The processing time is calculated as the run time, plus the **set-up** time (but excluding time in queues, waiting and moving times).

Shrinkage

'Shrinkage' is a commonly used term for the situation where an organization's physical inventory is less than that which appears on the paperwork or computer database. Very often this non-tallying of figures, or shrinkage, can be attributed to theft, loss, storage in the wrong place, delivery to the wrong location, or unreported breakages.

Simulation model

A simulation model would be used in operations management in order to allow the designers to experiment with this representation of reality. Computerized simulation models are often used for experimentation purposes when complex systems are being developed. The use of a simulation model can help organizations to address problems and also to identify any unexpected opportunities without having to physically construct the complex system first. Computer simulations allow a series of changes to be made and the use of them helps to ensure that the finished product has been carefully examined and tested for all eventualities.

Single minute exchange of die (SMED)

Shigeo Shingo developed this methodology and philosophy for Toyota for the fast change-over of a machine from the production of one product to the production of another. The single minute exchange of die (SMED) helps to reduce change-over times significantly and benefits organizations by allowing them to use short production runs more economically. This means that the organizations' inventories are lower, and they can respond more rapidly to changing customer demands.

The methods used in single minute exchange of die include an off-line system that enables the production process to continue to run while the preparations for the change-over are made, and the use of quick connectors that reduce the time taken for screwing and tightening bolts. The alternative quick fastenings, such as cams and slip-on connectors, significantly reduce the change-over times.

Single-period model

Strictly speaking single-period models or single-period inventory models are used primarily for perishable goods. They may also, however, be applied to other parts or components which may have a limited period of usefulness. The primary concern is to order only as many of those items as will be immediately required or can be used or processed by the organization prior to the time when their perishability becomes an issue.

Single-piece production

Single-piece production involves attempts by manufacturers to maintain the costs of producing a product, regardless of the volume of any particular **batch**. In other words, single-piece production suggests that the costs should remain constant regardless of **lot size**, provided the **set-up** times are kept to an absolute minimum. Single-piece production is an integral element of both **just-in-time systems (JIT)** and the **Toyota production system (TPS)**.

S

Six sigma

The concept of the six sigma was designed by **W. Edwards Deming** and Walter Shewhart and is related to the maximum satisfaction of external customers, which in turn maximizes the financial returns. The six sigma system aims to reduce the defect rate to no more than 3.7 per million.

The underlying concept is that fewer defects mean lower costs, which leads to enhanced customer loyalty. Six sigma seeks to define, measure, analyse, improve and control the manufacturing process (see Figure 29) and can be considered to be an integral part of **total quality management (TQM)**.

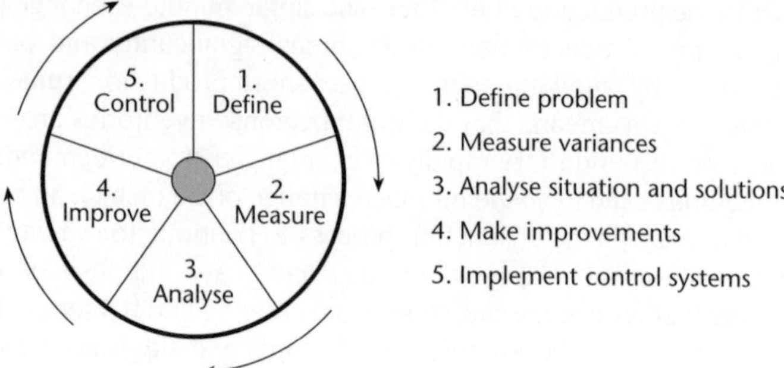

Figure 29 Six sigma system

Burton, Terence, *Is this a six sigma, lean or kaizen project?* At www.isixsigma.com/library/content/c020204a.asp

Alternatively http://mu.motorola.com

See also **process capability ratio**.

Slack

'Slack' is often used to describe the amount of time by which a specific job is ahead of schedule; it can be measured in terms of the number of hours or days early that the job will be completed.

In the context of project management, 'slack' is taken to be the difference between an activity's earliest start date and its latest possible (critical) start date. In other words, should the slack on a given activity be zero, then the activity is said to be on its **critical path**.

S

Slack time

See **critical path method**.

Specialization

'Specialization' can refer either to a manufacturing organization or to particular elements within the facility which aim to deal with a single product or service. Many organizations will seek to specialize in a number of different areas. One of the major means by which this is achieved is the establishment of a **plant within a plant (PWP)** where specialization can take place while other parts of the manufacturing facility can deal with more generic products and services, adapting and providing a manufacturing base for a wider variety of different items.

Standard cost

Standard cost is the means by which manufacturers seek to measure the exact cost of processing and delivering a single unit of a product or service. The exact way in which the standard cost is calculated differs from organization to organization, but the underlying principle is that the standard cost is the ideal cost. In reality, of course, the actual cost will differ over time as different circumstances impinge upon the associated costs involved. Typically, there may be fluctuations in the price of raw materials, parts and components, or there may be an increase or decrease in the number of defects. Note that the standard cost may not, necessarily, be the ideal cost.

Standard elemental times

Many manufacturing organizations, rather than using current data, or data derived from **motion study**, will choose to determine the amount of processing time by using historical data. Although this methodology may not provide the organization with an up-to-date assessment of the production time, the figures derived are, perhaps, more realistic, particularly given the fact that they can be averaged over a period of time, to take account of fluctuations in efficiency and productivity. This may not be the case from simply considering current data.

Standard normal distribution

Standard normal distribution refers to situations where statistics have a mean of zero and a variance of one.

Standard time

In process planning, standard time is the amount of time that it takes to process a part or a component. The normal time is taken first and then adjustments to this time are made for rest periods and breaks, resulting in the standard time.

Standardization

The term 'standardization' refers to an organization's efforts to ensure that all the workers are performing their tasks or activities in a consistent manner. An organization striving for standardization would do so to assist in ensuring consistent levels of safety, productivity, and quality. The term 'standardization' may also refer to an organization's desire to standardize the parts and components which it uses.

Starving

Starving occurs when a part of the manufacturing process runs out of input materials. Starving is particularly critical if the part of the process being starved is a **bottleneck**, as this will have a knock-on effect along the entire process. Starving a non-bottleneck may often mean that employees will need to be redeployed in order to deal with the starving problem. Ultimately, if a stage of the process is starved and not immediately dealt with, unless it is recognized as not being significant, then it will have a detrimental impact on the entire processing system.

Statistical process control (SPC)

An organization using a statistical process control (SPC) system would apply a series of statistical methods and procedures that relate to a given process or to a series of given processes. They would do this to analyse and control the process, and often work to a given set of standards or statistical techniques, by the use, primarily, of **control charts**.

Statistical quality control (SQC)

SQC aims to ensure, by statistical means, that manufactured parts will conform to specifications and requirements. While the parts, components or products are in manufacture, the manufacturer will use **statistical process control (SPC)**, but once the process is over and the products are being sent out to customers, then other statistical methods will be employed such as **breakeven analysis** and sampling.

Stock out

'Stock out' literally means that the organization has no stock of a particular item. During a stock-out period, the demand for the item cannot be fulfilled, the alternatives being to turn customers away or to convince them to allow the manufacturer to place the items on **back order**.

The stock-out percentage is the number of orders which have been either lost or placed on back order, due to stock outs, divided by the total number of orders actually received, expressed as a percentage. The percentage can be used as a measure of the level of achieved customer service (particularly in the case of a **make-to-stock** situation).

Stock turn

Stock turn is a widely used measure of inventory performance; it is expressed as the ratio of the cost of units sold to the average value of stock.

Stopwatch time study

As the term implies, this is the methodology used to determine the **standard times** of largely repetitive tasks and activities. It is still a widely used work-measurement methodology and is based on the work of **Frederick Winslow Taylor**.

Straddling

Straddling is, in effect, an attempt by one manufacturer to copy the activities or the features of another organization or its products. Straddling may involve the addition of new features, technologies or services to the business's own existing activities. Often, however, straddling takes place in a haphazard manner and is considered to be something of a knee-jerk reaction to a competitor's introduction of a product or a process which is deemed by the outside organization to be capable of giving the competitor an edge. For the most part, straddling may well cause more problems than it solves, as new processes which had not been developed within the organization are squeezed into the operations. This, in turn, may cause other conflicts which are not wanted and had not been anticipated.

Strategic capacity planning

Strategic capacity planning is a long-term approach to the deployment of resources, aimed at addressing the organization's overall competitive strategy. Long-term capacity issues may involve the acquisition of expensive machinery, or other capital-intensive equipment. In order to ensure that these investments are made with due concern as to the overall long-term aims, the purchase and implications need to be minutely addressed. In strategic capacity planning the projected requirements of the business, in terms of capacity needs, are directly related to the acquisition of machinery and other equipment which will facilitate the achievement of these goals.

Strategic partnering

Strategic partnering has become an increasing trend, both in manufacturing and in general business activities. Many organizations recognize that other businesses, which may have hitherto been considered to be general competitors, actually offer complementary products and services, or have been long-term suppliers or distributors. In effect, strategic partnering is a less formal version of ***keiretsu*** in as much as the organizations involved will maintain their close association and relationship for as long as synergies are enjoyed, and the relationship is mutually beneficial. Strategic partnering is very much based on the assumption that strength, economies and efficiency can be achieved by cooperation, rather than confrontation or competition between the partners.

Supplier quality assurance (SQA)

SQA seeks to assess whether suppliers are capable of (and are) producing supplies and/or services that conform to contract quality and technical requirements.

Supply chain

The supply chain is simply a generic description of the processes and organizations involved in converting and conveying raw materials to the end-user. The supply chain may involve organizations which extract raw materials, others who carry out a basic form of process upon these raw materials, which are then passed on to a manufacturer who will turn them into usable parts. Parts are then converted into components, which in turn are assembled or processed into a form of finished goods. These finished goods may then pass through the hands of distributors and retailers, before reaching the end-user. Supply chains may involve several suppliers, several more manufacturers and a related distribution system. In other words, the supply chain incorporates all the costs, time, transportation and packaging that may be associated with the various stages of the process of conversion. Increasingly supply chains take into account the return journey which many finished products undergo after having spent a considerable time with the end-user. Therefore a reverse supply chain is often in operation alongside the standard supply chain. This reverse system incorporates replacement parts and their flow, as well as the disposal and **recycling** of parts, components or whole products.

Supply chain management

The supply chain management approach involves the integrated managing and control of the flow of information, materials and services from the suppliers of the raw materials, through to the factories, warehouses and retailers, to the end customers. The benefits to an organization involved in supply chain management should be lower inventory costs, higher quality and higher customer-service levels. These benefits will only be gained, however, if all those involved in the **supply chain** are conforming to the standards set.

See also **bullwhip effect** *and* **value chain**.

Supply chain operations reference model (SCOR)

The **supply chain** operations reference model (SCOR) was designed by the Supply Chain Council (www.supplychain.org). The SCOR aims to standardize the framework of the entire supply chain operation. Its aim is to combine design, best practices and **benchmarking**. Typically, the SCOR model seeks to link the planning process from the initial design of a product or service, through its processing and delivery, and incorporating its possible return to the manufacturer, as a holistic planning process. The key elements of SCOR are described in Table 24.

Table 24 Key elements of SCOR

SCOR describes	SCOR covers
Standard accounts of management processes.	All customer interactions, from order submission through to invoice payment.
A framework of relationships between the standard processes.	All market interactions, from aggregate demand to the fulfilment of each individual order.
Standard metrics to measure process performance.	All physical material transactions through the supply chain, including field service **logistics**.
Management practices that portray 'best in their class' performance. Software tools that enable best practices.	

S

The four generic processes or sub-processes of SCOR are described in Table 25.

Table 25 SCOR processes

SCOR process	Description
Planning	Assessing supply resources, aggregating and prioritizing demand requirements, conducting inventory planning, assessing distribution requirements, determining production, material and capacities for all products, through all channels. SCOR allows management to make decisions, configure supply chains, plan for long-term resource and **capacity**, as well as product life cycles and product line management.
Sourcing	SCOR allows for the sourcing, obtaining, receipt and inspection of all materials and components. It provides the organization with copies of certificates and contracts and initiates the payment system to suppliers.
Making	This covers the request for materials, the manufacture and testing of products, packaging considerations, as well as calculations as to the best release time for products. The SCOR infrastructure allows for engineering changes, monitoring of production quality, **assembly line** scheduling and sequencing, and short-term capacity management.
Delivering	SCOR allows for forecasting and promotion planning, including sales campaigns and point of sale data. It also allows customers to place orders and the organization to monitor customer satisfaction levels by executing an **efficient/effective consumer response (ECR)**. SCOR also provides the organization with order management, warehouse management, transportation management facilities, as well as more specific delivery considerations, such as delivery inventories and the management of delivery quantity.

Stewart, G., 'Supply Chain Operations Reference Model (SCOR): The First Cross-industry Framework for Integrated Supply Chain Management', *Logistics Information Management*, vol. 10, no. 2 (1997), pp. 62–7.

S

Synchronization

Synchronization, or synchronous manufacturing, aims to produce a harmonious production, where all employees and machines are fully utilized. Achieving synchronous manufacturing implies that all parts of the production process are fully supplied and employed at all times and that there are no breaks in the production which have an impact on processes further up the **production line**. In achieving synchronous manufacturing, or synchronization, the manufacturing process is deemed to be working at the most efficient **capacity** level.

Taguchi methods

Genichi Taguchi carried out a series of experiments in Japan, developed to improve the implementation of **total quality control (TQC)**. Taguchi's conclusions and recommendations are used in manufacturing industries within Japan and the US to improve processes and products. It is claimed that Japan has experienced an 80 per cent increase in quality and in the US the Taguchi method is also known as **robust design**.

The Taguchi method makes quality decisions about cost effectiveness by the use of key words, which are explained in more detail in Table 26.

Table 26 Taguchi's key words

Taguchi method	Description
Loss function	The organization has to identify and recognize the importance of associating quality with the financial loss imparted by poor quality.
Orthogonal arrays	The organization has to design efficient experiments and analyse the conclusions of the experimental data with the use of, for example, linear graphs.
Robustness	The organization has to specify the cost-effective combination of factors which affect variations in the levels of quality and which are feasible and practical to control. This will help to minimize the influence of previously uncontrollable factors.

According to the followers of the Taguchi method, research is the key, as is testing products on a trial-and-error basis. This will give the organization a completely full picture of the product, and provided the business focuses on all aspects of this methodology, it stands a high chance of gaining a **competitive advantage**.

Peace, Glen Stuart, *Taguchi-Methods: A Hands-on Approach*. Reading, MA: Addison-Wesley, 1993.

Takt time

Takt time is the daily rate of demand divided by the number of available working hours over a given period (usually a day). Takt time can be used by an organization to estimate the **cycle time** (how long it will take to meet the level of demand). 'Takt' comes from the German for a conductor's baton, with the inference that takt time regulates the rate at which products are finished.

Task time

Task time can either be simply calculated, or may involve long-term observation and investigation into the processes involved in carrying out a particular activity. There is no reasonable definition or set of parameters which determine what a task may be, or how complex the steps involved within the task may become. None the less, a manufacturer would seek to identify the ideal or average task time, which may relate to a series of activities or an individual activity related to the manufacturing process. It is by aggregating these task-time figures that an accurate estimation can be made as to the full process time involved in producing a part, component or product.

Taylor, Frederick Winslow

During his research, Taylor (1856–1915) began with the assumption that employees only work for money. He developed a series of work study techniques which he considered would enable employees to reduce the amount of time it would take to carry out different tasks, leaving the planning and organization of tasks for the managers and supervisors. He believed that encouragement to work harder and the promise of additional benefits, such as money, as a reward for this would make employees sufficiently motivated to work harder.

Taylor, however, was proved wrong. He discovered that employees would only work harder when they were being supervised, but would return to their normal pace of work once the supervision was removed.

Since Taylor's writing on 'scientific management', much emphasis has been placed on **job design**. Henry Ford developed Taylor's principles into what has become known as **Fordism**.

Bratton, John and Gold, Jeffrey, *Human Resource Management: Theory and Practice*. Basingstoke: Palgrave Macmillan, 2003.

Kanigel, Robert, *The One Best Way: Frederick Winslow Taylor and the Enigma of Efficiency*. Boston, MA: Little, Brown, 1997.

Taylor, Frederick Winslow, *Principles of Scientific Management*. New York: W. W. Norton, 1967.

Theory of constraints (TOC)

The theory of constraints (TOC) states that an organization's **capacity** is limited by the **bottlenecks** in a production process and that these bottlenecks need to be identified and eliminated in order to improve capacity. Alternatively, the organization can seek to either circumvent the bottlenecks or utilize them to its own advantage.

The theory of constraints was designed by Dr Eliyhum Goldratt and is, in effect, an application of **Pareto's Law** in process management and improvement. As far as Goldratt was concerned, in order to improve performance an organization needs to identify the constraints placed upon it. In the short term it needs to exploit these constraints, but in the longer term it needs to overcome them. The theory of constraints is typified by having the following elements:

- An identification of the constraints in the system, as no improvement will be possible until these have been discovered.
- A decision as to ways in which the constraints can be exploited, making them as effective as possible.
- The deployment of resources to support the constraints, even if this means diverting resources from non-constraint areas.
- An evaluation of what the system constraint is, and the acquisition of whatever is required in order to ensure that the constraint is no longer an issue.
- Once the constraint has been eliminated, there should be a repetition of the process, as the next weakest link in the chain will have become a constraint. In other words this is a process of continuous improvement.

Dettmer, H. W., *Goldratt's Theory of Constraints*. New York: McGraw-Hill Education, 1996.

Scheinkopf, Lisa, *Thinking for a Change: Putting the TOC Thinking Processes into Use*. Boca Raton, FL: St Lucie Press, 1999.

Therblig

Frank and Lillian Gilbreth invented and refined the Therblig ('gilbreth' backwards) system (1908–24) as a means by which the motions involved in performing a task could be minutely analysed and investigated.

The system was designed not only to identify the individual motions involved in a task, but also to note the moments of delay in the process.

The Gilbreths' major concern was with identifying unnecessary or inefficient motions and then utilizing or eliminating wasted time.

In the period 1915–20, the Gilbreths began to identify around 15 or 16 motion cycles, but at this stage the system was not comprehensive. After Frank Gilbreth died, the full Therblig system appeared in two articles in *Management and Administration* (August 1924, pp. 151–4; September 1924, pp. 295–7). The categorized methods, including the unnecessary and fatigue-inducing motions, now amount to some 18 categories. The Therbligs, which can be seen in Table 27, are plotted onto a Simulations Motion Chart with the time that it took to carry out each motion.

Table 27 The Gilbreths' Therbligs

Therblig	Colour	Symbol/Icon	Therblig	Colour	Symbol/Icon
Search	Black		Use	Purple	
Find	Gray		Disassemble	Violet	
Select	Light gray		Inspect	Burnt orange	
Grasp	Lake red		Pre-position	Sky blue	
Hold	Gold ochre		Release load	Carmine red	
Transport loaded	Green		Unavoidable Delay	Yellow ochre	
Transport empty	Olive green		Avoidable delay	Lemon yellow	
Position	Blue		Plan	Brown	
Assemble	Violet, heavy		Rest for overcoming fatigue	Orange	

Where relevant, the motions of both hands and feet were plotted and the chart was then examined in order to identify Therbligs which were taking too long, or could indeed be eliminated by reorganizing the task itself.

At the time, the Therblig system was revolutionary and aspects of the original system designed by the Gilbreths have remained within the overall concept and application despite the passing of the years and the development of working practices. If nothing else, the system, based on time and motion studies, continues to be developed as a concept, which was exactly what the Gilbreths had always intended.

Mogensen, Alan and Barnes, Ralph, *Common Sense Applied to Motion and Time Study: Motion and Time Study*. New York: John Wiley, 1980.

Third-party logistics (3PL)

'Third-party logistics', or 3PL, is a term used to describe the use of a transport-dedicated organization, effectively as a partner or subcontractor, for the movement of inputs and outputs. Third-party logistics may also refer to warehousing, handling and processing which is carried out by an outsourced organization.

Many organizations have discovered that by streamlining their transportation, supply and delivery systems by effectively **outsourcing**, they are able to concentrate on their **core competencies** of production, rather than transport and distribution. Typically, the third-party logistics will be permanently attached to the manufacturing organization and effectively run by the third party, who will liaise with the manufacturer in order to make vehicles and drivers available as and when required. The flexibility of the system allows the third party to redeploy assets in situations where transportation is at a low level and yet to bring in additional transport assets during periods of high activity.

Third-party order processing

Third-party order processing is a form of external procurement which is achieved by presenting a purchase order to a vendor. The vendor is instructed to obtain the material or services on behalf of the originating business, from a third party.

Three Mu

See **3MU** (see p. 264).

Throughput time/rate

The throughput time is the average time a single unit takes to pass through the entire production process. Throughput time can be differentiated from **lead time** in as much as the latter includes the throughput time in addition to the time it takes to process the order, and the delivery time. The throughput rate is the average output rate which a production process can be expected to achieve over a given period.

Time bucket

Simply, a time bucket is a unit of time. Time buckets are used to measure the duration of a process or activity associated with **material requirements planning (MRP)**. Typically, the measurement of the time needed for receiving or releasing an order, or the **lead time**, would all be calculated in terms of time buckets.

Time fence

Time fences are lines which are drawn vertically through a chart according to a chosen period pattern. Time fences are boundaries between different periods in the planning horizon, aimed to define short-term regions within which there are planning restrictions designed to minimize costly disruption to production and supplier schedules.

Time fences provide guidelines to establish where various restrictions or changes in operating procedures will need to take place. There are three main types of time fences:

Planning time fence – bordered by the current date and a chosen future date, this is a period within which the planning process does not alter the current material plan or master schedule. Within the planning fence, the planning process does not reschedule any order due dates or create new planned orders for the item concerned. It does reschedule or cancel orders in cases of excess supply.

Demand time fence – bordered by the current date and a chosen future date, this is a period within which the planning process does not consider forecast demand when calculating actual demand, it only deals with actual demand. Outside the demand time fence, the overall system does forecast demand and it is possible to instruct the system to take the demand time fence controls into account.

Release time fence – bordered by the current date and a chosen future date, this is a period within which the planning process will release planned orders as discrete jobs or as purchase requisitions. It is possible to specify the release time fence within the overall plan.

http://sandbox.aiss.uiuc.edu/oracle/nca/mrp/index.htm

Time-based compensation systems

See **output-based (incentive) systems**.

Time-based strategy/competition

As the term may imply, 'time-based competition or strategy' aims to position manufacturers to be able to effectively shorten the **lead times** for their customers. There are three reasons to seek this **competitive advantage**:

- First, it may be valuable for the manufacturer to identify and categorize customers who are either time sensitive or price sensitive.
- It is always desirable to drive down the costs associated with carrying a finished goods inventory.
- Thirdly, the approach aims to minimize activities which do not add value, and as such, time-based competition and strategy have many features similar to those of **just-in-time systems (JIT)** and **lean manufacturing**.

Stalk, George Jr and Hout, Thomas M., *Competing against Time: How Time-based Strategies Deliver Superior Performance*. New York: Free Press, 1990.

Stalk, George Jr and Hout, Thomas M., *Gaining Time: Executing Time-based Strategy*. New York: Free Press, 1993.

Time-phased order point (TPOP)

T

Effectively, a time-phased order point is an extension of the **reorder point** system. TPOP uses a demand forecast in order to estimate and plan when the inventory will reach the **safety stock** level. The TPOP will alert the organization to the need to ensure that an order arrives to replenish the stock at that time. Normally the TPOP will be set in conjunction with the **lead time** required to complete the processing of the products or components in the manufacturing process.

Time-series forecasting

Time-series forecasting involves the identification of patterns in historical data which can then be used to formulate forecasts. Time-series forecasting can be approached in one of the two following ways:

- Univariate time-series forecasting uses a single time series from the historical data as the basis for future forecasting.
- Multivariate time-series forecasting looks at the historical data and any other related variables which are applicable, both to that historical data and to the period in the future for which the forecast is designed.

See also **weighted averages** *and* **exponential smoothing**.

Tolerances

Tolerance is another means by which **quality of conformance** can be measured. In consultation with a customer, the manufacturer will determine an acceptable range of values for measurements in respect of a particular part, component or product. The tolerance range incorporates slight variances beyond the ideal, which naturally occur as part of the production process. The tolerance would, therefore, measure both the maximum and minimum degrees of variation of the norm.

Tolling

'Tolling' is a term used to describe a contract manufacturer, or the process of contract manufacturing. Contract manufacturing involves the subcontracting of another organization to carry out the manufacturing of parts, components or products on behalf of the major manufacturer. Tolling can be differentiated from either **outsourcing** or normal customer/supplier relationships in as much as the contract manufacturers never own the materials they are working on.

Tooling

See **dies**.

Tornado diagram

A tornado diagram is an effective method of displaying different parameters of output measure. The parameters are sorted from top to bottom, from the greatest range in output to the smallest, so that the diagram actually looks like a tornado, or an inverted cone shape. Each parameter is usually estimated as having a most likely value, a lowest value and a highest value. The results are displayed as horizontal bar graphs. The tornado diagram does have one serious defect in as much as it does not show the interaction between the different parameters.

Total preventive/productive maintenance (TPM)

Total preventive or productive maintenance (TPM) combines the ***kaizen*** concept of continuous improvement along with standard **preventive maintenance** issues. Rather than simply seeking to repair faulty equipment, TPM seeks to maintain it – in other words, to ensure that the equipment is not gradually becoming less efficient and more prone to defects. TPM aims to maximize the performance of the equipment within the production system over its entire life cycle with the organization. In doing this TPM seeks to pre-empt possible losses in production by generating a schedule of regular maintenance for each piece of equipment. Attached to the system will also be a full repair and maintenance history.

See also **overall equipment effectiveness (OEE)** *and* **preventive maintenance**.

Total quality control (TQC)

Total quality control, as the term implies, is a process by which a manufacturer embeds and instils in the entire organization a comprehensive quality control programme. TQC is applied to all areas and all levels of the organization, making quality a responsibility of every employee in every task, activity or function.

See also **total quality management (TQM)**.

Total quality management (TQM)

The concept of total quality management (TQM) has been stimulated by the need for conformance by organizations with regard to quality levels. This need has been brought about in essence by an increased demand by customers and suppliers for higher-quality products, parts and components. The fundamental principle behind total quality management is that the management of quality is addressed at all levels of an organization, from the top to the bottom. Improvements are made on a continuous basis by applying the theories and approaches of management theorists in an attempt to improve quality and decrease organizational costs. The emphasis, primarily on quality, is also very much on people and their involvement, particularly with regard to suppliers and customers. The fundamental principles of TQM are summarized in Table 28.

Bank, J., *The Essence of Total Quality Management*. Englewood Cliffs, NJ: Prentice Hall, 1999.

Oakland, J. S., *Total Quality Management*. Oxford: Butterworth Heinemann, 1993.

Table 28 Principles of total quality management

TQM principle	Description
Committed and effective leaders	A commitment to and a belief in the principles of TQM by those key decision makers at the top of the organizational structure is essential. They have to portray this commitment to the lower levels of management in an effective style of leadership by providing resources to make changes happen.
Planning	It is imperative that all changes are planned effectively, particularly as the TQM approach may differ fundamentally from the approach currently adopted by an organization. All planned changes must be integrated throughout the whole organization, with cooperation throughout all levels and functions. With quality, or improved quality, as the key dimension, a longer-term strategy will be adopted throughout the organization's functions, from new product design through to getting the product to the end-user.
Monitoring	A continuous monitoring system will be put into place so that the process of **continuous improvement** can be supported and developed. Problem identification and the implementation of solutions will be sought.
Training	Without education and training, employees and management will lack expertise and awareness of quality issues. It will be difficult to implement changes in organizational behaviour unless there is a comprehensive and effective educational scheme which not only seeks to provide the initial information and understanding of techniques, but constantly updates those techniques in order to reinforce understanding. Without this investment short-term TQM benefits will be difficult to achieve, as will the long-term impact of TQM through conventional measurements, such as increased efficiency and general growth.
Teamwork	The development of empowered cooperative teams is an essential prerequisite of TQM. Under the system, teams are encouraged to take the initiative and often given responsibilities which would have formerly been management roles. Without the involvement and **empowerment** TQM is almost impossible to implement as it requires both the participation and the commitment of individuals throughout the whole organization.

⇒

Table 28 Principles of total quality management (*continued*)

TQM principle	Description
Evaluation and feedback	It is imperative that individuals within the organization see the fruits of their labour. TQM requires that there should be an integral system which not only provides positive feedback but also rewards achievement. The evaluation and feedback of TQM will invariably involve the measurement of achievement of both internal and external targets, notably through **benchmarking**.
Long-term change	As TQM becomes embedded and very much a fact of life in the ways in which employees think and processes are carried out, there is a permanent change to the ways in which attitudes, working practices and overall behaviour are approached.

Toyota production system (TPS)

The Toyota production system is a much lauded **continuous improvement** system. It has successively shown increases in quality and productivity and is considered to be one of the fundamental **benchmarks** as far as **lean manufacturing** is concerned. TPS has been a much copied system and has led to a proliferation in different forms of production methodologies based on the fundamental principle of TPS. True TPS incorporates waste reduction, **empowerment** and respect for employees, coupled with customer satisfaction.

T

Tracking signal (TS)

One of the simplest ways in which to create a tracking signal is to use the following equation:

$$R_t = R_{t-1} + E_t$$

where R_t = the running sum of errors; and E_t = the forecast error over period $_t$.

The tracking signal is used to identify a forecast error which is appearing on a consistent basis. Having received the tracking signal the organization will need to change the parameters of the forecasting model in order to achieve more accurate results. If there is a significant bias in the forecast, then the **mean absolute deviation** is used.

Trade union

Trade unions protect the interests of their members in areas relating to wages and salaries, working conditions, job security and welfare benefits. They negotiate with the management of organizations on behalf of members of the trade union who work for the business. The national committee of the trade union is an elected group of permanent employees who implement the policies of the members. Regional and district committees are formed around the country, with branches in the larger towns, and each union member is attached to one of these. Trade union representatives negotiate with the management of an organization during the documenting and implementation of collective agreements and collective bargaining, and take part in dispute resolution. They would also be entitled to attend disciplinary and grievance interviews, as well as being involved in discussions regarding dismissal.

See also **industrial union**.

The Trade Union Reform and Employment Rights Act contained measures to continue the Government's programme of reforming industrial relations and employment law. The Act gives employees the following rights:

- to obtain a written statement of their main conditions of employment, including pay, hours and holidays;
- a minimum of 14 weeks maternity leave, and protection against dismissal on maternity-related grounds;
- protection against dismissal or other adverse treatment on grounds related to health and safety;
- protection against being unfairly dismissed for exercising any statutory employment protection right.

With regard to trade union members, the Act covers the following aspects:

- freedom to decide which union they join;
- a postal ballot before a strike;
- protection against fraud and abuse in trade union elections and finances;
- not to have union subscriptions deducted from their pay without their consent.

Controversially, the Act also addressed unions and competitiveness:

- requiring unions to give employers at least seven days' notice of industrial action;

- protecting businesses against the damage that strikes can cause;
- providing customers who are deprived of goods or services as a result of unlawful industrial action the right to take legal proceedings;
- abolishing the Wages Councils;
- introducing new Careers Services.

www.legislation.hmso.gov.uk/acts/acts1993/Ukpga_19930019_en_1.htm

Traffic management

In itself, traffic management is a complex series of operations as it involves the organization and control of incoming and outgoing items related to the manufacturing process. In other words, traffic management is the management of the physical inputs and outputs required by, or produced by, manufacturing organizations.

Transformation process

The transformation process is the essential function of the manufacturing process. Literally, the manufacturing process transforms a series of inputs (parts, components, machine time, employees and other factors) into a series of outputs (finished or part-finished goods and services).

Trend

The term 'trend' is associated with the technique of forecasting and a trend should show the average rate of change in demand. Typically, the trend will be a visual representation of the fluctuations in demand, which will appear as a slope on a graph which is either ascending or descending.

Two-bin system

Simply, a two-bin inventory system is a visual **reorder point** system which should alert the organization, without the need to physically count the stock. In a two-bin system a main bin is used for the normal inventory, and parts and components are taken from that normal bin until such a time as it is empty. The reserve bin is opened only when the main bin has been exhausted and this reserve bin now becomes the main bin. The task of the organization is now to replenish the reserve bin in the knowledge that there is sufficient stock in place in order to cover the business over the period it will take to secure the new stock.

Some organizations resort to locking the reserve bin and use the request for the key as a signal that the normal bin is empty and that an order needs to be placed.

Type I and Type II errors

These two terms are most closely associated with conclusions which may be drawn from inspections or quality audits, either during or after a manufacturing process. A Type I error is the incorrect assumption that a process is producing an unacceptable level of defects and is therefore not performing correctly. A Type II error, on the other hand, may lead the manufacturer to conclude that the process is in control and that there are no serious defects when, in fact, there is cause for concern.

Under-utilization

The generally accepted explanation of this term refers to situations where an organization fails to make full use of the resources it has available in the form of assets such as labour.

An alternative definition of the term 'under-utilization' refers to a situation that exists when a department of an organization, or the organization as a whole, employs a smaller proportion of protected ethnic or other minority groups than are found on a regular basis within the organization's labour market as a whole.

Uniform commercial code

The uniform commercial code, or UCC, is a standard set of regulations which apply to commercial transactions in the US. The uniform commercial code covers bills of lading, letters of credit, and bank deposits, amongst other key transaction documentation.

Uniform plant loading

Uniform plant loading aims to stabilize and level the production systems, by creating a uniform load on all work centres engaged in constant daily production. One of the means by which this is achieved is to establish freeze windows to prevent changes in the production plan. Manufacturers may also deploy mixed-model assemblies (producing roughly the same mix of products each day and using a standardized sequence for several products on the same line). This allows the manufacturers to meet demand fluctuations through their inventory rather than through stepping up their production levels.

Using the fundamentals of **just-in-time (JIT)**, the following procedures are often used to assist the manufacturer in achieving uniform plant loading:

- The reduction or the elimination of set-up times (aiming for single digit set-up times (under 10 minutes) by better planning or process and/or product redesign.

- Reduction of **lot sizes** as the reduction of set-up times allows economical production of smaller lots. This requires the closer cooperation of suppliers as more frequent deliveries will be needed.
- Reduction in **lead times**, moving work stations closer together, applying group technology as well as cellular manufacturing. This also involves a reduction in queue length, improvements in coordination and cooperation between processes and again the cooperation of suppliers in terms of reduced delivery lead times.
- The introduction of **preventive maintenance**, which will reduce the idle time to a minimum.
- The introduction of flexible working practices such as the training of employees to operate several machines, and to perform maintenance tasks and quality inspections.
- The introduction of supplier quality assurance methodologies and the implementation of a **zero defects** quality programme where errors which lead to defective items are eliminated. The concept of quality at source (***jidoka***) is implemented to give employees the responsibility for the quality of the work they carry out as well as the authority to stop work when problems are encountered.
- The introduction of small-lot systems and the ***kanban* system**, which is capable of conveying parts between work stations in small quantities.

Unitization

Unitization involves the bundling of products, parts or components into cases or pallets in order to facilitate easier transportation and containerization.

Universal Product Code (UPC)

A UPC is a standardized number used in the USA which is designed to allow the unique identification of a material. The UPC is always related to a specific unit, measure or type of packaging. The Universal Product Code corresponds to the International (formerly European) Article Number (EAN), which is used in other countries.

Upper control limit (UCL)

An UCL is a horizontal line on a **control chart** which represents the upper limits of process capability. The UCL is usually depicted as a dotted line.

Utilization

Utilization involves the creation of ratios to compare output with design capacity. In other words, utilization looks at the resource productivity and attempts to apply a measurement. Since productivity is normally seen as being the difference between inputs and outputs, utilization seeks to improve this ratio as far as is practicable. In essence, the higher the utilization, the higher the **value added**.

Value added

Value added, or added value, is an increase in the market value of a product, part or component which excludes the cost of materials and services used. In other words, this is a cost-plus-profit concept, defining 'value added' as either the difference between the cost of producing a product and the price obtained for it (the selling price), or an additional benefit offered to a purchaser in order to convince them to buy. Added value is the key concept in both the internal and the external accounting systems of an organization and is a useful means of identifying the relative efficiency of a business. It should be noted that the value-added concept looks at internal input costs in such a way that they are not confused with the external output costs, which may be beyond the control of the organization.

The value of the goods or services supplied may depend on a number of different variables. Obviously, if the organization is processing raw materials into finished products and is responsible for all stages of the production process, then it has a relatively high degree of control over the level of added value involved. Organizations which buy in components or part-finished products do not have this depth and length of control. They purchase products which have had value added to them already. The supplier will have gone through a similar set of calculations prior to selling the components or part-finished products on to the organization, which in turn will continue their processing. In the final analysis, the level of value added to the goods or services supplied is directly related to the price the customer is willing to pay. An organization may decide to add value which would raise the price beyond that which the average customer is willing to accept. In such a case, the supplier would have either to accept that it cannot receive the expected price, or to drastically reduce its costs, which have contributed to the end-user price.

The most common definition of 'value added' is profit. Before the profit is realized, however, it is necessary to be able to cover the directly applied or overhead costs of the organization. If the organization is able to cover the various costs, then it has gone a considerable distance towards being able to **break even**. It is only when added value exceeds the **breakeven point** that the organization moves into real profit. It is, perhaps, this part of the value-added concept that is most important. Profit means a number of things to an organization, for example, additional investment potential, expansion, reorganization or acquisition. The nature of value added has a tendency to push up the end-user price from the moment the raw materials are extracted. In stages, some more dramatic than others, added value will be heaped upon the product. Each layer of the **supply chain** will demand its rightful profit in handling the product or service. Consequently, if an organization is not involved in the total extraction, processing and sale of a product or service, then it may not be able to curb unnecessary levels of added value elsewhere in the trading cycle.

Value analysis/value engineering

Value analysis and value engineering require the services of a cross-functional team, in order to identify specific aspects related to a product or a service. The team will identify the primary functions of the product or service and assign a value or worth to that function. The next process is to generate alternatives which, whilst they are true alternatives and will accomplish the same ends, are cheaper to achieve. In other words, the analysis or engineering revolves around cost reduction while maintaining the functionality, quality and other attributes of the product or the service. This process aims to simplify both the product and the processes, leading to lower costs for the organization whilst, perhaps, improving the performance of the product, but cognizant of the fact that the product needs to be as good as it was before the analysis took place. It may be necessary to redesign parts of the product in order to achieve these cost-saving goals.

Value chain

The term 'value chain' was coined by Michael Porter in 1985 and is used to describe the activities of an organization and how they are linked to the maintenance of a competitive position within the market. The value chain can be used to describe activities both within and external to the organization, relating them to the organization's competitive strength. The analysis itself values each activity which adds to the organization's products or services. In other words, it considers the organization's employees, available funds, as well as machinery and equipment. The supposition is that the ways in which these resources are deployed determine whether the organization is able to produce products and services at a price which customers are prepared to pay. By successfully organizing the resources, the business may be able to achieve a degree of **competitive advantage**.

As can be seen in Figure 30, Michael Porter identified five main areas or primary areas related to the delivery of a product or a service: inbound logistics, operations, outbound logistics, marketing and sales, and service.

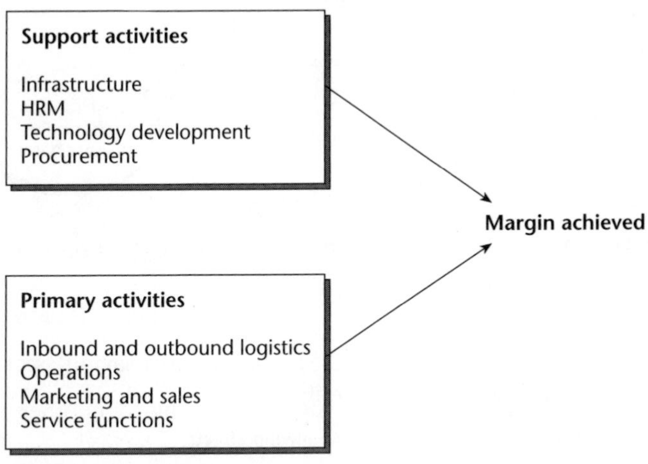

Figure 30 Organization of resources

These activities are supported by procurement, technology development, human resource management and the overall infrastructure of the organization. On this diagram, the activities contribute towards the margin, which refers to the profit margin between the costs of the primary and support activities and the price which the customer is willing to pay.

In the majority of industrial sectors, however, the organization's value chain is simply part of a larger structure, which incorporates the supplier's value chain, the channel's value chain and the customers' value chains. The position of the organization can be seen in Figure 31.

This more holistic impression of the overall system suggests that the progress of raw materials, components and products across the entire value chain requires consideration of the other elements' requirements in terms of a profit margin. In other words, depending upon the relative strength of these elements within the value chain, margins can be squeezed or enlarged. Internally, at least, an organization can seek to improve its margins by adopting tactics such as a **just-in-time system**

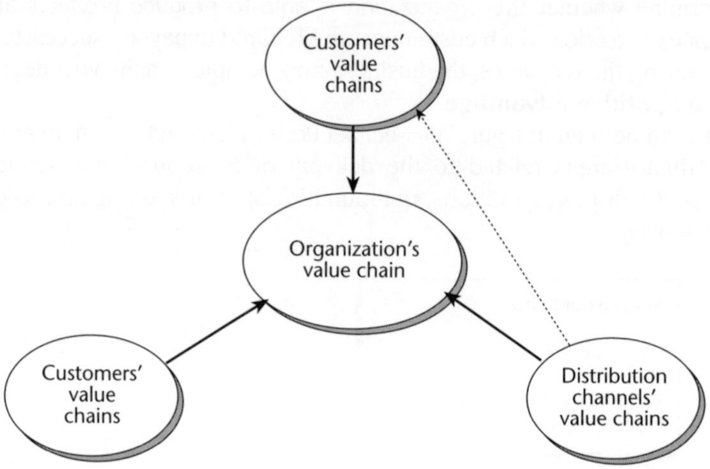

Figure 31 Position of the organization in the overall system of value chains

(JIT), whilst not passing on any of the associated cost saving, but retaining that as an additional profit margin.

See also **supply chain management** *and* **bullwhip effect.**

Porter, Michael E., *Competitive Advantage*. New York: Free Press, 1985.

Variable costs

Variable costs, in contrast to **fixed costs**, can be considered as those costs which are incurred in direct relation to the amount being produced, for example, labour and raw material costs. In order to make one unit of production, an organization would incur an accumulation of labour, raw materials and variable costs. In other words, certain production costs come into operation only when they are required. Variable costs are costs which are increased or decreased in line with production. In this way, as output increases so will the variable costs incurred, as more of these factors need to be incorporated to increase output. Variable costs increase proportionately with output and will always do so.

Variable manufacturing costs

Variable manufacturing costs are changes in the operational costs which are normally associated with the changes in the volume of production. They can be differentiated from fixed costs as the latter remain static whatever the level of output.

See also **variable costs.**

Vendor managed inventory (VMI)

VMI is an inventory management system in which it is the supplier who makes the decision as to whether the customer needs to restock. The supplier either physically visits the customer or requests stock-level information in order to make an assessment as to the usage rate of stock and the probable point at which the customer will reach zero stock. Usually, as there is an inference that the supplier will be keen to ensure that stock is placed with the customer whatever the circumstances, the customer only pays for that stock when the stock has been used or sold. In other words, when the supplier visits the customer or receives information about the stock levels, this triggers an invoicing system which addresses the difference between the current stock levels and the known stock levels at the previous vendor enquiry.

Vertical integration

Vertical integration is a business acquisition process which aims to secure adjacent levels of the **supply chain**. Typically, a manufacturer will seek to acquire either a supplier or a distributor or retailer in order to gain firmer control over the supply network.

Vertical loading

Vertical loading is the stacking up of jobs at a particular work centre. They are loaded one at a time according to the organization's rules regarding priority.

Virtual factory/organization

In literal terms, a virtual organization does not exist. However, the term is used to describe a flexible organization which does not have a physical presence or central organizational structure and relies on a network of remote employees engaged in a variety of telecommuting and telework activities. It may also refer to an organization which employs outworkers, paid on a piece-rate system. The virtual organization acts as a provider of work and a fulfilment service or intermediary between the outworkers and the customer.

Waiting time in line

'Waiting time in line' describes the usually non-productive time which customers have to wait before being served or having their orders processed. There are essentially two costs, the cost of service and the cost of waiting, that must be balanced in a waiting-in-line system, as well as the cost of a scheduling system. Theoretically, a scheduling system is a management strategy designed to avoid waiting lines.

In cases where the cost of service and the cost of waiting are known and measurable, the organization can attempt to determine the optimal, or close to optimal, waiting-system configuration and rate of service. However, the cost of service has a positive relationship with the rate of service; conversely, the cost of waiting has a negative relationship with the rate of service. In other words, the faster the service rate, the higher the cost of service and the faster the service rate, the lower the cost of waiting. The opposite applies with a slower service rate, meaning a lower cost of service but a higher cost of waiting. Options could be summarized as in Table 29, taking into account the differing options available according to circumstances.

There are operational characteristics of waiting lines, which are:

- the possibility that no customers (or units) are in the system;
- the average number of customers in the lines;
- the average number of customers in the system;
- the average time a customer spends in the line;
- the average time a customer spends in the system;
- the probability that an arriving customer has to wait for service;
- the probability of *n* customers in the system.

See also **queuing theory**.

Dshalalow, Jewgeni H. (ed.), *Advances in Queuing: Models, Methods and Problems*. Boca Raton, FL: CRC Press, 1995.

Yao, D. D. and Chen, H., *Fundamentals of Queuing Networks: Performance, Asymptotics, and Optimization* (Applications of Mathematics). New York: Springer-Verlag, 2001.

Table 29 Means of balancing costs of waiting

	Single-server model	**Multiple-server model**	**Finite-source model**
Customer population	Infinite patient	Infinite patient	Finite patient
Waiting lines	Single line, unlimited length	Single line, unlimited length	Single line, limited length
Channels Phases	Single channel Single phase	Multi-channel Single phase	Single channel Single phase
Priority discipline	FCFS	FCFS	FCFS
Arrival distribution	Poisson distribution mean arrival rate = λ	Poisson distribution mean arrival rate = λ	Exponential interarrival times, mean = $\frac{1}{\lambda}$
Service-time distribution	Exponential mean service rate = μ	Exponential mean service rate = μ	Exponential mean service rate = $\frac{1}{\mu}$

Waiting time in the system

See **waiting time in line.**

Warehouse management system (WMS)

A WMS is a software system which is used in a storage facility for a number of different purposes, including:

- keeping track of the numbers and location of products held;
- the generation of picking lists for warehouse operatives;
- the creation of complex lists for major outbound deliveries;
- the organization and placement of products which have been delivered to the warehouse.

Weighted average

Weighted averages are used in **time-series forecasting**. From a practical viewpoint an organization will seek to place a greater emphasis on the latest data, rather than aged data. In order to achieve this, the organization weights the later, or more recent, values compared with the older values, thus making the overall time-series analysis far more representative of current **trends**.

WIP

See **work in progress.**

Work breakdown structure (WBS)

WBS is used in project management and is displayed as a tree-structured or hierarchical graphic representation of how the work has to be done. Work related to the project is split into its various components, which in turn can be broken down to specific actions or activities. The management of this work and the related activities can, therefore, be assigned by the management, who can compare current progress of the project with the overall structure. In this way any deficiencies in translating the theoretical construct into actual actions can be picked up at the earliest possible point.

Work centre

A work centre is a specific location in the course of a manufacturing process. At the work centre a series of tasks are performed upon each product or batch of products before they are moved along to the next work centre on the **production line**.

Work in progress (inventory) (WIP)

WIP refers to all of an organization's inventory which is currently being processed or has been assigned to a process within the organization. This would include items in the inventory which have been allocated for particular jobs, ready to begin the manufacturing process, or items which are currently a part of a product being processed, but that is not yet complete. The work in process inventory is a total count of all of the items which fall into this category.

Work measurement

Work measurement is concerned with the determination of the time that it should take to complete a specific job. The fundamentals behind this measurement are the **job design** (which determines the content of a job) together with a **methods analysis** (which determines how a job is to be performed).

Work measurement, or job time, is invaluable for manpower planning, the estimation of labour costs, scheduling of work, budgeting and the design and parameters of incentive systems. The process of work measurement involves the inclusion of time for probable (average) delays. A standard time is calculated for an average (experienced) employee to complete a task while working at a rate that is sustainable over a period of time (the shift, or per hour, etc.) The measurement also takes into account the assumption that standard methods will be used to complete the job, with standard tools and equipment. The measurement does assume that the materials and components will be available to the employee and that the working conditions are suitable for carrying out the work.

Traditionally, work measurement uses either stopwatch time study, historical times (based on averages over a period of time), predetermined data (perhaps derived from supplier information or ideal times which have been worked into the schedule, or **work sampling** (which involves estimating a mean from a series of observations).

Work sampling

Work sampling involves an observer making a series of random observations of an employee or of work taking place on a machine over a period of time. The observer notes the nature of the work and counts the number of times that the observed work took place (using different categories of work type) as well as noting non-work periods.

Work sampling is used in ratio-delay study and the analysis of non-repetitive jobs. Essentially, the process is typified in the following manner:

> Work sampling aims to provide a value ($\hat{p}$), which allows the estimation of the true proportion, p, within an allowable error, e.

In other words, the estimation can be characterized as $\hat{p} \pm e$.

There is a normal range of variability in larger samples and therefore the estimations can be shown as a normal distribution curve showing the confidence interval (see Figure 32).

The degree of the maximum probable error is a function of both the sample size and the desired level of confidence. However, in larger samples, the maximum error e (as a percentage) is calculated using the following formula:

$$e = z\sqrt{\frac{\hat{p}(1-\hat{p})}{n}}$$

where z = the number of standard deviations required to achieve the desired level of confidence; $\hat{p}$ = the sample mean; and n = the sample size.

In solving the formula for n, it is possible to determine the appropriate size of the sample (using the confidence level as well as the amount of allowable error decided by the management). This formula is:

$$n = \left(\frac{z}{e}\right)^2 \hat{p}(1 - \hat{p})$$

In cases when there is no sample estimate, a preliminary estimate may be made by using $\hat{p} = 0.5$.

The process of work sampling is therefore typified as following these six steps:

1 An identification of the employee or employees and the machine or machines which will be studied.
2 Notification of those involved as to the purpose of the study so that bias associated with observation is not a factor (e.g. **Elton Mayo's** Hawthorne Effect).
3 A calculation of the initial estimate of the sample size p, or the use of $\hat{p} = 0.5$.
4 The framing of the random observation schedule.
5 A recompiling of the sample size during the observations (a double-check mechanism).
6 A calculation of the estimated proportion of time spent on the specified activity.

Work sampling can be differentiated from time study as illustrated in Table 30 by examining the advantages and disadvantages.

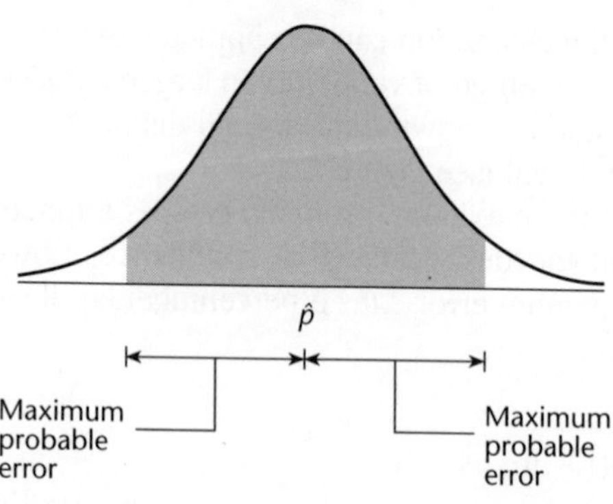

Figure 32 Work sampling distribution curve

Table 30 An assessment of work sampling

Advantages

1 Observations are spread out over a period of time, making results less susceptible to short-term fluctuations.
2 There is little or no disruption of work.
3 Workers are less resentful.
4 Studies are less costly and less time-consuming, and the skill requirements of the analyst are much less.
5 Studies can be interrupted without affecting the results.
6 Many different studies can be conducted simultaneously.
7 No timing device is required.
8 It is well suited for non-repetitive tasks.

Disadvantages

1 There is much less detail on the elements of a job.
2 Workers may alter their work patterns when they spot the observer, thereby invalidating the results.
3 In many cases, there is not record of the method used by the worker.
4 Observers may fail to adhere to a random schedule of observations.
5 It is not well suited for short, repetitive tasks.
6 Much time may be required to move from one workplace to another and back to satisfy the randomness requirement.

Source: Adapted from Richardson, Wallace J., *Cost Improvement, Work Sampling and Short Interval Scheduling*. Reston, VA: Reston Publishing, 1976.

Work station

A work station is a single-employee area where the individual carries out his or her job using specialized equipment.

Worker–machine chart

A worker–machine chart illustrates the amount of time a worker and a machine are either working or idle during a job. The chart itself shows if the worker or machine is idle for an excessive amount of time.

Worker–machine charts can be used for teams of workers interacting with machines and with each other, in which case the chart is called a 'gang process chart'.

Worker–machine charts are vital to job analysis as they can assist in the study of work methods used in a job alongside **flow process charts** and **motion studies**.

Workforce agility

Workforce agility is a measure of the flexibility of employees, enabling them to be deployed in different roles or on different shifts, or indeed involved in different activities within the organization. The workforce agility can be measured in a number of different ways, as can be seen in Table 31.

Table 31 Workforce agility

Agility purpose and measure	Explanation
Efficiency	With improved efficiency the organization should be able to meet deadlines, reduce **cycle times**, and achieve a lower level of **work in progress**.
Flexibility	Costs associated with the payment of **overtime** and the loss of **productivity** as a result of employee turnover or absenteeism can be reduced by multi-skilled employees. These individuals will be able to take on the work of absent employees. In addition, flexibility also offers opportunities to rapidly adapt the production environment.
Quality	A higher-quality workforce means that employees will be able to notice and take remedial action when there are problems. With improved quality of the workforce comes improved quality of the manufacturing process, as well as the prospect of employees being more prepared to suggest methods which would further enhance or improve the processes themselves.
Culture	Workforce agility should bring improvements in job satisfaction and motivation, particularly if the working environment is constantly upgraded and improved.

Hopp, W. J. and Van Oyen, M. P., 'Agile Workforce Evaluation: a Framework for Cross-training and Coordination', *Proceedings of the 2001 NSF Design and Manufacturing Grantees Conference*. Tampa, Florida, 2001.

Working Time Regulations 1998

This is a very detailed set of regulations, which apply to 'adult workers' (over 18) and to 'young workers' (over compulsory school age). The regulations cover working hours, night work, daily rest periods, weekly rest periods and annual leave. The regulations are summarized in Table 32.

Table 32 The Working Time Regulations 1998

Regulation coverage	Summarized details
Working hours	A worker's working time, including overtime, must not exceed an average of 48 hours in each 7 days. If the worker claims this right not to exceed the 48 hours, then he or she must not suffer any detriment because of it. A worker can agree to work longer than 48 hours per week, but this agreement should be made in writing with the employer. Employers are obliged to keep records of the hours worked.
Night work	Normal hours of work, for night workers, shall not exceed an *average* of 8 hours for each 24 hours. If the night work involves 'special hazards' or heavy physical or mental strain, then this limit is reduced to 8 hours worked in any 24-hour period.
Daily rest periods	Adult workers are entitled to a rest period of not less than 11 consecutive hours in each 24 hour period worked (12 for young workers). This rest period may be interrupted for certain types of work where the activities are split up over the day (or are of short duration). Where an adult worker's daily working time is more than 6 hours, they are entitled to a rest break (at least 20 minutes, 30 for young workers, for every 4.5 hours).
Weekly rest periods	Adult workers are entitled to at least 24 hours uninterrupted rest in each 7-day working period or two rest periods of 24 hours in each 14-day period worked, *or* one 48-hour rest period in each 14-day period (young workers 48 hours rest each 7 days).
Annual leave	Workers are entitled to at least 3 weeks leave per year (4 weeks from 23 November 1998). Workers should be paid at the rate of a week's pay for each week of leave.

www.hmso.gov.uk/si/si1998/19981833.htm

Working Time Regulations 1999

Statutory Instrument 1999 no. 3372 was an amendment to the Working Time Regulations 1998. The most significant changes were the removal of the need for employers to keep records of the hours worked by individuals who have opted out of the 48-hour week, and the extension of the scope of the 'unmeasured working time' exemption.

www.hmso.gov.uk/si/si1999/19993372.htm

Working Time (Amendment) Regulations 2002

These regulations amend the Working Time Regulations 1998 to implement the Young Workers Directive, protecting workers aged 16 and 17.

www.legislation.hmso.gov.uk/si/si2002/20023128.htm

Workplace (Health, Safety and Welfare) Regulations 1992 (UK)

These regulations cover a wide range of health, safety and welfare issues, including heating, lighting, seating and ventilation, welfare and work stations. The Workplace (Health, Safety and Welfare) Regulations 1992 completed a series of six sets of health and safety regulations to implement EC Directives (replacing a number of old and detailed laws).

Under the terms of the regulations, employers have to ensure that workplaces meet the health, safety and welfare needs of all members of a workforce, including people with disabilities. Several of the regulations require things to be 'suitable'. Regulation 2(3) clearly states that things should be suitable for anyone (including people with disabilities).

www.hmso.gov.uk/si/si1992/Uksi_19923004_en_1.htm

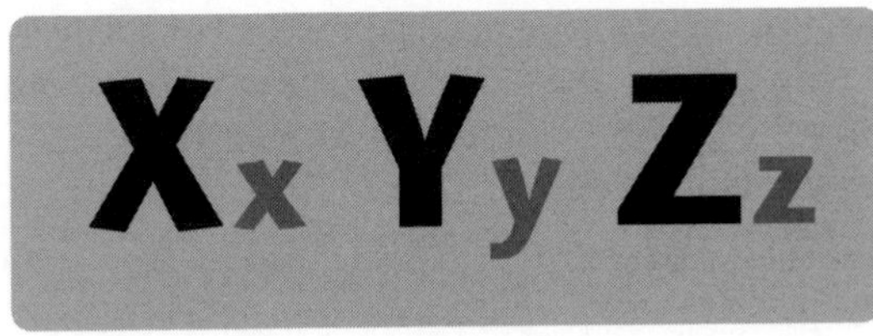

X-bar chart

The X-bar chart is used to control processes where a statistic under study is based on 'variables' data. The X-bar chart is developed from the average of the data for each subgroup, usually the mean and standard deviation of a sample.

Yield management

'Yield management' is real-time demand forecasting, which is also known as revenue management or real-time pricing. It is used by organizations to calculate the best pricing policy for optimizing profits. Yield management is based on real-time modelling and forecasting of demand behaviour per market segment.

This methodology was first adopted by the airline industry in the early 1980s as a means of comparing supply and demand with differentiated pricing and control of the inventory for each price category. The concept rests on the premise that the producer gains in increased turnover and revenue, whilst the customer enjoys lower prices for the same quality of service.

Yield management is a tactical weapon which aims to ensure the profitability of manufacturers in a competitive environment. From the early 1990s the concept began to penetrate other sectors of activity, initially in the United States and then in Europe.

Zero defects

For the most part, it was considered that the concept of 'zero defects' was a goal that could not be achieved; in many respects it was also considered to be unnecessary. It was always thought that at some point in the course of production a defect would inevitably creep into the system, and that provided the product reached the customer in a fit state and that defects were minimized, then this would be sufficient.

Both **Crosby** and **Shingo** have been credited with developing the concept of zero defects. Shingo certainly developed the concept of ***poka-***

yoke as a way of achieving zero defects. Reducing process variability is a second way to achieve zero defects. The desire to achieve zero defects became a specific goal during the 1980s, particularly amongst manufacturers producing complex products.

See also **Crosby, Philip B.** *and* **Shingo, Shigeo.**

Zero handling

Zero handling in **just-in-time systems (JIT)** means eliminating or reducing (namely by redesigning) all non-value adding activities.

Zero inventories

In **just-in-time systems (JIT)** inventories, including **work in progress**, finished goods and sub-assemblies, aim to be kept at zero. Under the system, there are no sub-assemblies, no work in progress and no finished goods. This implies a radically different way of approaching manufacture, which traditionally viewed inventories as a **buffer** against fluctuating demand or unreliable suppliers. Traditional manufacturing tended to be built around the non-stop use of expensive machinery running at full capacity in order to keep the costs per hour down to a minimum.

Zero lead time

Zero lead times derive from the concept and use of small lots and increased flexibility in the manufacturing system. In **just-in-time systems (JIT)** there is recognition that some markets cannot have zero lead times, at which point the focus turns to the reduction of the **lead times**.

Zero quality control (ZQC)

Zero quality control has three essential components which aim to lead to the elimination of defects:

- Source inspection – involving checks for the factors that cause errors, not the resulting defect.
- 100 per cent inspection – involving the use of a ***poka-yoke*** (mistake-proofing) device to inspect automatically for errors or defective operating conditions.
- Immediate action – involving the immediate termination of operations when a mistake is made, and their not being resumed until it is corrected.

Collectively, the key elements of zero quality control can be said to have the following weightings in terms of their importance and contribution to the system:

- Source inspection achieves a 60% reduction.
- 100 per cent inspection (*poka-yoke*) achieves a 30% reduction.
- Immediate action contributes the remaining 10% reduction in defects.

Zero set-up time

Zero set-up times aim to reduce the set-up times to allow more predictable production. Zero set-up times lead to shorter production time and production cycles as well as lower inventories.

Z-statistic

A z-statistic is used to look at probabilities in a normal probability table, which aims to illustrate the normal deviation of the standard normal distribution.

Numbers

3Mu

3Mu is shorthand for three Japanese words related to **total quality management** and **just-in-time systems**. The 3Mu are ***muda*** (waste), *muri* (strain) and *mura* (discrepancy).

3PL

See **third party logistics.**

5S

5S is shorthand for five Japanese words which describe the workplace and individual cleanliness. These are:

- *seiri* – straighten up your workplace or desk;
- *seiton* – sort out your equipment;
- *seiso* – sweep and clean your workplace;
- *seiketsu* – spotlessly maintain your appearance and character;
- *shitsuke* – self-discipline to follow rules, procedures, and standards.

5W2H approach

5W2H is a shorthand means by which the fundamental questions surrounding process improvement can be posed. The 5W element refers to Who? What? Where? When? and Why? The 2H element refers to How? and How Much?

By addressing these seven issues, an organization is able to take into account all of the key factors related to process improvement, establishing the parameters of that improvement, and assigning a time frame, costs and responsibilities.

6 sigma

See **six sigma.**

7 zeros

See **seven zeros.**

Index

Note: page numbers in **bold** indicate major entries